W9-ANY-900

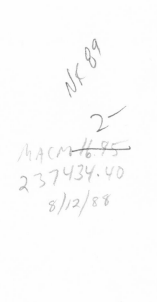

NK89

2-

MACM 16.95

237434.40

8/12/88

Also by Theodore Weiss

Poetry

The Catch   1951
Outlanders   1960
Gunsight   1962
The Medium   1965
The Last Day and the First   1968
The World before Us: 1950–1970   1970
Fireweeds   1976
Views & Spectacles: Selected Shorter Poems   1978
Views & Spectacles: New and Selected Shorter Poems   1979
Recoveries   1982
A Slow Fuse   1984

Prose

Selections from the Note-Books of Gerard Manley
Hopkins   1945
The Breath of Clowns and Kings: Shakespeare's Early
Comedies and Histories   1971
The Man from Porlock: Engagements, 1944–1981   1982

From Collected

Princeton Poems *of*

One Theodore

Autumn Weiss

Afternoon

From Collected
Princeton Poems *of*
One Theodore
Autumn Weiss
Afternoon

Collier Books
Macmillan Publishing Company
New York
Collier Macmillan Publishers
London

I would like to thank the Guggenheim Foundation and the Princeton Institute for Advanced Study for helping to make the preparation of this volume possible.

Copyright © 1987 by Theodore Weiss

All rights reserved. No part of this book may be reproduced or transmitted in any form or by any means, electronic or mechanical, including photocopying, recording or by any information storage and retrieval system, without permission in writing from the Publisher.

Collier Books
Macmillan Publishing Company
866 Third Avenue, New York, NY 10022
Collier Macmillan Canada, Inc.

Library of Congress Cataloging-in-Publication Data

Weiss, Theodore Russell, 1916-
    From Princeton one Autumn afternoon : collected poems of Theodore Weiss.
      p.   cm.
    ISBN 0-02-071020-8 (pbk.)
    I. Title.
[PS3545.E4735A6 1988]   88-11910
811'.54—dc19   CIP

10 9 8 7 6 5 4 3 2 1

Printed in the United States of America

From Princeton One Autumn Afternoon is also published in a hardcover edition by Macmillan Publishing Company.

For, to, and with Renée

A Note

Though this volume of poems is called a collected, it is not complete. Some poems, fit for one flight of publication rather than for the long haul, have been excluded. A number of those remaining, especially the longer ones, have undergone a close rereading: a combination of sympathy, criticism, and new perspective. Since writing for me has constituted something like a work in progress and since with time poems may show weaknesses as well as new possibilities, I have attended to these developments. Revision has been an increasingly integral part of my writing life. One early long poem here was some twenty years in the making. A making which has continued in this latest round. Thus reverberations, deliberate and inevitable, sound throughout the volume. For, to some deep degree, each new poem is a reinforcement and realization drawn up out of and for its predecessors.

Over a lifetime the voice of a writer, as it changes, with luck also grows more unmistakably his or her own: the changes, bearing out earlier premises and promises, come home again. That voice strengthens itself by its very accommodating of others and the other. So from the start I was after a voice that could give voice to the many people inside and out, to the drama of their collision as well as to the larger music of their harmony. These people derive from my past and present, but also from history and the arts, as from poetry itself. An ideal I have held before me is a poetry, a language, absorbed in and exploiting its own immense resources yet, at the same time, transparent to the world at large.

Contents

Gunsight 1962   107

From The Medium 1965

From The Last Day and the First 1968

From The World before Us *1970*

From Fireweeds *1976*

From Views & Spectacles *1979*

From Collected

Princeton Poems *of*

One Theodore

Autumn Weiss

Afternoon ℰ

From Princeton one autumn afternoon, 1986

Dear Zbigniew Herbert,

Someone said all poems compose
one poem. Who's to judge him wrong?
Have I not long been occupied
with speculations having to do
with those in your "The Old Masters?"

So, while our fall is at its peak,
trees galleries jammed with jostling
masterpieces, I, though we've
not met, feel called upon to write
to you.
      Because they never thought
to autograph their work, you,
envious, urge those Old Masters

    make the serpent scales of pride
    fall from me

    let me be deaf
    to the siren calls of fame

I I

Could you and I believe the God
we aimed to please was watching, angels
too, fluttered over angels we had
newly hatched, we'd also slight
our names.
      But if these works are real,
their angels, their events, the light
they shed secure in each, why should
they need to be identified?

Once it's done a great painting seems
to have produced itself and waits
on us, orphans that we are, to claim,
proclaim it and so name ourselves.

3

Even now we can appreciate
what miracle those works achieve,
each one a meeting (mating) place
for heaven and earth their makers,
making, slipt into.
                As you say,

    uttering no frightened cry
    no plea to be remembered
    they drowned without a trace
    in golden firmaments

III

And even here and now like them
I'd press this gallant bustle—
trillion bushes burning, burning
babes in rushes, crucifixions
by the bushel dangled from sumacs,
maples, sycamores—between my pages.

Gladly too I'd drown in it.

This windfall should remind us of
many a painting's sky-borne company.
Incarnation of the local light,
they match up with the amber of
a roisterous beer, an auburn glance,
hair in a rush, a flashing thigh;

their flying up and down inside
the landscape seems to flourish it
forth.
          Among the candle-flickering
saints highnoon itself is caught.
Or else, as now, sunset's draining
out of clouds and banked-up foliage.

I V

Leaves, crackling pungent under-
foot, in lustrous green, a clustered
host, must rise again.
                    As will
that youngling, loved of the sun,
become a crimson flower, every
spring repeating its exact,
black "Ai! Ai!"
                    One listening hard
can hear, muffled among these leaves,
yet willed enough to rouse a storm,
Milton, bowered by Vallombrosa:
Keats and Hopkins, still at harvest:
reading aloud, Perkiomen Stevens.

V

Paradised Adam and Eve, I'm sure,
smack in the middle of, and busy
looking after, ripe, self-multi-
plying words, hardly brooded
over their own names.
                    Not till
the snake woke fears, those vine-
thick-choking doubts, and lust
for that which they at best
already had.
                    You and I mid-poem,
words flown headlong out of us
resembling in our minds the trans-
port—dancing
                    fiery-still
as any sumac, maple, sycamore—
of seraphim, never stop to harp
upon our names, the likelihood
of everlasting fame.
                    At loving
you know this: too much to do,
thinking and the senses overborne,
to fuss about yourself.

VI

                  Such loving
's relative to love collecting,
nectar, inside words, especially
for the likes of you and me
who work in them.
                  Diligent as bees,
we'd, milking flower after flower,
distill a cargo, fragrant-mellow
as those names the ancients wrested
out of time, celestial agents,
and themselves.
                  Tang still in them,
those names abounding on our tongues,
are we not instantly in touch?

A touching, love, that teaches us
the meaning and the strangeness of
ourselves, the future flamed before
us in their gone, still robust past.

VII

Imagine a God Who made by uttering,
fruits full-globed, the eloquence
that is sun and moon and stars,
burst sparkling
                  from His mouth:
the swift-limbed sundry—antelope,
newts, butterflies—shot forth,
shapen breaths:
                  soft words warbled
into birds, beruffled melody,
in turn melodious:
                  and next,
the lumbersome, as if the earth,
humped out of itself, like hillocks
tossed, ox, elephant, rhinoceros,
should shake the very earth:
                  swarming,
from within, vast swarms on swarms,
until the Lord declared Himself
in man and woman.

VIII

And then He,
seeing that what He'd said was good,
bade Adam finish off His speech
with blessings of a name for each.

At that, burnished by his heart-
warmed breath, so benimbused rose
the horse, the eagle, and the bull,
the lowly too,
        the tittle flea
and nit, motes mica-like in sun,
the prickly rain, the wobbling sea,
restrained as Adam's twilit will,

that Job, such marvels dazzling him,
as they would do those Masters, shed
his grievances, not to say his name.

If but for one brief heavenly spell.

God- and poet-wise like Job
we'd better pause to contemplate
admiringly the wonders He had said.

IX

This mid-day, out as if to see
all things, snags onto bottom twigs,
then jigs, a halo, round each grit,
a bug gem-embered in the grass:

lovers, struggling out of sleep,
inspired by each other's body,
leap to kiss's precipice:

a lonely-girl-sighed song flares
up, a sufferer's racked "O me!",
maggots, blissful in a pot of sun-
warmed pus:
        and asters, staring
back at that which opened them.

There snagged until the world
turns into nothing but a smoldering
gold that obliterates all words
and every gnawing doubt.

X

                    But then,
as does wide-shadowing fear, that
darkness radiance breeds, the daily,
walleyed, settling back, oppresses
us,
      like that giant carrion-
fly in the foreground, hunkering
high above the painting's scene,
ready as it glares to swoop down
on the crucifixion tiny many miles
away.
      Struck by an acrid smell
that daily spreads of melancholy
and decay, no wonder we clutch
names.

X I

      In former ages daylight,
despite the horrors it had shown,
also geysered out of everything,
out of those Masters' fingers, eyes.

And they saw that they must lend
a shaping hand to keep it. Saw
to it that asses, cattle, shepherds,
basking, shone forth, company fit
for cherubim.
          It may be true
that earth and heaven never coupled
more enthusiastically, not even
in hoary Greece.

XII

A wilderness
for paradise, the burning bush
their golden rod, on Jews alone
did God bear down more searingly
and therefore more endearingly.

Obedient to Him, abhorring
graven images, their heartaches
scored by every breath, breath
it was—
        crammed into rugged words,
mind's images, mind's luminous
Jerusalem—
        they prized the most,
but after that, His breath still warm
on them, His touch, the worldly goods.

XIII

And still we make our way by words.
Any sudden ailment, however raging,
once the doctor's labeled, loses
half its terror;
        names assure us
that the mystery, beast monstrous
though it seem anonymously,
has been, if not completely tamed,
at least corralled.
        But learned doctors,
fixing names to that they've learned,
names mostly what they've learned,
know too, for what they've learned,
the cost and loss they must sustain.

XIV

In the anatomy lesson, itself
a still life for the faculty
and students concentrating, first
a finger—that had sprouted as if
to beckon on the first of spring,
then, stiffening in its own winter—
went,
      and, finger after finger
by their ligaments,
           the hand,
apt at plucking apples, capons,
a guitar, at patting an old cat,
a child frightened by the dark,
a woman, gathering the treasures
from her body similar strokes
composed into a work of art:

last, clutching itself, an agony
expertly rummaged among the limbs
as though become one with the body:

and then the orbic eye, in which
clouds had dallied, towered cities
drifting, mountains camel-humped,
and days daylong shifting views:
finally, the heart, that stamping
ground a savage brood had trampled,
each one interested in nothing
more than its own ravagings
until it had devoured itself.

And so the body and the person
disappear.
      After that, the year
ending, the annual ceremony due,
before the assembled doctors, staff,
and relatives, the hospital priest
repeated the dismembereds' names.

A number of the doctors wept.

X V

The body and the person disappear.
But names and names (files on files
of lists) remain?
                    Christen the leaves,
each one, at large, the tipsy waves—
O wine-dark, wine-drunk sea!—each
twittering wind?

                    How many lost?

Like leaves long crumpled, animals:
great auk, aurochs, pterodactyl,
woolly mammoth, every year
ten thousand species:
                    herds on herds,
bodied in words alone, slink rustling
along the windings of the tongue;

ancient, colossal civilizations,
Phrygia, Mesopotamia, Assyria,
a swelled mirage of variegated
butterflies the winds swept off;

the rifted continents; the stars,
aeons ago erupting, flares now
fitful in the sky;
                    abandoned, long
dead gods, Melgart, Marduk, Eshmun,
awesome to their votaries,
yet intimate too;

X V I

                    and those, people
once, the mythic ones, collecting
power through the centuries,

admirers added to them as to
the population of a country,
as a star needs time and space
for the fulfillment of its shining,
enhanced by what it shines upon,
Moses, Jesus, Lao Tse;
                    but now
we tend to idolize those few,
Einstein, Weinstein, Finkelstein, Bohr,
who've tied their names to whirling
particles, to more and more
of less and less,
                till like Lucretius
they know the bliss of nothingness.
Or how many scientists can dance
on the head of a non-existent pin?

Women too, adored for the visible,
hoarded in their names, of charms
the mind can feed upon: Helen
who bore the whole matter of Troy;
Cleopatra who turned the world
into a harum-scarum, name a morsel
luscious still upon the tongue.

(Try comparing Cleopatra, even
Mata Hari or Marilyn Monroe,
of a certain glamor if not
stature, with a Mrs. Thatcher!)

Whatever glorious fuss past ages
might have made over holy relics,
they kept no better than Cleopatra
in a flask.
           And yet their names
alone, do they not enliven us
more than people I have known:
Max (Moxie?) Charkov (Sharkow?),
Annie (Marnie?) Picon (Simon?),
Cohens, Cohans, Cones, Kohns,
Kahns, Kuhns.

XVII

Meeting Delmore Schwartz
when we were asked to record poems
(late for him, battered, ragged,
grey), I said, "Well, here we are,
the Schwartz and the Weiss of it."
And he, silent, stared at me.

Our parents, aspiring for us,
sought romantic, Christian names:
high-toned Delmore, Theodore,
euphonious together.
                           "In Hungarian
Weiss occurs almost as often
as Smith in English."
                           Theodore Weiss
the Congressman, Theodore Weiss
the Trumpeter, Theodore Weiss
Director of Bellevue, Theodore . . .

XVIII

And those closest to me, parents,
teachers, friends, like water slipping
through my fists, can I recall
their telltale gestures, any words?

Great-Aunt Jenny, the worldly one
among her sisters, the last time
I saw her, head bobbing, floated
on layers of fat that jammed the room.

Great-Uncle Morris, the cap maker,
little round man with large doe eyes,
hunched over a sewing machine,
weeps so his tears entwine the thread.

My socialist grandfather, fresh
from Warsaw, believing his landsmenner
wise in the ways of the Big City,
their "You can't be an American,

Herschel, with a name like Hallam!"
promptly changed it to Harry Weinberg.

A phrase, your own, would conjure them,
at best does little more, myopic,
speckled mirror, than reflect
exteriors, your giant ignorance.

And yet, like spring-fed rivulets
insurgent through the lurching sea,
is not their breathing ever current
through our breath?
          As the Ur-breath
swells behind us all, and waits,
a stillness gathered in the air,
until the Voice, no longer able
to bear it, bursts, a conflagration
needing everything to feed its lust.

XIX

Fix eye on clothes, jewels, hair
that stuff a room; on watches ticking,
gleaming teeth; then try to ferret out
the names entangled there.
          On bodies
tossed about like birds in a cat's
playful clutches, deft knives probing
them for "Names! Names! Give us
their names!"
          Then dumped like logs,
like water poured.

XX

          A body, person
disappears. The names, ripped up
with records of their owners' past
and burned—
          "Hair we save, golden
trinkets, teeth, but every other
vestige of this trash we blot

from off the face of the earth as if
they never were!"—
                    belched into sky,
a cry's last crackle.
                    "My parents?"
the young woman shruggingly replied.
"Dying in a concentration camp,
by now they would have died anyway."
Anyway and anyway and anyway.
                              Mother,
a suicide, asking that her ashes
be "strewn to the four winds," joined
the others
          long disguised as air,
dear ones mixed with distant kin,
the doubly ghosted, naked even
of their names.

XXI

                    Such ghosts, their cries,
in a day lucid as this, should they
not shower round us, thick as flocks
of leaves, cold, ashen flakes,
the breeze shaped into syllables?

They had, looking, loved till looks,
blending with the birches, lent
a deeper tint to flowers, sunsets,
dawns for those come after.
                          Touching
some one body, they were borne
beyond all speech except as they
sighed out the other's name to feel
their moment everlasting, the only
wholly now.
          Then they died nameless.

XXII

Consider our sad inadequacies,
the countless species we have failed
to name and those we stint

15

(“Christen
the leaves, each one, at large”?)

So we, unlike the Eskimos,
tuck snow, whatever its mien,
into a single word,
                    coop birds,
droves on droves, into “robin,”
“sparrow,” “crow.”
                    And yet this thrush,
trilling in the holly, though
it differ from the feathery rest,
sings as if its body were a bill
a trillion thrushes warble through,

as if indeed forever’s forest,
all its generations waiting,
nestled in the first small seed.

XXIII

Still for things figuring strongly
in our lives we strike off many terms.

So Edmund Wilson soberly collected
104 synonyms for “intoxicated”;
the prudent Franklin, 228.

Joyce, having read that a man,
Cycle by name, had married, said,
“Now he should be called Bicycle,
and when a child comes, Tricycle.”

“Oh, no,” I interpose. “Popsicle.”
And then, the cycle starting up
again, dub him, melting, Icicle.

A name by any other name, it’s clear,
whether Rosencrantz or Guildenstern,
Rosenstern or Guildencrantz,
Hermanus Posthumus or Herbert
Holocaust, and settling in,

will prove as personal and smell
as sweet.
        Broadway, Fifth Avenue,
and 42nd Street bespeak a poverty?
With time how fragrant they become.
Not even numbers, bodiless things,
long balk imagining.

X X I V

                But then,
as if the denizens of earth
and sea and air were not enough,
we must invent terms for our hungers,
mind's dream-fantasies:
                elves,
spooks, chimerae, minotaurs,
the heavenly host, its hierarchy.

But have any of the minor ones,
beyond a Puck, an Ariel,
attained a first or private name?

As Donne said of "these little stars,"
though they possess a goodly part
of heaven, fame is not for them.

Even the big boys, though Hebrew,
Gabriel, Michael, Raphael,
had to make do with Christian names.
And yet lit up as in italics,
they were instantly recognized.

X X V

The feelings too: do you, privy
to their inner lives, adorn
each with a special name? And do
they, changing, ripen and decay,
at the beginning Juliet Joy,
Jezebel at the end?

17

                              Or among joy's
divers offspring is there one
that needs no name, like a child
at play, while Jeremiah Grief
and Lester Lust go their mad way?

Also, those mental things, those high-
blown abstractions we try pinning
names to, Soul, Truth, Liberty.

Or faceless words like teleology
or epistemology, resistant
to any attempt at Thouing.
                              Yet
for such as these, less than shadows,
men, passionate to worship, bent
on fleshing them, gladly hack
the world to pieces.

          X X V I

                              Like natives
adopting names that only tribal
members share for fear strangers
cast a spell on them,
                    this student,
tired of her ignorance of trees,
resenting too their public stance,
christened those most neighborly
with names she alone could know:

the one outside her window Linda
after her best, if far-off friend;
that longhair overlooking the rest,
Elmer; slender, swayed, a shimmering
sheaf of smiles, Mable.
                              However,
observing Mable's mercurial moods,
her bewildering, assorted dress,
she saw she should have called her

Sheba, Shulamite, Badroulbadour.
Or rather every season change
her name.
        As a colleague and I talk,
along his office window streaks,
swift as lightning, an elm just felled,
all autumn falling, very glorious
Babylon, in the dust.

XXVII

            The arrogance
of names? Surely you must realize
those Old Masters no less vain
and no less envious than the rest
of us.
        With this fellow craftsman,
that, they vied, for contracts much
as for the purest azure, spotted
first in eyelids (under which
angels might have sought out shelter).

Where one stood among the choir
God bade His dominions congregate;
sunbeams, each a gnat-big rainbow
for the stained-glass windows,
wreathed—
        row upon row of martyrs,
shaken for their torments, squinting
astonished at him; prophets, gape-
mouthed too; below, her calm, solemn
smile arraying her, a young woman—

vaulted, echoing chords he loosed,
a paean of pride, but also praise.
At once the church became a many-
cell-brimmed honeycomb.

XXVIII

                For that
alone there is abundant cause
to envy those Old Masters.
                But we,
though inwardly and out benighted,
also are attended:
                you by memories
of ruthless police, stark terror,
the unpredictable become the law;
and yet within that grinding maw
like Szymborska and Różewicz
unswervingly you serve the truth;

and I—a goulash, one part Polish
the rest Hungarian, spiced up
with Jew, so three times screwed—
by the West's complicities of greed.

XXIX

So now and then we must believe
that one remote age or another,
more coeval with our longings
than the present, for its heroes
and their storied deeds has left us
far behind.
                Among the mind's resorts
old paintings, bits of, if not portals
to, a sense of paradise,
make our world more tolerable.

Still, however fabulously jeweled,
as if buried in mines, to blazon
forth they need the sun, our dark-
addicted eyes.

X X X

But as the newest
critics tell us, it's a mistake,
if not a downright fake, to think
a work, whether it be painting,
poem, song, belongs to anyone.
By godly language alone it's done.

And anyway would a rose or one
of these accomplished leaves be rosier
were it, beyond its own intricacy,
like a curled-up scroll, a painting,
proudly, plainly signed by its maker?

In any case, I judge the Old Masters
lucky because they knew the only
certain fame wholehearted striding—
sumac-, maple-, sycamore-wise—
barefoot into glory,
                    instantly
immortal, in their name-free works.

Yours,
Theodore Weiss

From The Catch *(1951)*

The Hook

The students, lost in raucousness,
caught as by the elder Breughel's eye,
we sit in the college store
over sandwiches and coffee, wondering.
She answers eagerly: the place was fine;
sometimes the winds grew very cold,
the snows so deep and wide she lost
sight of people. Yes, she was well
satisfied with her work, expected—
while the quarry's owner was away—
to do another year of it.

I I

She is hammering. I hear
the steady sound inside our dry,
noisy days. Sparks fly; the mind,
so taken, mighty for a moment,
becomes quarry and sculptor both,
something caught like love and war
in this golden mesh: and daring
caught that flings like sparks girls
and boys, flagrant cities prompt
to daring's will, love and war
its burly seconds.

I I I

I see again three kids we passed,
three kids lounging at the edge
of a forsaken quarry like something
they had built; in its sleepy pool
they found the whiteness of their bodies,
the excitement like parian marble.

IV

Such the waters we find ourselves
in. We sit in the college store absorbed
in food and talk. Eagerness seizes us
like love that leaves its best sailors
in the mighty waves, love the word
for hook whose catching, and the struggle
there, is one great musical clash
of minds—each wave a passion and a mind—
a possessed, tumultuous monument
that would be free.

V

                    We strain forward
as to some fabulous story. Incandescence
springs from her, the hammer of remembrance
fresh, the young woman, bulky graceful body,
face shining, who sculptured all winter
alone near the source of her rock,
digging down into the difficult rock:

the young woman who lost a day once,
talked to her cat, and when the mirror
of her art became too clear, when dreaming
seemed too big for night alone, took long
walks back to people, back to speech,
and time:
                    the woman, who at last—
"I do not use live models"—sculptured fish—
"I remember long lonely holidays at shores
when the spray alone defined green shapes
approaching"—has just seen (her eyes
still gleam with the gleam of it,
blink like the making of many
a take) a great catch.

VI

April, we say,
is the time for fish, for reaching
in its sea-like waftings one
of earth's original conclusions
like the leftover gill slits
the singing student told us about
in this very spot just two days ago . . .

we are in the middle of a great catch,
there collected as from her year-long
lonely rock, the thrashing, clean-
scaled, clear-lit shad in the net.

Cataract

In the falls, music-woven,
clamorous coils as of cymbals
and shields, I see features
purer than my own: desire
lithe and riding, breaker-bearded,
as the wanderer. I see the first
son of my wish whose thews
were tissued of the sea.

And when my hearing tries
the billows of the wind, back
to its snowy crest and back
to its warring mouth, again I meet
the stranger of myself, the one
that sleeps with restlessness
as the distant mutter of drums
the water cores:
                in jagged fast-
nesses of fire turmoil strides
one with earth's progenitor.

Astonished, I have struck
the rock that moors these seas;
and I am one with the marching
men, possessed as one, their
dazzled minds obeying potions
of the moon, proceeding
by incessant crags, their eyes
reflections of the cataract.

Already gone, the priests
of war, they go to meet them-
selves, to crash into the center
of the drum, the humming waves,
the fiery rocks where
the sirens of the senses,
cold, cold, O burning cold,
calmly thrum the air.

A Brown Study

by the waters Venus raised . . .

I

Amid ocean of wish—
and the dolphins of whim
with slippery fins flick up
the playful swishing spray
in my comber-briny face—

amid ocean of wish,
shaped no doubt like pine-
apple, bristling and resolute
on its dish, carapaced
as any crab, crabbed
as any apple can be,
                amid swirl-
ing and so certain sea (palms
to the right no doubt
as the stalk, saw-toothed,
tusked worthy of a snout, roots

out a night-borne chough
chattering as the sea, bruited
from the daysprings of a voice
beyond appeal) with me
the root
         I suddenly see
her rising a resonant, a serene,
the dolphins flipt around her,
pips of spray punctual in sea-
green eyes . . .

II

              I see—
with me the root—her coming,
heart's thump the consequence
as of the fruit that split

          the world.
Through that gape—the parted
lips, the earth upstarting—
dark's naked tread. The bottom-
of-the-deep with all the days deep
sunken crowns pursues.

          Dainty
dreadful step as she that plummeted
from earth's fell grip rose up again,
winter still on her,

          winter
and its whites and, last, maddened
sleep in step: a pomp that holds
the world together worm to star,
orders bedlam in the sky . . .

III

          I see,
so that my head, pineapple head-
hunter-shrunk, spiked with frowns,
its carapace pricked and scaled,
crossing daggers on all sides,

concentrating studied
brown and bite, racks bitterness
into hardest core of succulence:
rowdy sweet seeing is.

          Amid ocean
of wish and a leaky day, blue-
blotched shadow to this
loneliness, the commotion—
blowing spume like pips—
of my horny notion

          turns
into her nation, obedient
as waves, bowing whites, vestal—
in devotion, tidy, to the tune—
maidens to the sluttish moon.

A Sum of Destructions

The amities of morning
and the buxom habits of birds
that swing a bell-bright city
in their intelligent wings;

last night's squall has
drawn off like anger's tide,
the remote and muffled waters
beating solitudinous rocks

and murmurous
in the hidden parts, ebbing
and beating, of the mind
as some half-forgotten name . . .

the rain has withdrawn
like the tents and the Greeks,
like the hard-to-believe-
in days of our childhood.

Light moves, the whole
massed flotilla of morning, kin
to the upward flight of birds
returning;
                and brutality,
the hungers and the hatreds
seem fabulous, seem members;
the gouty rat and straggly

root collaborate. Earth
in wounds, deaths, decays—
past hours its rutted crusts—
with the billowy sky

is the field-
upon-field, and all one,
of one master observing
the various fruits:
                        somewhere
a child in a cage, inferior
bodies making a passable
road, a girl passionate

with pain, an old man
watching the earth escape
like his once endless
strengths, his poems head-

long. And one fills
with awe—as the town
with morning, every cranny,
the birds brimming fire-

escapes and broken windows—
that the earth like some wise
breath never balked, a many-
membered bird-flight,

should include all,
must be a terrible good.
The eyes passing,
contracted from night

and war the stars
undertook, finally emerge
the topgallant of morning,
and those eyes roam

free as the Greeks:
wherever a drop of water
is, spindrift city of water
gleaming, there is home.

Panoramic Sue

Add Susan
as a nook of sight, of looking
on the sly: add "ho!" to blue,
"O" sedate and "how?" a stare,
the thrusting of her chin,
till windy sky is racing like
her pond ("hepatica" her father,
pointing, says) "patacake! patacake!
clap your hands!" and we see
beyond beyond.

Her chuckle is a huckle-
berried hill, as is her run-
ning and her fall, the ruddy ball
that bounces through her hands;
and all the wily sea resounds
in this tipt shell: an April-
rain is not so gay, so
round. As Renée, tying Susan's
shoelace, bends, Sue gravely

pats her on the back:
"I pat my mother, when
she's good . . . now you
pat me!" and her chortle
is as puffed, yes, sprouts
a cherry-blossom tree
in spray round buzzing saw
and zooming boom of bee
beside the droopeared
rhododendron patch "Susan-

sized," next to the azalea bush
"big as Bobby—he's our brother,"
and another poised as "Pete—
he's our dog, sniffing at
someone else's tree . . . that's
G I A N T and that's mother
bending to kiss me
when the curtains fly,
fixed to a whee, and the night
comes in bigger than me!"

and it did, out of the O
of her eyes and the huddled
corner of her voice, bushy one
touching unknown sudden shores,
till sky's bright as a ball
your wishing dare not have,
redcheeked day snatched out
of your hands by "come to bed!"

To Penny when She Comes of Reading Age

Your eyes are full
of windy distance; caught
between two times, you sit
on your father's lap.

We smile to you
and, all of a comeliness
like light collected, you
smile back; then, head
cocked, look at us intently.

As we gaze, you slip again—
a perfect recollecting—
into a whorled solemnity:

briny sounds, bright pebbles
tossed, bubble forth, self-
sufficent things, yet words
of need,
        like breathing
or the tears burst out
from timeless roots far
below the crusty phrases
of your elders.
          Awed,
we listen as to a sudden
utterance of some ancient,
mysterious, lost tribe;

the myriad selves we have
forsaken, frowning, plead:
the wish, mired long before.

We are back, sea split,
dizzy ark, where all
the constellations—Bear,
Lion, Dog, and Scorpion—
commingle. . . .
                Taking down
the little I overhear,
I write this poem
                that you
perhaps will read it
when these days will be
to you as you are now for us.

Let this poem be a dusty
yet still whispering shell,
remnant of that moment

like a wave's crest—
like the blue eyes
of your rag doll echoing
you—now washing out to sea.

The Dance Called David

How could I know
how beyond this love
which held me to him and
by its very hold blinded me?

Hours of many days
we walked, past the reputable,
through scenes, people, past
street-names and corners,
                              deep
through poverty with its charming
air of things half-dropping off
into oblivion.
                    Words from me,
pointings to oddities in color,
sudden, explosive sights
and sounds,
                    recalled him
as those that burned in hell
steadied their flames to answer
one earthbound.
                         Like something
mattered out of air, a smile—
did it reflect the morning
songs that once enlightened?—
would flicker, then go out.

How could I know,
I who loved him, viewed
the world around us as phrases
visible of his unmoving lips,
a music incredible, illuminated
as a battered hurdy-gurdy
by the love he simply woke,

how could I know
how right I was: windows
strewn behind us, swirling
traffic, parks bouqueting lovers,
children burst from school,
all movements in the meaning
mysteriously clear he was for me.

Only now, years after
his death, do I know what
terror I called friend, what
wrestlings I walked beside, what
anguish—dance of madness, gaiety—
he adorned,
           the total city
with its grey wizen streets,
each ash-pale puddle, its thin
furtive faces, and the tiniest
broken straw looked after.

Only now I see
how much he deserved—
if love must deserve—whatever
love I could attain, and more, I
speechless, ignorant as a child.

These years between, now
that he is with what we are not,
time and the multiple wild fears
have helped me recognize what
first must have frightened me
away.
      Time that cut us
off sharper than space can
holds out again generous hands
as he, the harmonious blacksmith,
leads me through the depths unroll-
ing, these scarred years that are
journeying and pity, of myself.

After Five Years

Beside the lumber
recently cut, some men
struggling up a muddy, snow-
ridged road, and five-stories-tall
in your peak-roofed apartment
where warmth was common,

I, after these years
wondrous about returning,
fearful a little,
more than a little hopeful
before the host of possibilities,

I, anxious for revival,
standing at your porthole
window, the latenoon sky
sullen above your sea,
                              ships
puffing along, humped peddlers,
so that I cannot, do not care
to, pursue romantic thoughts
of their cargoes, voyages,
extravagant adventures,

I, a raveled thread
at the needle's eye, asquint
after the flashing pattern
of my silent partners, try hard
to think of you spun back,
gathered into your imagery:

this sky not yet beginning
to ripen your excellent moon,
the mindless sea adrift
with its abstract boats.

And try with disappointment.
For nothing happens, no north
of thunder scours my hearing,
no lightning hallows my thought
or brightens my conscience,

not even this fruit, here
in this bowl as it used to be
promising incredible secrets,
stirs its ruddy lips
to the words of love
and acknowledgement
we somehow always expected;

not the books where we left
them, dusty, close-mouthed
as the phrases we mixed,
sometimes beat into a blow

that swirled this room,
crow's nest, back
to first seas breaking,
furious exultant pain.
                            Only
five nameless unshaped men drag
along the turning, muddy road
next to the new wood, raw,
awkward, an eyesore,
five men for the moment
flickering
                (even as flakes
of snow begin to prick the sky-
light we used to praise,
a god's view, so we said,
for our eyes raised),
                            then
slipping—hardly anguish—
through a narrow break
in the grey fence just below;
                        and they are gone.

A Commonplace

as the silly shepherds
after their first radiant scare—
sheep and cattle at their munching
with the winter
               bent yet spin-
ning lilies—forgot . . . hunched
puttering over our benighted star,
we lose track of tears.

See him stamped there,
come down into the common-
place who let himself be stabled
in the blood.
               His walk
brought sea, salt, fish, bread
of his body. Yet within his memory,
each breath travail,

did loiterings of his past,
in sleep perhaps, cajole him: pride,
when as a child he confounded
the learned elders;
               lust:
touched by a woman long possessed,
he knew his virtue troubled
in him;
           or pain itself, simple-
minded pain, did it perhaps reduce
him to the pulse of immediately
suffering man?
             O garden
of agony, so dry it drank his blood,
grew in him, till he cried with a man
mouth and a man mortality . . .

but the garden had its malt as well.
For the shepherds, far inland, blood-
warmed, the star faded into a stone
their cattle sucked for salt.

Shades of Caesar

(a meditation at Bard College by the Hudson)

Speakers:
The narrator
Caesar
A soldier in Caesar's army

> *Yet Caesar shall go forth; for these predictions*
> *Are to the whole world in general as to Caesar.*
> *When beggars die, there are no comets seen.*

I

Come out into this moment
of clearing and sit on this bench;
come from the files like a man
in the toils, his eyes
hardly his own with staring;

sit and stare, mortuary
for the vine-veined chapel peering,
a battered sundown, through the trees.

We smell the air, do nothing
but smell the air, pungent round
a smoke-shaped bird whose prospectings
echo seconds of the dead:

the ancient scholars
and the ministers-to-be in stiff,
black gowns, remembering with bowed
heads in this clearing the Greeks
and the Romans, mixed with the Christian,
muttering dry prayer:
               disreputable
old Rip Van Winkle, bowled at the bias
of his spouse's tongue, stumbling in
on the sport and the peace-piped
Indians.

An absentminded wind
from the Hudson no doubt, descendant
of a blow sails once grappled, worries
the leaves in dry-scented eddies.

           *

We do nothing, we who ponder
thieves and murderers, bawds
bountiful of flesh, trading
in need and pride and lust,
we the isles bound
by such common trafficking:
                    do nothing
but search the dry shadows under the maple
—maypole once, and after the jubilant
circling, the sugar milked from it
into the guzzling sprawled mouths below—
for the luxuriant shape, the long-sleeping
imperial theme—call it thyme—of myth,

the leaves that are falling
                and
                    falling
round and round like burnt days
ript from the calendar
of what a leaf or two ago
seemed endless:

           *

          O fierce felicity,
the air gross with diadems,
sleek-headed sounds and winds,
ritual like nude runners,
                the seed
of darkness a relentless fertility
whose holy touch, we thought,
a feast of shepherds, would enable us
to strike off sterility's curse.

How in the fields, peasant
with wind and rain, the hours
of light have labored;

now light pauses
before the hail and the fire:
charred wind swept over,
a desert mouth,
                one groan,
one wound, a swarm of jiggling
bones the far-off, foreign city,

mountain of fire sinking
into the sea,
         falling
           and
              falling
deeper and deeper till we drown.

               *

Now amid the swaying
leaves-and-lights,
            the city
near us, wandered in with the wind's
mixed murmurs, caught in its commerce,
unaware of the sickness welling
within it;
           yet despite all complaints,
all obvious omens, the people remain:
the sociable beast, the terrible
touching,
          a hospitality
for strangers and songsters: the blind
man groping toward us, chanting
into the noises, cuts a path

through dowagers and worn men,
veterans from new wars done with life,
boys and unwed girls, children
exposed, a wilderness like autumn
awaiting the big wind.

               *

            The towers
of their worship around them, I toss
till, legs dangled alongside its banks,
my first stream appears:

                  those presences,
the Little Lehigh, lounging a long
distance from the lofty Hudson, counting
over and over the wealth of that sun-
squandered day, the hot grass
and prickly slum the air's become
like a strew of new senses.
                        Heavy
boughs canopy waves coiling mid-
forest: satyrs these flashing
cars and burled faces,
melancholy party of pleasure
lusting to be flames bursting
and the sovereign of ruin
chaired on the sun's shoulders.

                        *

Amid the leaves-and-lights we drowse,
and I think of the burning and the brevity:
thirty years now and at least half
eaten away
            (when I consider that Alexander
at my age had conquered so many nations
and I have done nothing memorable,
have I not just cause to weep?).

Shall I, in this sleepy campus,
with the rest having forsaken all colors,
in passivity's pride neither cold nor hot—

these limbs that looked sturdy,
longer than time, consumed
by slow flame—
                not even rouse
(in the camp of Mars, Venus and Mars
intertwining) a wiry, wind-conspiring
smoke expanding into huge air—
wind Shelley forged, blasting tyrants:
"Look on my works, ye Mighty, and despair!"

And Milton's storm, rooted
in the Muses, inspired by his passion,
that, driving two ways, cleared

the sky of corruption, blew down
the devil's horde, evil's harvest—

hinging a blue, god-lunged blast? . . .
nothing shall burgeon from these limbs?

II

Caesar, had the knives
not dressed him with generous wounds
like imperial autumn, not done him
kind service of cutting him down
at his *floruit,*
            would have seen
his vision dwindle, surrounded
by the abiding faces, unctuous, meek,
of betrayal—and broad, brightest
above them all, his own—
                      he who pushed
his name and his terror to the outposts
of barbaric speech, nomadic towns swept
together, till the world seemed
a province of Rome.
                (He was only
the latest, the last, and the loftiest
wave of that tide and that city
that might, had anyone money enough,
be bought, for a time.)
                   At last violence
found its dandy.
               But what of those forces
pride and success little prepare for,
gathering as they winter within him?

Unabated, the sly stream flows on
that first exalted him. His vision
drowned, he would have stumbled
on to absentmindedness,
his former greatness, a stream
of mirrors,

        *

                    mockingly sinuous
before him:
                    Cleopatra
(snug in his best friend's arms),
the barge a blaze of motion, in her
eyes new beckons of conquest
                              (could they,
the never-daring, know, they who called
her serpent, Circe, whore, what splendor
sped in her toils?),
                    the river,
were it Lethe, eyed by her,
caught on the point of wonder,
would forget itself forever
in her memory!
                    (how she came
to me in that troubled dusk, the ships
burnt behind me, hemmed in on that island,
mind overburdened with schemings:
                              my bed
untouched, tucking my gown around me,
I paced the tower: how, wrapt
in a flock-bed),
                    proper vehicle
for one of her trade,

                    *

                    (bound like mere
merchandise, she came: emerging, she fell
before me, raised eyes and a sight
I never dared admit:
                         years and years
march along the scarred dusty body,
past Mars mighty in our bravest fight,
past his most manly nakedness,
upon another front, in different
arms, suddenly to emerge
                         into air
a site of thyme, the fabulous realm
of childhood like a god buried deep
in the heart.
                    My battles, those past,
those recruiting me? Her beauty, her dark

brow bright with long-rooted eyes,
caparisoned rivers and trees.

But what charm was hers let a year—

winter it was, winter within the walls
of a well-provided, sly enemy,
and only a handful of men by me:
I trusted to the report of my exploits;
was I expected to anticipate this?
kitchen conspiracies and vast conquest
idling, nations put by, moldering armies—

attest.
    Death itself to our solemn
employment, the roaring engines
of our siege, yielded its passion,
a pure torrent I, confounded, could
only submit to.)

*

      Seven years Calypso
kept Odysseus by her, seven years
coiled in the golden loom
of her hair and her spell-weaving
body:
    despite his unbroken lament
by the sea, moments, cogent beauty,
must have held him—

        as the Nile
winding—the sly stream flows on—
its mysterious and redolent
source, headlong over his triumphs.

*

And no issue or comment
came of this year as he zealously
carried the empire past the known
world.
    (Beauty was terrible, too much
upon us, sheer terror; and terror at last
denying desire, arresting hate, dictated
an end.)

Even we realized
what he saw in her, our clumsiness
but the rough side of the silken
feelings she spun within us.

              (My roots
held, the first voices, the very forces
she summoned out of me; let a woman—part
divinity though she be—dangle and dungeon
me with a shiny hair?

             What empire
can one pluck from dalliance? Retire
from the world I labored to build?
Man and the universe were
my specialty.

         Hers also, angling
to satisfy her mildest caprice;
like kittens my men tumbled around her,
sucked in as by the sea.

           How long
could any man's back show above this
whimsical will?)

          *

       The sly stream
flows on . . . those few that grumbled,
protesting him caught by an old
salt fish, were jealous or impotent;
we knew what battle our general had
on his hands.

       But we, being
what we were, forgot who he was,
what he had done.

         We could drown
our wounds, our women, all the towns
we spoiled in a cup of wine.

Not Venus herself, though he went
where love's warfare waged thickest,
could distract him long.

          His cleverness
did not fail him, nor his awareness
of facts: his age, his nature
(hardly cut out to be an Antony),

what price he must pay.
So let us say a year was
an heroically short time,
                          nothing
he cared to entrust to the public
page beside the Civil Wars: a year
dismissed, as his whole private life
would be by the future:
                          absentmindedness,
his own as well as the world's:
one day an old man scarcely
thought of . . .

                    *

                    still we loved him,
all his honors and riches—
the vast delicate loot—he shared
with us.
        So the enormous debts
he incurred for the people.
Bribery? Old frost-faced Cato
himself admitted that in a time
like this bribery under certain
conditions was for the public good.

Consider the excess common
in our city, taken for granted.
How many really objected to the war,
any war?
        Only he looked after us.
The same diet he had of hardships
and dangers, avoiding no labor.
Marching, he with us, days and nights
without pause in all kinds of weather
and enemy country, and this just
before battle!
            We loved him,
his shifts of temper, his quickness.
Example he was of what we—common
enough, good with a spear, liquor,
women—could be and in him were . . .

                    *

an old man scarcely thought of;
then as history, futility;
no longer hated or envied;
victories forgotten, doubted
(my own or somebody else's?),
by spittle betrayed, by gout.

Who knows his motives
any better than he did? Ambitious
but the ambition of the mob, his sons
and his sires.
    Only what he thought
he was—the sly stream flows on—
snatched out of his feeble hands,
pushed aside by the glittering,
arrogant, ruthless young man
of himself straining upward,
the world before him and he ahead
of the whole world,
       pushed aside
like a thing for the nursery.

      *

Rather than the slow, unceasing
blades met in the ambushes
of flesh, this death *(a sudden one)*
unexpected, yet a death earned,
made with his own hands, body
hacked by knives he recognized.

Let a bosom-friend *(O traitor,
what dost thou, thou my son?)* batter
death's door, Charon him,
the salt crust of grief clamped fast
to his jaw, over the last stretch
(the stream flows on)

      *

    like the Rubicon
—at his delay a noble-faced stranger
appeared out of nowhere, piping.
Soldiers and trumpeters (I was one
of them) flocking around him,

our general snatched a trumpet
from one, ran to the river
and, sounding advance, plunged in,
saying, "Let us go whither
the omens of the gods
and the iniquities of our enemies
summon us. The die is cast."

Like children or birds quick
to the falconer's call we followed—
into Lethe and into the dark
continuous wood: into his own
blood-finished monument.

*

                   He, last
heart of this bloody wilderness,
struck, became a tumult
of mouths,
         his last will
and long-lasting testament
(the wound in his loins was fertile):
all his wealth, palaces and arbors,
torments and fervors, he left
to us.
     For such a one
should hands that bore deaths,
victories, festivals, love bursting
violent leaves as summer hived
in the seed,
       not be a torch
to demonstrate amid the seethe
of honey poured through roaring
civil cracks (O sociable beast!)
the imponderable dark stalking
the palsied streets?

I I I

          Fittingly
the blow-crowned, arms outstretched,
climax in the royal line, returns

us to a denouement of Caesars:
such the diverse will of an age's lust:

returns as the wheel must,
as the season; one role
a mask for the other: one aimed
at heaven, the other hanged
by the heels, cut down lest they
wither on the bough; in this rack
all crimes ecstatic.

*

        "Those we raise,
risen too high, we seek to humble:
see, he bleeds, is mastered
by such straits as the meanest
carpenter hews his life to.
                  Great men,
time's motley, exceed our need:
consider the lilies of the field,
the common, unnamed leaf.
                 Men, rifled,
the mines dug up against themselves,
founded and scummed and pounded
into the base—battlement,
momentary tower, kingdom
come—of war."

*

        This the way
they redeem themselves, the way
a Caesar charms them:
one moment out of the mire,
the luminous moment becomes a halo
of hate, their knives and faces
flashing.
        O melt all beggars
into the bold bright image—the die
is cast—of Caesar: pour them
(Rome enough) into tribute
of an embossed coin soon spent:
such a thing is Caesar.

I V

We wake, our sleep a falling
mire of faces, a ring and a rack,
the taste of our father strong
in our mouths, sting of his death
upon us, we who bore him,
                                        denied
him, who bore him and broke him,
hating the love he demanded,
the death he proved for us.
Hate is the bright sword
that reflects faces crooked.

What light of noon—the betrayer's
smile gold for it—can tell those who
killed Caesar from those who chaired him?

When we adore love, hate stabs us;
fallen before hate, the dove
impales us . . .
                            was the morning
so different after the killing
of Cock Robin, the babes
in the wood, the apple whose
bite split earth into serpent pain?

V

We, are we not equipt with faculties,
with hands, hearts ("slight he was,
subject to attacks and fits
of all kinds of weakness"), equipt
for the labyrinth as the best of them?

Caesar's chief fortune we were;
he used us, leather, mortar, iron,
battering rams, battlements,
momentary towers . . . we loved him,
with groans were willing.
                                        Confounded
in doubts *(better than a long life*
of trembling a sudden death

and a noble one), cowardice
came to manhood within us.

Is it so much worse, eating
roots like tumors, drinking
horse-piss and rotting water
that shows us beasts, than living
with old inescapable fears?
                What good
hiding in the mountains or rushing
home from the fields? What sanctuary
a world-husking kiss?
                (Behind us
stood the Ethiopian Mountains
of the Moon where the Nile issued,
whispers of the undiscovered country,
and the slinky creatures of Isis.)

Where the heart is, there the muses,
there the gods sojourn, a great
guest in small houses!
                O heroes,
shall one moment of oblivion overcome
centuries of striving, pervert all valor?

          *

Appetites—bitter teeth
of beasts the air, fanged poison
the dust rising, the sea—
grope for shapes.

This our nakedness, our secret
lust, come to embrace us.
                  All men,
breathing as one, bound in one
brotherly season of terror
and hate, in the winter-late
sun falling together,
                  mere son
of man, our hope, our hate putting
greatness upon you, Caesar, govern us
with the whore you espoused.

          *

                                    Very glorious
the city sits in the midst of the seas
worshiping lust
                        ("age cannot wither you . . .
for vilest things become themselves in you,
that the holy priests bless you
when you are riggish").
                              Hear the midnight
streets dizzy with drink, mob of stinking
breath and sweat, loudest at the gates
welcoming chaos.
                        What sheaves
are these, what unity of desolation?
Into great waters your pilots have
brought you, O city; your fairs
are heaped, riches sacked from every
cranny of the world:
                              stumps, like the garden
trim with murder, loom as this proud, blood-
clot city ("sinking into the sea's midst")
of execration, Caesar's last province.

Alexander, the Greeks said, went as far
as chaos. Have we—faculties, desires—
not pushed beyond! . . .
                              those of us
that shall survive this, cowards
(neither hot nor cold), die
a thousand deaths.
                        And yet the core
storm in the robin, is not the hardiest
heroism of all enduring it, its blows
and slights so daily-constant?

                        *

Odysseus at the end,
recalling his toils, the mad
stream he had dared to ruffle,
shed ambition, divine loves,
immortality,
                        and through the ruddy
weather of wound and time sought
a private life and, the sea
settled, oars taken for scythes,
a kindly death.

What better,
amid the sudden flare-up
of berries like trophies
of one's own fabulous past,
than to sit on a mound
     watching
the goat at its shaggy song,
the tragedy so deep around
one is completely part of it,
apart like faun and goat
from history,

    *

like old Rip
listening to those Catskills,
swift-footed mountains of time
moving more subtile than clouds,
the sly Hudson, leaves . . .
      in honeycomb
noon, like women around, they led
out the songs (daily words once)
from cloud and brook, the music
of the small folk and the dances:

in the waters of that falling
melody many faces shone,
time itself idling there
where the suns drink, one broad-
faced Dutch interior . . .

    *

      twenty years
thirty, we wake from our dreams
of the mountains, gradually
leave the green knoll,
     the lordly Hudson,
steeped in a purple cloud, a sail
like a drop of sleep aerial on it,
losing itself in the color-quaking
highlands;
     pass the heady blue melting
into apple green, into grey vapors,
our joints rusty as the shining fire-
lock we started out with

(from roaring
mountain cataract to rutted river bed,
the sly stream flows on); push
through the tangle of birch, sassafras,
witch hazel,
        out into the city,
into the strangeness, a snarling of dogs,
stiff row after row of houses, familiar
haunts of maples and sun once, files
staunch against noon.

             *

        Yet forest-
muffled, midway, the wistful faces
of old desires peering at us, there are
clearings;
        hidden in the shadiest,
shabbiest tree, boughs still thrive,
buoyant with foliage all gold:
                these daily
streets, the church like a rock
dispersing dawn, the young woman
bountiful of flesh, lofty on high
heels, her painted features
turned to the sun,
          prefaced by sparrows
bathing delicately in dung.
Their loves are private.
          But who now—
no interstices to slip through,
the jealous blows coming
closer and closer—shall know
contentments of such privacy?

             *

          Let me go
down, down to the bottom of my people's
bestiality and doom; there on the sodden
floor let me grovel, dire mien

of their dreaming. The gods,
whatever they are, are ruthless,
unforgiving, taking full pleasure
of their punishment no matter

how we turn. Any goddess
Paris had favored, his end would
have been the same. All we can do—
our dignity—is decide

who shall destroy us. Let me,
with my people, spurning the one
talent I have, pull down the temples
and palaces.
        Then at last
the gods will warm us; winter
we can by their ruinous burning.

      *

            Smashed
the gadgets between us and what we are,
the desert of the sociable beast flooded
by the ravenous tide, wide as wind
and snow, of the senses,
            self's animal
breaks loose: the gardener of prayer,
praise's champion: the wisdom
of tooth and claw,
          as in voracious
carnation, rose, these berries
strewn, pursed mouths in the grass,
fang-light and the sea: the star
apart, by strangeness taken in.

Licking honey from the murderous paw,
out in the open, reason made
commodious,
         only then peace
like stone (the lion hot within),
a rising chapel of stone, is reached
again: around it, desolate earth its pit,
by the roseate window of sunup, the flesh
of apple and peach, of burgeoning limbs.

From Outlanders *(1960)*

Preface

"Sonja Henie," the young girl,
looking out of the evening paper,
cries, "just got married!"

"I don't care if she did,"
the mother replies. "She's been
married before; it's nothing new."

Darnel, Ragweed, Wortle

And turning to me, the young poet
tries to say once more what weeds
mean to him—
              luscious weeds
      riding high, wholly personal:
      "O go ahead, hack away as much
      as you like; I've been thrown out
      of better places than this"—

his face just come back from staring
out the window into a day
wandering somewhere in early fall
and a long quiet contented rain,

the sky still on his face, the barn
out there, green-roofed and shiny,
gay in a wet way with its red
wet-streaked sides.
              I read his poem,
mainly about how much it likes weeds,
how definite they are, yet how hard
to come by.
          I say, "Like all the rest
only their own face will do, each
a star squinting through 30,000 years
of storm for its particular sky."

And as though a dream should try
to recollect its dreamer, we look out
across the long highways of rain,
look out

Darnel, Ragweed, Wortle

61

I do not say what we both are thinking
as we see it flicker in that rain-
soaked day: the face exceeding
face, name, and memory,
yet clinging to our thoughts.
                      Black
against the sky, a flock of cranes
shimmers, one unbroken prickly rhythm,
wave on wave, keeping summer jaunty
in its midst.
        And Sonja Henie,
the star, the thin-ice skater,
after many tries, tries once more.

"The poem's not right. I know,
though I worked at it again and again,
I didn't get those old weeds through.
I'm not satisfied, but I'm not done
        with it yet."

There in that wheatfield
of failures, beside all manner
of barns, frost already experimenting,
the slant of weather definitely
fall, lovely scratchy

Darnel, Ragweed, Wortle

Phenomenology of the Spirit

I

When the first grass to be cut,
the season's ripening plot, suggests
the sea, try, though it be risky,
radishes and peas;
        then bid
your children, flip as the breeze is
wide and frisky, sun to daisy,
stamp the ground.
        Last April
you, arms flapping like a scarecrow,
shooed them off your freshly
seeded lot.
        How could you know
carrots would prove responsible; how
could you tell that the spots
heeled would be
        the first—
and the only ones—to sprout, those
akimbo, knuckle-tough carrots,
coming up, tip-eyed,
        cocking
this frizz of laughter cloddy earth
must break loose in a tipsy
wind to know.

II

Hegel, trim, head-gardener
of logic's overgrowing whims, rated
Napoleon the Soul of the world,
but not the Spirit.
        Only as
he came through the process told in
a furrowed brow—Hegel thought—
the cocked hat,
        pudgy fingers
fixed, hidden beneath the taut coat,
could he be regarded real. Ah,
there was more to it

            than even
ponderous Hegel knew. That cocky
curious carrot, half in earth
and half in air,
            blundered on,
thunder's thought and stumpy consul,
till plotting time and place,
his soldiers mowed
            like grass,
wrought changes, trampled him under
to erupt, unhampered, a regal
root, the rugged
            link otherwise
always missing in the all-embracing
mind, that element-refining
sublime, of Hegel.

Sonata Pathétique

Let it be some sheets of music,
molding lamplight into the shapes
of music, and a fly, a last
survivor in this bleak November,
cross-legged on the page, humming
to itself like one of the black
notes come alive.
                              I listen
as though to overhear the strains
of a great green air it once
belonged to, archaic chord. Yet
flicking shabby wings that sparkle
in the haloing light, it sings
no plaintive tune.
                              Ah, fly,
about your composition what can
I say? But moments there are
undoubtedly so self-willed, self-
fulfilling, that the day of their.
emerging glitters, little more
than grit upon their wings.
                                        Then
they, outlandish, zither about
until they find some setting—
sheets of music in a lamplight—
they can be moderately at home in.
But one there was, old weather-
beat, much noted
                              for his feats,
like you a lone survivor, and what-
ever the measures meted out
to him, a dapper dancer, by his
clever footwork never too far
from his true estate . . . a scurry,
and you are purring in our cat.

A Gothic Tale

Framed by our window, skaters, winding
in and out the wind, as water reeling
so kept in motion, on a well-honed
edge spin out a gilded ceiling.

Fish, reflecting glow for glow,
saints around the sun, are frozen
with amazement just one pane below.

Skates flash like stars, so madly
whirling one can hardly tell which
is sky and which the watery floor . . .

one night two straitlaced couples,
a footman over them, rode out
in a dappled-horse-drawn sleigh
onto the river, a moonlit lark.

The ice broke and they—sleigh,
footman and all—riding in state,
rode straight on into the lidded water.

That winter all winter folks twirled
over them who—framed in lace,
frost the furs, the shiny harness
and their smiles the fire that keeps
the place—sat benignly watching.

"One foot out, one foot in,
are we real," thought one, "we who
wander sheepishly in dreams, or they,
the really sleepless eyes, under us?

And every night who knows (a laughter
troubles us like dreams) who skates
(a thousand watch fires the stars)
above, peering through the pane?"

Simples of the Moon

I

Though most people may deride
late shadowy walks in Bronx Park,
spiked railings and stone walls,
crumbling like a chalky skull,
cannot long suppress the will

of a seed. Like you,
Albert Ryder (the thin caul
of a wide-eyed moon between you
and the city, and a field, going
greenly on, its music abysmal,

massive, warm), slipt out
between newspapers, a codfish,
a dried bread, snug in their traps
mice partly decomposed, a lop-
sided pot simmering all day.

I I

These you lived by,
even as you studied inchworms—
any perch for saunters in the air—
from windows in your workshop,
shaggy-browed two casements

commanding an old garden,
kept going by some great moon-
time making trees, shadowing you
like the cat, nine-lives-cosy
in its corner, till things

entered—the wind, the wind,
the wind—that you could see.
Demeanors of the mind they were,
less than the faun scaring
the graces, spicy wanderings

III

like faun and flavor
of some violin, yet instinct
with a valor, innocent of failure,
taking any air as able to endure,
a passion equal to all hope.

To Yeats in Rapallo

It must have been there when you arrived; saints
are not such insubstantial things, surely not
the one called Sant Ambrogio. The paint
upon his face looked splashings of the vat
and what the poor folk of Rapallo rightly
ask of saints; they must be bright enough
to understand base needs, to make their white
as lovely as the sacks of seeds, the love
of goats and olives.
              There he stood, pert
as any drunkard's hope, head askew,
limbs akimbo as a local dance, a skirt
like flashing, wind-backed sea not much below
his vision. The steep slate path to him the course
a stone takes after a bird or a runaway horse.

Barracks Apt. 14

All must be used:

this clay whisky jug, bearing
a lampshade; the four brown pears,
lying ruggedly among each other
in the wicker basket; the cactus
in its pot; and the orange berries,
old now, dangled from their twigs
as though badly hung there.

Like the picture lopsided
on the wall, stalks wrangling
in a peevish wind, yet the crows
flapping out a harmony all their own.

These as well as the silence,
the young woman reading Aristotle
with difficulty, and the little girl
in the next room, voluble in bed:
"I'm talking in my sleep . . . laughing
in my sleep . . . waking in my sleep,"

all are parts hopeful, possible,
expecting their place in the song;
more appealing because parts
that must harmonize into something
that rewards them for being, rewards
with what they are.
                    Do this and do,
till suddenly the scampering field
you would catch, the shiny crows
just out of reach, the pears
through which a brown tide breaks,
and the cactus you cannot cling to
long like that thorny Aristotle
suddenly, turning,
                    turn on you
as meaning, the ultimate greenness
they have all the time been seeking
in the very flight they held
before you.

No matter what you do,
at last you will be overwhelmed,
the distance will be broken,

the music will confound you.

The Greater Music

All things turned to Orpheus' hand.
Narcissi bloomed—and all at once—
the burning loveliness far underground,
then bloomed a retinue of bees, all hived

as in a greater self, intent on hearing
the sweetness of their lives, stilled
in that welling strain; and animals,
rapt as plungings of the sea,

admired in that pellucid glass
what they might be. But only Orpheus,
when the fierce hand plucked his strings,
could not consent to the divisions

of the lute. His breath, greeting
the stone-deaf, eager stones (though why
those fury-flying stones did not hear
and build into a tower of hearing

round his air I cannot tell), delighted
to be ript and strewn like tortured
peace out of that terrible grip,
too rhapsodic for the mortal ear.

Yet as his head drifted down the stream,
the waters touched by that perfect lip
at once were set to dreaming, his course
the music they drank as from a golden cup.

Interview

From haselwode, there joly Robin pleyde,
Shal come al that that thow abidest heere.
Ye, fare wel al the snow of ferne yere!

I

In the sky overcast
                    (with cardinal
          combed, the wood in its own dark
                    middle lost)

faithfully the fires trace their course.

I I

Hunched into the dark (burst of cardinal
close the only chink), feet kicking
up a sough-like, several cry, I shuffle
memories:
              oh the verges, the snug
valleys promptly rising, ever-
green supple surprises with a "high
there!" and a youth upon me, an ancient
popt upon me, rhapsodic air . . .

no shore beyond our own, we play journey-
man to wasp and plum. All of summer
makes a rambling inn so myriad
we cannot prove its end.
                        But quickly
ages pass the boundless fields;
through cracks stony dampness shows,
damp and the rigid years: baneful iron,
gold more baneful, battleways:

III

                              thickets
deepening, the wood in its own dark
middle lost, time's musty smell

seeps through, a muttering of derelict
stars whose brute light briefly
crosses on its way.
          Held in that ruinous
glow, numberless frosts, defeats, old
men's councils and alarms, brothers
at arms quarry out the polyglot dark.

The cries will not be stilled;
bloodshot the water, its rheumy eyes,
bloodshot and seething in every vessel
of wood and stone; toads also, terror,
raining into our beds, our labors,
our most secret loves.
          The land stinks.
It rises, all the dust of it, into lice
and swarming flies: all the bodies
of beasts and men, lice, flies, murrain;
hail tries it, fire mingled with hail.

Then—for the cruelties still succeed,
the cunning: foxes sally from their holes
like lords—an east wind, locust-laden,
a cloud and a darkness
          over all,
the young deaths, a thick tangible dark
like the young deaths—their morning
hardly begun—in its own dark
middle lost . . .

I V

          within myself
I fumble for the stables of the sun,
the prancings there, the blade-whirling,
gem-like pageants,
          as a cataract might turn
upon itself, as moonlight's beast
morning-laired.
          Cardinal coigns
new sight, wind-cleaving river too
that raids the sundry dark deep
past the snow.

Stones I kick
like breathing, white sides flare
as on this grate of glance faces,
each flicker a face (the whole belated
litter of night). Then windows blink
fat, pompy blooms.
Point by point
the stars converse; their fire deepens,
a ripeness, core, of rock disporting
itself like cloud.
Upon the grate,
each grit a shining man, we rise.
Shattered bottles pouring over, children
tumble out, the road one whirling hoop,
a glut of gold as our first age.

V

Lost in looking back? The city lies
before me, a sprawl and rut
that, sweating all last night, gleams
now a salt lick, as much a ghost
as its parasites.
I know this.
Still like him, stronger than truth,
this luminous image of childhood,
in its night-lights of a child
eager,
neither good nor bad, but greedy
for the promise of its own dazzling
appetite, still like him the image
clutches me, a forever lost,
yet in its hope
a forever touching,
noble suppliant, haloed here, brimmed
in the single of my sight
(brisk
as the white-shadowing body
of a goddess in passing,
concert
of goddesses, extravagant hair
igniting spires)
of the overcast sky.

In This Tower

As the sycamore makes one thing
of the wind, and the birch another . . .
as these roses, four kinds of roses,
related in scent, yet as different
as their colors, make in the vase
out of their difference one fragrance . . .

so in your moods by the gamut
of glances, the narrow yet infinitely
many diapason of breath, you make
one concerted thing of the air. And I
by the strength of my senses, great
folly of love that will lead me

whence the hardihood of its caprice
desires, I dare it, this one concerted
thing of the air. And I hold it
within me as I move in the clear
bewilderment like mirrors of its mansion
as the sycamore—its hackles tingling,

deepening with the scent it is
bringing out of itself in the wind—
moves through the wind that radiantly
moves inside it. Linger, I cry,
in this tower, improvised as the flare
of my breathing, as the patterns

sheaved of the birch and the sycamore
in the curious wind, in this headlong
tower of my tuning, this valorous air
that swells through me, bowers round
for the person of you it supports,
enlarged in the song you sing forth.

So moved, I would hold you,
a racing—the leaves more fluttered
than fauns—as of trees deeply rooted,
clouds anchored, massive, ever moving,
the mountains are, I still at last
in the tempest birch- and sycamore-bruited.

A Local Matter

I

But who does us?
Who flexes like fingers, strains
in our sinews that they sing,
one felicitous agony?
These thoughts, these thoughts
thieving through night that things—
even hope and lust everlastingly
raucous—heckling locals
trying to distract us,
fall dumb.

I I

The cat all evening
lulled the mouse, licked it
and pricked it and loved it that
never a moment did it move
out of sight. O the success,
the bliss, the fittingness
of nature there; mouse
recognized its consummation, its all-
devoted, all-devouring heir,
where the future was
suddenly breathless.
Grin, claws.

I I I

Hum of mouths within me:
waters at their loom spinning
out the sea, the lilies
in their velvet skill break
stones, break stems for a somewhere-
rooted, roar-cored wind.

I V

And you, enchanting
the maddest din as winter

pears can pipe the speckled curves
in scented air of summer round,
do you not, like that lady
of the wild things, discover
in your bending
wells, a company of drinkers
borne up by the swell?

V

These the lines
I do not somehow have
to learn; they find their parts
at the moment of burning:
the appropriate pain, the fitting
grief. Meantime I cling
to things that belong:
shag-root of a dog
not the whole world can impress,
the sparrow tucked in the sky
ticking out fall.

V I

And yet the subtle
strings twang into us all;
I think of turtles in a bowl,
their shells like painted shields,
churning upon one another,
each overwrought by private music,
rushing together to one
gleaming doom.

V I I

Now in the lute-time,
soon brute, of the year I
slouch down, the silky lounge
of one in perfect health
(hear the chestnut
gayly crying in its country fire).

I lounge as I wait the advent
of one all sinew and strain,
the lunge. Like a string tautening
to the discords of precisianist
pain, I fit: come, windy
dark, like all the kingdoms
of the North and within the gates
of my Jerusalem set your serried
singing thrones!

VIII

In the state of weeds,
high-spirited undergrowth,
there congregate vast dynasties.
Themselves flashing armor and plume
before the shadow coming on
of the long summer light, locusts
clash their cymbals.
Again and again, mighty in leaves
as Nimrod, the mouse enters
that the seasons be maintained
as locally as a broken fence
beside a yawning dog,

IX

till I, skinned,
glistening, one of many
hides racked in a row, lesser
tale in a larger, from the lean-
to of noon, sink to mouse, catgut,
fiddlings of some nameless bog.
At work religiously, maggots welcome
me passing through, goodwill
from one end of death to the other,
into and through that minerals
know me, the odors use me;
how the hum becomes me,
once and ever the household
word of the air.

Homecoming

I

Like that old-timer who has kept by me
I know the place of danger and of change
and most, most tellingly, when they jut forth
their avid face, the moments that deny me
a staple of the place.
                    That old-timer—
rope bloody through his hands, coursing
as the cordage sings: dog's lope and grace
of the deer, faun like a woman's love,
meat-scent fattening whatever air;

that song also like his chambered bow,
twenty years' music coiled waiting within,
catching on comrades, harnessed together,
winter and summer caught in the toils,
driving the sun, from east to west
one wheaten swath, his goddess winged
in this weather;
                    love likewise enduring
(twenty years not able to take its measure,
not chimerae, not orgies, able to make it
forget) its own lulls and forgettings,
surges of hunger the sea shrinks away in—

that old-timer, buffeted as he was,
gripping twisted planks in a rampant sea,
clutching the last shreds of his wits
against rock and brackish brutality,
saw still this was his native element.

I I

This and not sea-nymphs, not floating
islands centered in a season made of wish;
not noon with air the tissue of a voice
winsome at its loom,
                    spinning out
along the ample warp of boughs a spell
that tangles men fat thrushes in a net,
knots them, fawning claws or bristle set,

in one appetite.
                    Like him mast-pinioned,
flung by stormy words out of the sea,
hot blood in the lungs of a blinded cry
or grist for a bird song they become;
but only his ears open to homespun hunger—

"feasts and vistas of love, the struggle's
gaiety: her voice in all its changes,
in division strongest, ranging over peaks
and losses, leaf-tossed island in her voice"

(like him golden liar she was, lyre
strummed for their amusement by the gods,
loom too in its weaving night and day,
spinning him nearer home)
                              "in our room
the changes come, zodiac in its restless
pride, its creatures here to suck selfhood
from our interbreeded breath;
                              she the sea
under me, dolphins arch a sleek summer
by our side, the poplar and the birch
whirled in their autumn"—

        I I I

                              rooted, yes,
as his old tree, but flowering in open love,
in boughs that branch a household, season
air and crown, as it is crowned, sky-
high change.
              In the top-greenery
the gods, looking down, dumbfounded,
at our strangeness with vast unblinking
incredulous eyes,
                    envy us that we forever
change and, by our changing, settle
in this whirling place.
                        Better driftwood
swirling in the sea, an olive's litterings
over a battered body, than the ample warp
of boughs that snags us—thrushes in a net—
out of the complicated, mortal text.

The Fire at Alexandria

Imagine it, a Sophocles complete,
the lost epic of Homer, including no doubt
his notes, his journals, and his observations
on blindness. But what occupies me most,
with the greatest hurt of grandeur, are those
magnificent authors, kept in scholarly rows,
whose names we have no passing record of:
scrolls unrolling Aphrodite like Cleopatra
bundled in a rug, the spoils of love.

Crated masterpieces on the wharf,
and never opened, somehow started first.
And then, as though by imitation, the library
took. One book seemed to inspire another,
to remind it of the flame enclosed
within its papyrus like a drowsy torch.
The fire, roused perhaps by what it read,
its reedy song, raged Dionysian, a band
of Corybantes, down the halls now headlong.

The scribes, despite the volumes wept
unable to douse the witty conflagration—
spicy too as Sappho, coiling, melted
with her girls: the Nile no less, reflecting,
burned—saw splendor fled, a day consummate
in twilit ardencies. Troy at its climax
(towers finally topless) could not have been
more awesome, not though the aromatic house
of Priam mortised the passionate moment.

Now whenever I look into a flame,
I try to catch a single countenance:
Cleopatra, winking out from every spark;
Tiresias eye to eye; a magnitude, long lost,
restored to the sky and the stars he once
struck unsuspected parts of into words.
Fire, and I see them resurrected,
madly crackling perfect birds, the world
lit up as by a golden school, the flashings
of the fathoms of set eyes.

An Egyptian Passage

Beside me she sat, hand hooked and hovering,
nose sharp under black-lacquered hair,
and body, skinny, curving over a brownish big
thick book.
          I glanced past her hand to pages
she checked; there, beside strange symbols,
curious hawk-beaked little birds at attention,
gawky beasts, stiff plants, which I, despite
rail-shuttling shadows and battering light
at the end of tunnels, gradually made out
as items in a German-Egyptian lexicon.

Then red- and black-brick tenements; billboards;
excavations; three boys with mattocks, digging
by a squat, half-finished, bushy hut;
tumbled-together shacks, drifting in the way
of winter; smokestacks; near the bank,
its wharf rotted through in several places,
a gutted house like something done by fire,
slowly floating (so it seemed) out on the river;

and the dumps, one burning in three spots,
lurid like old passion among heavy, piled-
up boxes and black, banged-in pots, and birds
floating above like ashes.
          Birds too
on the Hudson: ducks in strict formation,
gulls—like lungs—working their great wings
or perched like dirty, jagged lumps of ice
on the ice caking the shoreward waters.
And all fashion of ice, from shoots in spray
to zigzag rows, waves at their apex trapped.

Along the shore a shaggy, red-brown brush,
so thick partridges must be crouching in it,
as in the Hudson, under an icy lid,
a brood of clouds. And heavy-headed, long,
thin, flaggy things like the stuff we think of
growing by the Nile.
          The trees across the river
rigid, bare, through them the early light

already deepened, purpling. As through
the little crate-white houses, quiet enough,
but indoors, I knew, no bush for its morning
birds busier.
           Still her eyes never left
the ibises that fluttered under her fingers.
Deeper and deeper she went, like the sun
unfolding fields, forsaken spots, and towns,
the dirty sharp details of, always more
and always clearer—like the river itself,
the roads agog with golden high-legged going,
song-sparrows swept from their nests, their wings
praising the sun—the steeples, broken houses
and smoky streets, kids dashing in and out
of hide-and-seek, the billowy wash on lines.

And I thought of sitting on a polar star
a million miles away, looking down at this earth
surrounded by its tiny nimbus of a day.
And I saw the days—each hour a speck, twelve
motes combined—like waves like sparks like bushes
burning, lined up one by one, for its intricate
strokes each a kind of word.
               "Poughkeepsie,"
the conductor said as he took her ticket
from the seat. Several times he tapped her
on the shoulder before she looked up, fumbled
for her coat and bag, and lurched out.

Descent

I

At least another time believed
there was an age more golden,
golden age when men could move
the raging beast, the stolid oak,
and rocks like notes upon a lip.

Yes, it believed earth, flame
and river, vying, in reflection
of ceremony-charmed and -charming
mates forgot their differences.

Even time, through woods
and wilderness of cities, down
to the dark iron rungs of death,
forgot.
　　　　Grief humming, agony saw
itself in another light. So far
music swelled.

I I

　　　　　　　Another time
believed . . . and what discovery
was here, those great first days
in woods, in walleyed back bed-
rooms, your lips a live coal
to my mouth, warbling
holy, holy, holy,
　　　　　　　O my Adam
and O the glory that thronged
our wayward dingy dangling town,
each dawn a steeper mountain-
top for the night's deep-
ening climb.
　　　　　　In your hands
songs so erudite they found out
the lordly dances, olive branches,
of my body.

     Kings and queens
like owls and cardinals stood by,
royal lovers, the jealous dead,
that we should have found out
their sovereign secret and come
abed to their godhood, to lie
in such fixed state.

   I I I

     Generations
of martyrs rose, a Francis
shining, hymned hawk-eyed songs
pining to compose the world—

nothing of old, no cold, no wind
or hail or snow, not flailing sea,
not brokenness could withstand
the slight smooth wield
like a long light
     flying,
wild bird crying, of your wrist—
to compose the shattered world
into one field of love.
     O strew
these backroom beds with violets
and rue; fill them with rumpled
cries as of creatures thrashing
in the underbrush, creatures
flashing in the sea.

   I V

     Ten years
ago . . . we have, through strength
and through weakness, through love
and indifference, unerringly come
to this time when we no longer
need—
   at least so we say—
the emulous lovers of old,

that gilded company of kings
and queens, the gold-gross bull,
the snow-fierce, arrowy swan.

The determinate music moves us,
will we or not. Sleeping, awake,
it moves us. We are what we are—
not as we would be or once were—
satisfied. At least so we say.

We have now seen the dead
several times, wrested some pity;
we have come abed like two wooded
children, lost, afraid and yet
trusting,
       wrapt in the sodden
dark, the war and the city-blind
wilderness of windy snow, lost
and yet trusting.

     V

          Let us not
lose ourselves in personal pity,
in private awe. The marks of travel
on us, still some haven there has
been, some truth and some joy
in our journey.
          But loved ones,
time's chimerae sucking them into
what shape they will, melt as dawn
before the black wind.
            Another time
believed? An age more golden
when man could move? That harmony
is broken. The charm flutters
and smokes. Disbelief reverberates
through the hollowness

V I

                    of all space
and time to be confirmed. Let us
not lose ourselves in self-pity.
We have come a long way.

Let circumstance rebuke us;
let emptiness puff up a power
the ram and leopard stamp,
bedded ram and raven of our sins;
and then let evil like an alien
cry over us, mirroring its fixed
and aimless fate.
                    (These people,
these places, that should compose
a legend where truth is met,
where solemnity would know itself
for all the rest performing it,
storm like foreign tongues,
the dark's own voices.)
                            You,
bending—a recognition—to me,
light the hollow, as another woman
led another man to their resource.

In our embrace what comprehension?
Love, the rest depend upon this union
that estrangement by its strength
approves the worth of, and the force.

The Giant Yea

. . . who can bear the idea of Eternal Recurrence?

I

Even as you went over, Nietzsche,
in your last letter, as ever, you tried
to reach him:
                "Dear Herr Professor,
When it comes to it I too would very much
prefer a professorial chair in Basel
to being God; but I did not dare to go
so far in my private egoism as to refrain
for its sake from the creation of the world."

The past before him, the hateful present
stifling no end of futures with noisy smoke,
what could the Dear Herr Professor, magnificently
sober Jacob Burckhardt, do or do for you;
how thrust pitiful hands into what proclaimed
itself a sacred solitude?
                          Maybe too at times,
syringa blowing through his classroom (gape-
mouthed angels Paracelsus pressed into his lectures
in this very room, throwing all Basel
into an uproar and a hatred that finally
drove him out,
                familiars also like a rout
of mornings bickering to swell the retinue
of Dr. Faustus after breakfast), trumpeting
through the profundity of his pauses,

maybe he could let that host, with nothing
to lose in being, be themselves, especially
as there sprang among them heroes out of Raphael
with everything to gain.
                         Even now Astorre
the horseman, in the twinkle of that scholar
eye, spurs quarrying the dark, falcon-plumed,
plunges, a warrior of Heaven, to the rescue
of a youth, fallen with copious wounds,
by this aid exalted.

I I

Alas, for all Astorre's
audacious charging down the margin of the page,
the Professor's age, parading with its Sunday
family-walks and the thundrous drummers of Basel
in trim, upholstered parks, benumbed him.

What was there for him to do who saw
his begetters, fighting men, furious, mighty
in their pride, tumbled to such petty end?

That beauty being slain on the high places
in the midst of its noblest battle, should he,
exclaiming, dare to tell it, publish it
in the streets so prim and polished, to see
the daughters of the philistines rejoice?

He let you go, best emparadised,
or so you said, in the sparkling shadow
of a sword, retiring into frozen heights,
a terrible loneliness, enhanced by sun.

I I I

At the end, rocks breaking their doors for you,
out poured the shaggy men, hordes of flame
and drunkenness. Solitude, dressed in winds
and falcons, rang, a honeycomb of voices
hailing:
          dancer David; Agamemnon, amethyst
with proud and deadly twisting; Dr. Faustus;
Borgia and Astorre, those human hours,
sowing splendors with their wily wrists.

The peaks, much moved, conscious of the love
that guides by the same capricious path as stars
the agony, the maggot's tooth, hurtling
to your beloved town, stormed its arcades
past the drowsiest beds. God was dead,
long live the gods.

In that third-floor room,
still going about in your academic jacket
and down at heel, all the heavens rejoicing,
laughing, lifting up your legs,
into the middle of the rout you leaped,
a satyr's dance, as always, the conclusion
of the tragic truth . . .

I V

You in what we are,
alas, and by your effort that had to fail
have reached us.
And we go, perhaps as the Dear
Herr Professor did, saddened that we cannot
give ourselves,
the Greeks at last, Paul,
St. Augustine, Luther, Calvin too, surpassed
by the resolution—not time could tame it,
not the mob's indifference—of your fury.

A Working Day

After such a day, too cluttered
for clearing and no way out, no way
to grasp this nameless yet pervasive woe,
after such a day turn to *Genesis*:

ponder the sea before the waves began,
ponder bdellium and the onyx stone
(gold of that land is good), the beasts
got of man's solitude, till woman,
aspiration of his breast, is made. One
flesh, time loitering there.
                    Then "Cursed
is the ground for thy sake." The taste
of the brow's sweat mixed with stubborn
bread this Book knows too well;
the fidgets in ourselves
luxuriate, deft creatures of despair.

Not even the flaming cherubim
could hold that garden in, the snaky weeds
and cankers, plotting and complotting,
avid for this their holiday.

I

                        You thought,
Thoreau, to sit it out while your giddy
trivial Nineteenth Century preened itself
to death.
            For a time, like a halcyon
perched on a spray, and only a few steps
between you and Concord, you settled in Walden—
long as the season of need prevailed;
your land's lord, you sat it out, secure
the valors you had witnessed, flight
of the seasons, daily in their several lights
remitting more clearly your singular truth.

Then, bold saunterer of morning, gaze fixed
forever on a fresher, greener time, back again,
more private than before.

II

We, in a wood,
dark, cluttered, just outside your field,
admit by the radiance of what you discovered
there, the order of beans in a row,
the sweetness of your clearing, the blight
of this we wished for: piper, pigweed,
Roman wormwood?
No name can cast a slowing
spell upon that ragtag army, backed
as much as we by sun and rain. We run
through our assets, friends and events,
the whole summer store.
No one, no thing
can help us. Least of all those who suffered,
tried grief and terror to what seemed their end.
We think, incredulously, of our first glossy
learning, our pride: not one of the past,
the great we assumed we could lean on
forever, has a word for this.

The day, slowly, like a blind idiot
picking in a rock-pit he thinks garden,
passes us by.

III

But you, Henry,
sitting there, going your own way—free
in a world of your own choosing, verge
like that vigorous bean crop between wild
and cultivated fields—were you out of it?

Those companions, mind and body, the populated
self you turned to, unctuous creatures bent
on their own careers, were they to be trusted
any more than the rest?
The rift
that should have made us whole, imperfect
from the start, multiplied first loneliness.
One flesh. At the end, foundering in the blood,
you sat it out, watching the inroads
of the darkening wood.

The Generations

(An old woman is working in her garden.)

Bent in the sun,
the long burrowing light on my back. Sixty
summers, thirty Augusts here, all borne
in this day. Look out far as the eye can see,
plain the triumph of the shadowless sun.
And John come to this point again between
seared corn and squash, their rows, wave after wave,
gone over him. Bend to the work, my hands
tending and tending.
Once it was things to be
righted; the dawn brightening to our gaze,
grapes to be propped, their vines, creeping
between our hands, no honeybee's labor
among the blossomings more sweet.
Late noon,
end of the garden John stands, looking out,
grey boy, to his dim grey youth, faded
denim blending with sky. Come to the kitchen
smelling of earth, mixed with lingering warmth,
arms full of the fruits of our toil, the good
we wrest from the earth.
Mr. Eckles, nodding,
passes; Reverend Hout pauses; always
the same text: crops and children, changing
weather. Long days spinning from these veins,
out into the bleached stacks of noon, to twilight's
quilt-crazed colors, tightening into knots.

Still at night, the body laid away,
once again the mind is free and upright,
swift inside the Good Book's evergreen leaves,
serene for breathing lovely Christian names
of that first fragrance—Ruth alone in the fields,
the Child joyous in His mother's arms.
The words, strangely humming seeds, brought
as if by wing from farthest lands to nest in,
swell the mind into an heavenly harvest.

Those words we first read, good, open, falling
away . . . in his father's field as we stood,
earth seemed to look to one sure light. Night
it was, but only night for moonlight, turned
as though to look to us. As I to him . . .

that light a burning dark, the laboring breath:
the face—not his, not mine—to be endured
for saving of souls, the making of men, the fiery
face bent over me. Patience, John says.

There he stands, still as any juniper
that crows might use him for their easy perch.
Shrugs, then smiles after the rugged wings
crackling out, blue-black, as dark's thievish work
inside the light. Looks at me, pale eyes
still flickering with flight, then looks away.

And yet content to stay forever in that
other world; content to dwell in their air,
his father and his father's father beside him,
so he thought; to sit by their window
the whole evening through, their rocker creaking
back and forth in the cracked boards. Content
to keep our boys there.
                                   Here in the town, alone
in this rocky garden, I prevailed. And he
said nothing, not after his long working day.
Keeps to the rocker, book sprawled on the floor,
rocks till the needle breaks inside my flesh.

But how the boys respond. Clothes I make over:
John to Joseph; to William; to Edward; then
back to John.
                     Slow afternoons, young voices
floating out, eyes caught in the needle's track,
I look up to the cries, my boys all noise
and racing. Like wild things they play. The bodies,
rising, hurl against themselves, playthings
in their game, then snarled in the failing light,
spin with the Eckles children and the Kulps
to the dark till each—behind doubled bush
and wall and tree—is only a dwindled sound.
I pull, cry out, summon them, hanging back, home.

The lessons still to be taught, the boys growing
like fields run wild, leaning wherever sun
and wind may blow, whims of the season.

He let it go, and I alone to set it right?
No place of mine escapes, not while a bit
of strength sticks to these bones, bent in the sun,
hands in the dirt, sweat glistening like luxury
in the dirt.
                    My boys, all noise and racing!
Joseph, frail, twisted by every wind,
and William, growing too fast, grasping—Will-
o'-the-wisp he is—the slenderest thistle-light.

Yet there was Edward, he at least strained up
to greet me as I bent. Roots he gripped,
the first bud, certain summer's whole procession—
ripening through his hand—could be dragged in.
My tenacity, John said. My will indeed:
to know, to do, to hold.
                              Read to him,
his face among the pictures—the animals gentle
in their alphabet—like something princely
blossomed there, naming after me
with first clear breath flowers, birds, and beasts.
Day by day his mind more avid, lighting
up whatever feeds and brightens it,
the Sabbath like the morning in a dazzling
river picks its promise from his voice.
The sons of Mrs. Eckles and the rest
poor copies beside him, the Church's speaking word,
his brothers in his splendor splendid too.

Will-o'-the-wisp pride is to light us by!
Once angels flew round men, in their wreathings
hymns, jubilations, to honor them. Such heaven
I thought to bend into my house. This earth
that should compose His word nestling us,
one round of seedtime, harvest, trees and hills
resounding, He Himself came down to walk in
and to hear, still mouth it is, all mouth
that—soft as moth and wren, the velvet rose,
the night in steady whispering—gnaws at me.

Down in the dark, down in the dust like Him
Who gave up all for us. Most given over,
as my garden, alone out here with the shiftless,
makeshift scarecrow. Not I given over.
The trowel, bone-fast to the hand, strikes
again and again. What plant my heavenly Father
has not planted will be rooted up.

But when? Hack away, with each blow
sweat turns to silvery coilings that, sprouting
fiendish numbers, eat themselves fat in my sweet-
smelling fruits.
        Even as I work who gloats
behind me but these weeds, my sons going,
slips of my will, who but the devil gloating
through these shoots, my sons, their petty thefts,
deceits, his glossy leaves, and whorish books
wherein his good luck lies.
        And Edward most.
The endless smut he sneaks into his room,
bird and beast and every creeping thing,
like toad-bunched idols at their hideous
delights, befouls the altar, my scoured vessels.
The sacred gift of God, His breath, our lovely
words, forced to couple with the serpent's
hissing blasphemies, their black spawn flaunt
upon a public page.
        Good books, he says,
our age's greatest, as in the Gospels heaven
singing in them, the Maker's world. Compare
such with God's chosen! What the purpose,
where the promised end?
        Silken words
to set off filth. O how condone "the snot-
green sea"! Like slugs, their slime smearing
over the shiny leaf, twined round and round
each other, one writhing brown obscenity.

Rip them out and rip though some good go.

And Edward there—pages crumpled in my hands—
O let me not think of it—to see the face
of that fury in him, flaring,
as behind him in the doorway flares

John, and all the gloating weeds I thought
I'd plucked, rows on rows, wave after wave
going over both, the Garden—leaves just before
their fall—crackling flames.
                            Only such slugs
can cross this rift? Pull down, stamp, they speed,
devouring, through the fields.
                            This ravage Eve
first birthed, Satan, spreading plague, the slugs
pitching far-flung tents even as they
turn the world to dust. They are what they
were meant to be, faithful their brief hour
to their given task.
                            And Edward no less faithful,
already begun the lifelong desert journey,

myself striding, monstrous, in his meanest
deeds! I reach out . . . he that is without sin . . .
not even him the late chance, the last hope, gone,
gone out of my hands . . .
                            my father rejected,
the first Father, and my youngest, father
of my future . . . are they to be merely
unfolding, thriving of my wretchedness—
my sons, my sins!
                            Flesh knows a will of its own—
weed. My will beyond my will, how much
can two hands do? Patience. The patience forever
demands. The husbandman waits for the precious fruit,
and has long patience for it, until he knows
the early rain and the latter.
                            But when the rains
fall so fast, so full, wilderness alone
prevails? Must we feel our way back all
the way of thorn and rot to glimpse the anger
of the flaming angel, else we push
God out of us, God altogether?
                            This separateness.
It stretches through words, chores, my mocking steps.
Clutch as I may, will nothing bend to me?

Lilies lolled on the breeze, the lordly hollyhocks,
more glorious than Solomon, they toil not,
neither do they spin—like him out there,
flushing the light. Nor the gnats, a gossamer,
heating in shameless lust the last of the sun.

Light failing at last, for all that I do,
down on all fours in this crowded bed, worm
and the dark, conspiring, leer at my back
(Eckles, Mrs. Eckles, oily Hout),
the glittering, unregenerate stars.
                            Look up,
old tattered scarecrow. Sky is earth, these weeds
white sides, tarnished, of a truth unending,
of men past ruth and time.
                            Patience? Forgive?
Blow, hack and pull that a clearing be made.
Pluck the weed out, pluck now, or let flesh go.
Else why a soil with hands and mind, a will
of its own, if it must yield?

A Lesser Prophet

And here, the sun begun once more,
groping with me, bleary-eyed, through trees,
the wind, leapt into the forsythia,
its leaves a blowsy sibyl's tossing, rushes
from its midst a fire-snorting dragon-
fly;
     and as the codger next door cackles
to himself—then was he up all night to start
as early as he did disgruntling my sleep?—
that Greek in the flopping pages of my book
on a little boat, the Pteroti, is en route
from Piraeus to Poros on the trip I took.

At once he, white-haired, homespun, kilted,
white-wool-stockinged, on a whittled stick,
the breathing of his bitten crags about him

(Meet? Not we, not in Poros, Athens,
or Mycenae. And yet that Easter morning
as we climbed to Delphi's summit,
on the way, lambs turning crisply
on their spits, were we not greeted
by the gravely smiling patriarchs
at this work?),
          speaking, spreads an air
for flutes, children, fire-nimble lambs
and bees:
          "My father was a prophet famous
up and down the mountain. Next month
I once more practice what he taught me.
I am, so to speak, a lesser prophet.
Still people listen.
          The first six days
of August represent the twelve months
(the morning of the first day is January;
the afternoon, February; the morning
of the second, March, and so on);
then I note the little clouds at dawn,
the streaks at sunset of the heavens
and the wave-sown sea, the flocks
with watery bells welling over cliffs.

Looking down from my house at the ripples
of the moon, I shall observe the shiny path
of Venus, listen in the grass to crickets,
stow away certain phrases from my dreams.

Three days fasting, I keep strict account
of every leaf and flower falling due,
of dishes broken, those utensils lost,
the name of every child that hurts itself
at play.
         On the seventh day of August
I tell my family and the neighbors
what to expect in weather and in every-
thing.
        No tiny portion of the year
escaped my father. But I do best only
the first six or seven months."
             A decided
comedown? If only I could count on things
I see six or seven days!
         Still what if
the sky refuses to open; and if it does,
only fills with farther sky; if the bird
stubbornly sings robin, and stray words
from my dreams even as I touch them
melt like tracks in snow?
         Summer's air
supporting flutes and flowers, crickets chirp
in key, dishes briskly break, and children
hurt themselves in play.
        And pages
flapping in the sun enable me, O mantic
words, to be with those I never met
an instantaneous one.

A Trip through Yucatán

You have, in a sense,
been through it all; each experience
has known you, like a Swiss clock
in the middle of the room, forcing
all things to its rickety breathing.

Abruptly then the one out
that you see—rather than swinging
in and out, forever, on a crazy
and precarious stick, pretending
to be another hour, another place,

one of you for one time, another
for the next, and never meeting—
the one out is a breakdown.
Then all things can, with a sigh,
forget you . . .
                    yet after days
of snow, too swiftly falling to be
accounted for, in the middle of it
a moon appears, absurdly beautiful
and warm . . .
                    like the dinner-
party you have just come from where
the speaker assured you your French
accent reminded him of his trip
through Yucatán:
                    a group
of Americans, a few Spaniards,
and several French, all insisting
they understood each other's speech;
only he, interpreting, knew the truth.

Madly, the epitome of tact,
he hopped about from one to the next,
trying to keep their ignorances
from them . . . I have stopped jumping;
and moon-wise, in a sense, arises

that last, implacable light-
heartedness, like emerging mid-jungle
into a jubilant calm, a clearing
of florid birds and plumaged flowers
that set the feastday of the storm.

Godspeed

. . . *blood*
That has not passed through any huckster's loin
Yeats

Huckster's loin? Butcher, peddler,
their god and kingdom jogged among pans
in the hump on their backs. No poets,
no prophets, no hard-fighting men.

Canaan enough the curded milk-
and-honey of their mouths, the groin's
leaping houses, lusty jokes a drench
against drought. Huckster loins

indeed and every weakness flesh
is heir to, whatever idolatry this seed
gropes out, industrious, to survive.
But though no statesman heeded

my forefathers, nameless at best,
I am not dismayed. Several were wily,
calloused fingers capable in the pockets
of the world and clutching willy-

nilly, with the gripe of Jacob
for his wrestler, the slippery scruff
of living—call it God. Rejecting manna
in the sky, they eked out covenants

catch-as-catch-can, and no more
binding than a rainbow, with the desert,
took curses, blows, as the rocky base
to the pleasures of their day.

And when their sweat mortised
the pyramids—straw cribbing stars,
between life and death the jumbled bones
composed the imperial corridor . . .

no blue-bled shades these men,
not an outworn, story-ended royalty,
but spawning supplers in the spring tide
of the loins, gorged as the sea.

House of Fire

I

To burn is surely bad, to be
possessed by greed or lust or anger . . .

Down the pathway pebbles clatter
into brush more ashen than the rocks
that mount the cliff; beyond it windows,
flaring, flood the light through vines,
entangled with the thudding wind,
as litter, crackled underfoot, puffs
up the dust of countless little deaths.

And yet in the abandoned field
below, through this intense decaying
and its acrid breath, a freshness wells
as if an April, some forgotten day of,
starting up out of the time's debris,
look round amazedly.

I I

The man
Job squats among the soot and ashes,
his complaints mingling with the smoke.
He sifts with peeling fingers cinders
of that once his boundless joy:

sheep, camels, oxen and she-asses;
seven sons, three comely daughters,
the tender dewy branch unceasing who
guaranteed the generations of his name
as of his various unique features;
and his fame gone through the streets
a bounteous morning to proclaim him—

these sift, soft flakes, breaking
in the flurry of his cries.

III

Yet what lust or greed or anger,
what burning in this house of fire
beyond what becomes a man, that man
who girt up his loins according
to the Lord's command?
                And sifting
flakes, he strews them in a drunkenness
of despair about his head, the last
fruits of his efforts, the folly
of all living.
            Surrender all,
the Whirlwind says, whatever endeared
you even as it made Me dear to you.

No less lovely than the first arriving
leaves at falling; through the nakedness
the mighty music, unmitigated, enters.

Dew all night an ice upon the branch,
the cedars cleaving in the wind,
like a huge flock gathering
in the boughs, each tree achieves
its height the moment when it crashes.

IV

And yet that leveling Wind
did He not summon as witnesses
His freckled, much-loved creatures,
numberless as leaves, yet loved
for individual, self-willed features?

Mane flamboyant, hoof and nostril
bristlings of the mine of fire,
the horse that, leaping forth, saith "Aha!"
no less to battle than to pelting hail;
Leviathan grown tender, weltering
out his rage, the boiling ocean docile
in waves self-absorbed—

these, springing
like the hurricane, soft cooing words
around His lips, from God's own fingertips,
warm with them He warms, exult Him surely
in the grandeur and unique particulars
of their pride.

V

Sky and earth
are held in a twilight's rushing
furious fire, earth and sky the route
of pawing hoofs, till all the colors drain
into one conflagration.
But here
as I pause on the little wooden bridge,
the waters, shielded by two arching pines,
needles heaped below, purl into a cat's paw.

Coolly the ripples from one side,
pursuing their dappled course, are crossed
like a shuttle by ripples from the other
till they pour together—yet still
themselves—in the next step
of their streaming.

V I

And so the sea
is fed, and so the fire, the rampant waves
and flames flared up in stubborn homage
to their fathering first desire.

Gunsight *(1962)*

Gunsight

(An interior monologue that records, through the voices in him, the sensations and memories of a wounded soldier undergoing surgery.)

Squinting after morning, like a sentry
on a mountaintop, you lie. The hospital
sheets bank round you, drifted as your sleep.
And midnight, come and gone, ghostly in swaddling
snow remains.
          You wait who would be one
with the flowerbed, stretched out in the court
below, one with your leg, a frozen block;
summer it mocks, bundled in that vase,
the roses choking in the oppressiveness
of their own breath.
             By such route morning comes?
Now lies, flight fettered in the ice, wedged
against the pane, as though a pulse throbbed there.
And somewhere, hiding a few stubbed wings, your Robin-
Hooded Wood, leaves fallen like the fairy
tales you stormed through, fumbles in the wind
for berries, fuzzy low faces you once picked,
oozing from your fingertips.

*

          Yet lie here
stony as you will, time, unabated, whirls,
its stars more wily than the dark's snowflakes,
inside your flesh.
          Even as you drowse
the corridor starts up its echoing.
Morning blue-lipped on her rattling tray,
she, white-breast, black-capped, -winged and -clawed,
arrives. That gimlet look, how far it's come,
like something out of snow. Bent over you,
snow peering into snow, arch, starched,
stiffest nun she is.
          Be quiet, she says.
Quiet to heal this feverishness? Scraps
of peace, placid nights, best baiting, rouse it,
greedier as it feeds.

*

Needle-plunged,
the room begins to rock. A January
hillock knees, unblinking snow claws up.
Down corridor's funnel on a swooping knuckled
cloud, the suck and buffet of the sea.
Doors worked by whisper's hissing draft
swivel you to a crackling wilderness
of lights, explosive glare a gash of knives,
one vast black-lacquered eye.
Snowy masks
bent over you, voices flaking, falling,
falling, through the seasick smell

breath in

It's cold. Faces, walls fling up at you,
cavernous waves, snow-kneading hands.
Oh fie, that smell

breath in

deep
past breathing, stench of bodies rotting.

Distance, many-hooded, sidles in.
A mountain stoops. How far it's come!

Through the crack shapes, muffled, flickering,

Can't breathe!

For crying out loud, cut the shaking.
Want to wake the whole damn wood?

*

Voices,
billowed up and down the air, prickle
everywhere.

It's only sticky cobwebs,
twigs wrapped in mist. You got the gun.
You said you wanted to hunt.

                          Something, skittering,
flaps against your mouth.

                        The dawn wind blowing
up—will you look at that lake skedaddle!
Don't be a scaredy-cat, a momma's boy,
scrounge down; keep your eye on that crack.

There in the trees like morning, dew on them,

sparrows by the trillions,

                          squabbling,
the dew's own shrillness,

                        and a giant one,

the sun,

          see that in its beak?

                      Wings spout.

Now's the time. Charge!

                        Summer pitching
in its leaves, the wood a wilderness of lights,
of one bird zooming through another's flight,

what are you waiting for? Shoot! Shoot!

bullets ricochet—the flock like hurtling
stones—against each rock, each tree.
                              East,
west, the breaking lake, its waters lashed
to wings, all, echoing, roar.
                          Across the gunset
heavens redbreast day is falling, flushed
and falling,
            body through which morning sang.

                      *

Only a handful, take it.

It's still warm

(come, my love, and lie with me)

still struggling in your hands.

You wanted it,
now it's all yours.

Breathless, July storming
the mouth

*(we'll lip to lip in mastery
enlarge the airs our senses sing,
the hanging gardens fingers bring)*

and through the heart the heartless sea,
oozings from the fingertips,
that eye,
that glaring eye,
won't close.

You can't
get rid of it like that.

Still it stares
through feathers twirling, tumbled over drifts

*(the hills and valleys
hovering, the seas of love)*

down slippery
peaks to their blooming summit time . . . lolled
on a herd-browsed cloud of clover,

Laura!

*

*(Inside this spinning bed we rove,
delve into every treasure trove.)*

From her hands and mouth it swells

(In coiling
warmth we lie that love, untoiling,
forage in us, finding, share
its raptures in our blended air.)

Exultant, love, the looter, slams its waves
through you.

      (Our honey-suckled kiss
plucking us, we blithely crest
the tide; like a sprig in the beak
of a dove we, soaring, wake)

            to fall
head over heels

      (into the clover)
closing round.

      (Roses ring us, sweet sighs
mixed with ours.)

      Roses by a field, choking
on their breath and on the wrangling smells,
shit, groans, the rattled gaspings
on the ground,
      her hair alive, hissing,
twisting, rush of wings,

      (that glaring
rigid through your eyes!)

      The trees loop over,
tangled limbs, lips, cries . . .

          *

      reeling,
caterwauling, night hauling you to rocky
port, the sailors weave you in as they
are woven round with heaving breasts
and rouge-fixed faces,

      Birdie, Gertie,
Madge and Meg,

            making light of midnight
stark, mouths like wounds,

                        she wiggles,
hot stuff, sizzling on a spit,

                  sinuous
smoke, twigged and shagged with ice,
hands looking after, horror
in such white hands;
                and slyly winking
from your polished shoes as on the needle
in and out the olive drab, crookback
of the journey, tracked through cloth
like thread; its knotting torments.

                    *

Swept out in a reef of faces,
                  Mother
weeping, Father frowning, preacher, teacher,
foamy with questions

                  (say, how many feathers
on a ruffled breast? its songs, its load
of flights, where do they rest?)

                  Shore recoils,
dawn shipwrecked in the toppling clouds,
the breakers of a handkerchief, the cry
spun out into the heave and tumble of the sea.

The black ship, drenched with slops, tosses round
in sleep that mumbles, tide-like, over them;
the sea itself gliding, ghostly dreams,
below, a thousand men smuggle the spoils
of continents,

            souvenirs brought
for Birdie, Gertie, Madge and Meg,

triggers clicking; helmets; like a lidless
eye the ruby Joe hacked off a finger for;
and tight-packed voices, babbling lucid
as these waves,

snug in our packs
with brush and comb, tooth by jowl
with Gertie snapt, the spicy note,

they try to read between the scribbled lines
as in the sea; time billows to a white
unbroken, daze like drifting mountainous
snow . . .

*

weeks on weeks of olive-drab waiting:
dumped in a crummy town, a game's loose cards,
the crumpled dreams, the tattered jokes,
the hands stuck like a clock's.
Over the barracks
sparrows flying, sun reaped in their wings
as in the trumpets of the tootling band.
And by the drill shed, never breaking ranks,

soldiers, fall in; count off; now cock your rifles,
aim and . . .

flocks on flocks, dragging the world
away, a great wind blowing up behind,
round and round the company goes, shuffling
a million miles in one small khaki circle,
while dance fumbles after limbs, the pinup
slumped to rutted eyes,

come on,
boy, it don't mean a thing
if you ain't got that swing,

legs cast up
and away in the jig of war, the reedy piper,
death, blows through the lusts, the memories,
you and the rest lice sizzling on a leaf
in the wind's lull,

aw, I'm stuffed to the gizzard
with shave, shit and shinola. A roll in the grass,
that's what I'm for, the water far below
a bare-assed shimmy

(we crest the tide,
high on a jaunty worldwide
sprig in a bird's beak)

                         sweeping back and forth,
billowy heat . . .

                    *

              two-bit sweating Anacapri,
a morning long, a leaf. Sun sashays in
and poppies razzle-dazz under its feet,
grapes, plums and dames panting to be plucked.
This is where July shacks up.

              The town,
dangling from its mountain slope, a fleece,

it's a sheep's life all right, stinks like a goat;
but you got to admit the flock, flooding
down the hill, is flashing in the sun,

its backside in a clump of olives, teeters
on three lopsided streets,

                    wash smacking out—
and what a sail, a whale, a zeppelin maybe—
the baggy drawers of Poppa Zookie. His cheeks
popt with grins like fish flopping in
a net, the town, its kids and dogs, yipping
at his heels, he grabs us with his smoochy kisses.

And down below, splashing up,

                    the fat-assed
washerwomen,

             blue-backed, sun-whacked waves.

Smack them as you drink this vino, singing
O Sole Mio, sun blinking boozy through.
                   *
Now summer gluts, July hunched down,
relentless with its whorish herd of never-
closing blooms, its gasping days, the sunlight

raspy with the muck it's lapping, turning
into dust.
　　　　Dust everywhere: those old men,
squatting by the cemetery wall,
the world, its past, deadweight upon their backs,
like ghosts of ghosts wheeze up their ancestors.

Go digging down inside your dust, one poke
you're through.

　　　　　　The pebbles crunching underfoot
are bones; in moldy crusts, in cheese each munches
on the dead, wine gurgling down the throat
their guttural blood.

　　　　　　　　You think your town's so hot?
Smoky coal-and-iron dump, day and night
it vomits crap on everything. In these
old boys still many a jig is kicking up,
twisting through the dirt.

　　　　　　Twisted
bits of women, broken from the start,
these ancient wraiths, heads bent together, sigh—
black shawls like shrouds—through fingers,
bony needles in the middle of their web.
Their keening and that steady low-down roar,
the hordes complaining in a too small bed,
a voice, the past's, more nettling than war.

　　　　　　　＊

Grab the jug. A couple more steps up the hill
and, there, you're out of it. The wine,
the babes, that's the lake to dive into.

The knoll waiting, knees bent for an outing,
the war folded away in the light, a dog-
eared history book to prop the table, folded
away like paper ruins, the calendar
of shattered days and nights ript out,
of scattered cities dropt, the countless lives . . .

　　　　　　　＊

the nine lined up,
              the dunces,
                        faces
to the board at the teacher's order,

                              order!
Chalky days remote, humdrum as school,

secure as home, no bug snugger
in its grassy summer,

                         home? its stances
and pretences . . .

                    your Father can sit still,
hours on the stoop carving a peg leg
for that chick. But what time does
he have for us?

                    (That's the boat, Son,
I promised you. Take this paper, fold it
here and here, it's ready to be launched
to dare whatever waves the Creek can blow.)

Listen to your Mother; don't go near the water.

(Puff a mouthful, off it scoots.)

                         Phew!
A cargo of your Father's pheasants, pigeons,
cuckoo Noah's ark.

                    (Trust it, Son;
speedier than any line you draw,
McCreedy's Creek whips you into the Bay
of Biscay, Venice, and the open sea
where the West Indies dance like spicy leaves
upon a tree.
              That bobbing isle's the hideout
for the likes of me,
                    old Captain Kidd.
But first we got to shoot

            (no time, supplies,
for prisoners, soldiers, line them up,

the nine . . .
                the dunces, faces to the wall . . .)

bang, bang, bang

                    (tangled limbs,
lips, cries . . .)

                shove them off the deck
and hurry up; the shore, the morning's
just a step.
            Now jump!

                    It's too rocky
to land, too deep and dark.

                    You got the bird,
a gold leaf in its beak, to wing you to that
sacred spot: treasure buried where
a limb sticks out.
                My wooden leg'll stamp;
earth rattles and they pop.

                        (Watch it! Pigface
Sarge
        old Pontius Preacher
                        Teacher
                            is bearing
down on you . . .)
                        *

                Teacher scrawls a curve
upon the board and, Columbus gayly bobbing,
it is Spain, refuge of the dawn,
its winter gardens blossoming; another
wriggling stroke
                (like Pocahontas Susie's
pigtails, black and snaky, and her shaky
two-way jiggle as her garter, smacking,
sends you, sends.
            Now snap it.)*

117

Something's breaking
loose!

(only a flock of quail, Son,
winter white-hot, nipping, at their tails)

The world whips by like smoke and crumpled papers
from a train, scraps of cities, distance,
stuck to it, the crazy seasons wrangling.
And your country, spooky in the sun
with highways: miles and miles of no one, nowhere,

(better stay where you belong, Son, holding
on to what's your own,)

secure as home,
humdrum as school! That's not the rule you learned.
Even as you pledge allegiance

to trickery
in the cloakroom

whatever's clutched
soon snatches out of hand.

A face looms over?

*

Out of dirty books and bodies—lice sizzling
on a leaf in a wind's lull—the Facts,
acrid with their beetling look, the chalk

who dared to scribble that nasty word across
the board?

sour old teacher stinks, ink
and droning voices, sex and summer hum,
as through the barred-off window you are brightest
scholar of, remote in daylight swarming,
Gooseberry Hill lifts its violet text,
then tips, like birds wing-propt, rippling twilight—

Susie's eyes that wink at what she's thinking—

and into the woods it dives of crow-quilled words,
dumb now like dizzy numbers rubbed off the board,
erasers beating, puffed into a cloud
of chalk, into the dark and into the stars
as valentines are cheating in the desk.

*

There in the empty cloakroom the Milkman's Son

I'm an old cowhand

                 is skillfully working over
the pearl-and-ruby, eighteen-carat movements
of the Jeweler's well-set Daughter.

                              Get her
in a corner: you got a hell of a lot
of catching up to do.

                (In one second
I will teach you more than ten Dogfaces
can in a million books and a trillion years.)

Use this map, the pieces like a jigsaw
fit. That's the clue. You're getting hot.
The answer, treasure, 's at the end of that.

     It's Love, LOVE, L O V E makes the world go round.
     Get into the spin, boy, be jet-propelled.
     Here are the curves, boy, from which to spill.
     Here are the swerves, quick trip to the moon,
     He who won't take it's an ass-faced baboon.
     So come on, boy, kick your feet off the ground.
     It's Love, LOVE, L O V E makes the world go round.

(Just like your father, borne by every breeze.)

*

Her garter, snapping, starts a swell that rams
the air—a gap in nature—people popping.
Smoke and snowflakes craze the sky. An engine
batters on the tracks, its lonely nightmare
whistle shrieking, moaning. Midnight slouches
down the street.

(Or is it morning, stiff
and glazed,
　　　　the crack,
　　　　　　the narrow crack
where day and darkness meet?)

　　　　　　　　The recess
crams with yelling Polish kids.

PHEEEEEEEEEUW! There he goes
Momma's boy, Momma's boy
pants like a hog,
grunts like a frog,
can't turn around cause
he's stuck in a bog.

　　　　　　Mid-winter
dark, a thousand corners crouching, keeping
terror bright, a genius, it, coiling,
leaps.
　　　Run!

　　　Scaredy-cat, scaredy-cat . . .

　　　　　　　　　the cold

deep past breathing

　　　　　　is ripping through. Slopes
sliding under you, you stumble,
　　　　　　　fall,
　　　　　　　　　roll
like a snowman
　　　　　round and round
　　　　　　　　through drifts
to their blooming summit time. Everywhere
a peak frosting your roof, snow-lapped, earth-
lugged, leaf-snug berries, tangy through, the oozing
fingers of Gooseberry Hill . . .

　　　　　*

　　　　　　O.K.,
boy, grab that bucket and let's go.
Susie, you come too. We'll pick the big
fat berries on the way,

through
these thorny bushes, over these rocks,

these rocks
and rills, round templed hills: high time you learned
a thing or two.
Hunch down. Clutch
the hillside, kid; you're Jack in the Beanstalk.
And by the maple, trying out the seasons,
sweaty summer red-faced at the fence,
when you reach the hilltop

it's muddy here

and Mother

(listen to your Father: you
can trust me; be a man, Son)

your turn's next.
I'll warm things up. While we plan out maneuvers
in the barn, you play soldier.
And like a sentinel stick to your post;
anyone who sleeps or runs away
is traitor and must die

(must die and die

and die)

if someone comes you know the signal

her garter smacks

(count off, cock your rifles:
get ready, get set)

march

(then we drill
and drill till trees salute and birds—the redcoats
are coming, beware, beware!—stand at attention
mid-air)

*

see that white inside the door,
that gasping through the straw, the tickled cry?
Those hands reaching out,

horror in such white hands!

(twigs and sticky cobwebs . . .)
come on, scaredy-
cat, now's your chance. I fixed it . . .

(charge!)

Fee, Fie, Fo, Fum,

(the signal)

thrashing in the strawy dark?

I smell

Oh fie, fie!

the rutted sweat, the blood

Father, Mother!

(What's eating you? You got away.
It's only your own tracks hotfooting after.
Now, still oozing bloody from your finger-
tips, the batch of berries that you picked,
jam them in a jr, baptize with spit.)

*

Right behind their fuzzy low faces who's that
pushing through the bushes?

(a scarecrow)

shapes
like men of crusted snow, numbers slipping
from the night's blackboard

(a rash of stars
marching up Gooseberry Hill)

the Polack kids

(the nine, nameless, faceless, lined up)

snarling charge.
                    Your lunchbox clattering,
they corner you, pinned to the schoolyard wall.
Terror, lean, a genius, croons, the world
one giant wintry glare.

                    Give them your apple,
sandwiches, the cake.

                    Still they come.

There's more to you than that:
stumbling up the hill, throw them your gloves,
your hat, your coat . . .

                              get him,
                    fat little four-eyes,
                    teacher's pet,
                    momma's tit,
                    poppa's snot,
                    one cent the lot,
                              get him!

                    *

A shot rings out; the wood a sortie of dark,
trees loop over

                    hunch down and hug

                              (we all know
what you two are doing in the dark . . .)

faces, passion-twisted, flicker down the street.
Behind them, sprawled like crackling bugs
fallen from the corner lamp, the millhands
on their porches grunt.
                    Belching fumes,
dumped over their lumpy wives, they roar along
the chutes; through the molten heart of the mill
faces heap

            which way did the little bastard go?
Get him, get him!

                    Figures, hurtling, ricochet,
cries of fire,
          Father,

              where are you?

engines stutter, crushing iron cars,
the sputtering shells crashed over us,
light on light is breaking through . . .

              *

(just one step more we reach the top.
Hey, soldier, look. Behind that tree,
that scarecrow's come alive.
                 He's scooting
up the hill. After him!)

              Guns glint,
the world slashing like sun on water,
faces flaring, plunging.

            (Watch out,
he's turning. Shoot, shoot I tell you
while you can.
          Atta boy, you winged
him good. He's falling.
              Wait for me!)

His black eyes shadowing, his arms outstretched,
he's clawing through the air, into the dirt,
the rutted sweat, the blood, words spluttering,
caught by that endless moment, face to face,
horror in such white hands,
               and Mother,
Mother slumped into your arms!

July clogged, hunching over you,
a glitter as of snows mixed in with summer;

far below, the same light striking fire
from the waves, the black-shawled, wintry shapes,
bent at the town's one well, beat their clothes.

              *

Snow blinkless in his eyes

(the glaring rigid

through your eyes)

             the lightning on the stock,
the morning, focused wholly on you, lock:
the vast unblinking icy look,

                   watch out
for the gun!

          the lightning on . . .
                can't see,
I'll smash it,
       (don't use your gun for that!
All spies got to be taken prisoner.)

No time, supplies,
            the cake,
                 the hat,
                     the lies.

Strike it, crush that glaring eye forever:
the blow,
         again
             and again
                 and again . . .

how many men you trying to kill?

*

                 A shot
rings out, a sortie of dark,

              (hunch down and hug . . .)

crashing iron cars, sputtering shells,
a thousand clashing knives, burst round,

my leg!

       into the dirt, the groans, the rattled
gaspings as you writhe.
                   Frank, Frank!

For Christ sake, got to get you out of here.
Throw your arms round my neck,

                             not so tight . . .

down through roots and rocks,
                         a hornet's seething
mill,
    a beak.
               It stares ecstatic
over you.
               Oh the black lake's stuck.
Across the gunset heavens, redbreast day,
flushed and dripping, feeds a pulpy weed

    the roses by us, sweet and . . .)

                   *

                       choking smell.
A body lurches, cold, stiff, flight fettered
in the air as though a pulse throbbed there;
from some far mountain spring, a common source,
the drops, coursed through your eyes, mouth, breath,
collect.
          How cross this great divide?

                        It's only
the narrow crack where day and darkness meet.
Grab the bird and stamp;
                and as the earth
begins to rattle,
          jump . . .

                  cavernous waves,
the heave and tumbling sea . . .

                  here's the boat
I promised you . . .

          east, west, the ship
is tossing; billows clamber summits over you.
The ship is hoisting

    skull and bones!

                     And those
that smiled—

          butcher, baker, teacher, preacher
undertaker—

        swarthy faces, snarling
at the rail. There's nothing you can trust . . .

that bird, its gold leaf lighting up the way . . .

                *

You zigzag like a furled-out, wind-flopt moth.
The breakers, toppled, hurl you onto roaring
rocks.
      The stooping, ice-capt mountain shatters;
upright from its evil-smelling cleft
figures flit like smoke shot from your breath
straining for blood to cross the fuming gap.

Darkness belches round,
                a wild-eyed scream,

how dare you come below?

             The nine, shapeless,
nameless, mist of dreams clawing, charge,

no, no you must not drink, not you, not you,
your face, twisted, shifting with every look,
don't make me see it!

          Having chosen this,
you have no other choice,

             each wiping out
the last about to speak . . .

                *

           Frank, Frank!
how have you, a wound for mouth, sped here?

Not by what the flesh can do; your breath
North Wind enough, swifter than your black ship,
I, timely as the rites of spring, arrive.

127

Through these many months and through
the body's dead-of-winter?

> *Through body's cold*
> *and dead you build your winter.*

> Lament is nearing;
> swollen cataract, weeping wails . . .

*

your name!
The waters, surging, mouth you.
Flesh gives,
white-capt voices,
the Shrouded Ones.
Something sucks

(forgetting boasts them all!)

each act, each thought.

Expect to keep that churning pulse, the dark's
and time's, their rancorous secrets, hid forever?
You its one supply of breath, an instant crop:
woman gabble, dreams orgy-fleshed, the dead,
recent and old, fierce by their former fairness.

*

Mother, why do you, pale as hoarfrost glimmer-
ing on leaves, my blood upon your lips,
appear?

> *Well you may ask. Not even here*
> *can I embrace you. Your blood you call it.*
> *Your father's blood! Even before your birth*
> *its stranger heart, wrenching itself from me,*
> *sped off with him. Else you would hear*
> *my cry in every drop.*
> *Yet rightly your question*
> *belongs to me. The pain I knew above*
> *sufficed. I ended it. I am here now because*
> *I wished—no less than have—to be.*

Help me,
Mother.

Those outstretched hands cannot be meant
for me. Dead I am and, as you are,
dead to you. Much better so than waking
old torment.
                    But why pant after two deaths?
The dark haunts you as it haunted me.
My hunger, like these tears, real
in a shadow's eyes, groping, goes on.
And shall until you feed it in yourself.

Why do you who would never let me go—
talk to this fever, Mother,

                    but now
no mistake of shielding can be made—
by your own blood, first drunk of me,
I tell you—against the trials you have
to go through still,

                    tell this aching
a story as you used to, make it let me
go—why do you avoid me now?

                    Try hard
as you will you cannot touch me, any more
than you could, even in that final moment,
call me back.
            Farewell, farewell.
Much as mist can wish, I, once your mother,
wish you, still my son.
                    When, the last time,
I hold forth my hand again, you will
indeed be much embraced and, so gathered,
ever stay in me.

                    *

            Oh stay.
                    But who
are these following you?

                    A mow of women,
faces flashing, most naked of their names
as of their flesh. Not only those you know
but glamors of time your mind cohabits with,

imagination's grossness. Mainly those
who, trusting, gave themselves to you.

And do: as flakes they come, your breath
the blast that whirls them round
as once it failed them in its falterings.
Now through your will working their own, fierce
by their former fairness.
                              Last and fairest,

Laura, driving them!
                        O why do you,
like a new moon blazing through these clouds
it chars, lour at me?

                        Never can I forget
That moment's forgetting; see, it boasts
them all! This time you shall not leave

How bear that thrashing in my hands?

                        *

Even as we lay there, summer's aim,
the roses and the lambs become an ambush,
tenderness, the very moment that
it rose in me, drove terror near, a cold
ferocity, nimbler than the morning,
climbing your eyes . . .

                        don't go; don't forgive,
and so forget, me.
                        Wind slipt through my fingers,
smoke in the gust of her own sighs,
                                    she's gone.

But the others do not disdain to drink of me!

Who are you would batter your way down here,
and with your body on? No breaking bloody
bones, no tears of yours, can tide you through.

                        *

Faces flurry—fevers, buffets—against me.
You pale kingdoms glimmer as from a vault,

like cinders struck: my ancestors, all jostling,
peer.

    Not forgotten! The hacked and crushed,
as ashes recognizable, yet voices fleshed,
their gaze, their gestures fixed in speaking only.

Through the mist calls flicker:
                    my youngest dead,
the few I began with, many days feted,
stuffed like hay-fat oxen, then struck down
by a single blow as one butchers at stall
for a wedding banquet;
                  through the gashes fumes:
rotting breath of festered years, youth wasted . . .

                    *

aether through the suffocating flowers,
high in this narrow room, banked on a cliff
of lilies, a waxen body lies;
                the tangled
keening, birds beaked in my ears; the dead
weight aching in my hands,

                    birds, trillions of them,
and a giant one,

            the sun,

                through rushing trees

breaks loose

        and so do I,

                headlong as always.
Frank, wait for me.

            You're the one won't wait.

Round and round you, chortling, leap. The moment
a scampering, rowdy hill, the sunlight sweeps
the boulders on both sides of us like beams
in its abounding will.
            But time won't wait,
the slender body thrashing in my hands,

that and the sly elated betrayals, sweet pain—

worlds and years between, what can I do?

of helplessness . . .

         sinewy moaning winds,
salt-mouthed as the sea, O do not snatch at me.

       *

Striding like anger, a shooting star, Father!
why do you refuse to look at me?
You're not dead.

      No more, no less than he
has always been to you, scared of a truth
he might have taught.

      The openness: light
explodes. Help me!

      Worlds and years and fears
between, what can he do?

      He rams right through me.
Father, why don't you hear?

      Get out your hacker,
whack the old bastard, cut down the beanstalk,
the golden pecker,
      into the mouth and eyes,
that cry,

    the body struggling, warm

        (fumes
as from a slaughtered calf)

      face gone out—
still it stares—that eye, that midnight-black
unblinking eye,
    O all of them and all
these faces, clustered, jutting out, jeer
at me.

Break them, smash,
                    the lightning locks,
the world clots on the butt . . .

                    *

But the trajectory of that blow—how easy.
Fellow soldier, since you dare by act
and suffering to come this far, hear one
who knows and so can speak for all the dead.

Gone down into the harrowed, ice-gouged soil,
clods clutched in the ruts, the hammered looks
and screams, smeared on their mouths, in time crop
forth, grape- and lilac-fleshed.
                    Back now
with a naked truth the living are—even
with this hand clenching the sodden dog tag
round this neck—too sight-lashed for,
                              like you,
the keeper.

          I?

                    *

          The blow, beating the face
together again and
                    as I watch, a glitter
coils up, hissing, licking at my foot,

like something out of earth and out of snow,
you the keeper: father, mother, children
and their heirs—ghosts you must bear into life.

Oozings from my fingertips, all make,
heart's hammering,
                    the facets of one eye—
Father, Mother, Frank, the Shrouded Ones,
and . . .
          you, the one I killed, barely covered,
green still in the earth, storming through
the others!

          Only by this many come:
through your efforts to avoid me, home.
Shun as you will the violence in each thing,

most violently in hand and bird's bright-morning
song, do you think hiding long preserves?

No treasure for us past what we have buried:
passions, loves rejected, banking up
their light and fire in the earth like restless
gems, the bird, the gutted morning, mouths.

Lie stony as you will, relentless time—
its stars more wily than the dark's snowflakes,
their fire needing to be fed—still whirls
and, unabated, will inside the flesh:
pain seeks you; doubt and anguish yearn.

O do not stare at me with such desire.
Shall the wronged, wrong itself, know love?
Please take this, drink with the rest and bless me
with forgetting. Let me go. Through the earth,
and into me, have you not probed enough?

It breaks me

        like the gun-struck thing I am.
Admire sores, black gaping gums, these sockets
filled with nothing.

        No, no! do not stoop
in this fanged light

         *

      a wedding
banquet . . .
      picnic . . .
          fumy with manure . . .
it's roses, love
    (it's Love, LOVE, L O V E)

that frizzled grin, your eyes like owls, raking,
thrust a shiny darkness through me
          out
to a clearing—
      you, Father, Mother, blending,
bob, carcasses sizzling on one spit!

(Love makes the world go round)

It's bending over,
goading them . . . I don't want to see it!
Don't they know I'm here?

*Love realises
nothing but itself, cares for nothing
but itself.*

The mouth, the wound, the beast
all tooth!

*

Who, hissing like wild fowl, a storm
of sickles bristling through my side, are you?

Tribes of tens-of-thousands your blood recalls.

Fie, ravage, crime, decay reek from your mouths.

*Your frauds' familiars, those you sped by,
those who claim the life you've long denied.
Try to escape? So ingrained are we in your glance,
its far end clotted with our hair, looking
away draws us nearer.
Out of your breath,
crushed voices, trampled scenes, journeys waiting,
generations grating in one seed,
we burgeon now our summer's withheld might.*

Where the end of terror? Fleeing the furies

hauls them into sight.

The beast at me,
the tooth!

*

*Through the length of your whole being
know it, feel it; then go, look after my life
and yours. That snaky head, a kindred too,
you must not yet confront. Nor swaddle in,
sipping the maggot's milk, homespun of spider.*

*Some things—the crag, the granite sea, the slug,
this mouth that grinds incessantly in you—*

135

cannot be turned into the human. All
that we can do is try, while we are men,
to meet them humanly.
             That time will come
when it must come, the time that does not seek
us out by name and does not recognize,
forgive or smile.
             Now I, having served,
return to earth that bore me of which I am—
in all these years of wandering and dread—
return. You too return, to these I leave,
the living isle, the human hour.
             Where men
in cunning pass the wily fox, in skill
of greed exceed the swine, dawn also dwells;
still dawn tracks out her dancing-floor.
The night involved, the Hunter on his knees,
see the great flock nestling in that song.

Remember me and these, but locally,
like lilac, iris, thickly clustered grapes,
and in conspirings of wind and sea.

                    *

Remember you? Nothing can be forgotten.
To be a living vault, inheritor
of all your griefs, spring brings flowers to
and summer chokes with plenty; to feel them
thrusting over me, the roses, puffy
with my breath.
             Yet woods in every leaf
look away; even as I touch, in pools
blue-lipt water chars.
             How can I push
this body to the top of my corruption-
crammed and -trammeled journey?

                    *

                         The hillside,
rubbled cries, is tumbling down. A green
man, giant as he rises,
                    something monstrous
out of snow,

stalks reach out, July
bristling bayonets in shocks, a bellied
commerce, everywhere suckling a dead man's bones.

My name

I never heard!

multitudinous
in skittering leaves an autumn long, cicadas,
twisted sounds, in hail of skillful winds,
handling your black ship's shrouds.
By such gear morning comes.

Back now

as the earth once pivoted in your wrist

into the motion, complex music
of the Pleiades, one with Orion,
rounding up his game he once pursued
and fled, like bees herded into dawn.

*

The ship pitches, giving up one last
concerted cry,

no less than men and beasts,
sky and the creature sea ride in its hold
as in that cry,

slows to his bed.

Slobber
in every breath, through the hissing aether,
bit by bit, finger joined to finger,
the bird is gathering me.

I twirl in its beak,
a seed, a twig, burst at once into a wood,
the dawn perched askingly among its limbs.

Through the mist and through the hard scrutinous
light, thick flakes whirling, faces shape
again.

Soon, the window thawed, its frost
like mountain flowers strewn upon these day-
heaped sheets, the world, barefoot in my eyes,
as walking to and from my bed, once more
begins.

From The Medium *(1965)*

The Medium

Fog puffed from crusted snow, rain sputters
midnight over them. Her words, a kind
of browsing in themselves, rise, cloud-bound,
by him in the bed.
                She says, "I know
now why I have no memory. It's come to me,
a revelation. I must keep my thinking
open; I am not, like others, scribbled
all over by whatever happens."
                      He answers,
"Revelation? That's what you've always been
to me; by way of you have I not slithered
under the skin of things?"
                    "Cleansed of words,
my fears and doubts cast off, the fears
that words invent, I see each thing, free
at last to its own nature, see it free
to say exactly what it is."
                  "As for our primo-
genitor," he chimes in, "beside his twi-
lit doorway, bent after the long day's chores
on the seraphic visit, meantime calling
things by their first name again."
                  "You won't
believe that people waken in my sleep
and like the moon, self-enlightened, speak
a language I don't know, move in a language
so itself one needn't know."
                "Dreams,"
he nods, "do such things, like you attune
the dim as well as the emphatic phrases
I live in, the world become a bob-
bingly translucent globe, that round,
piped like Aeolus' impassioned winds
into a tiny bag,
                then popped, grape-
sweet, upon my tongue, for you beside me
sounding its fanfare. Such cornucopia
your lip and hand."
                  "How you do go on!
Unless you curb these peacock speeches you
love strutting in, how will you ever hear
another's words?

Now listen to me. My father
lives again, in the special space I keep
for him here in my sleep, as he really is,
nothing but his fundamental voice,
directness daylight always must obscure,
cluttered as we are with long dead habits
and with failures, rage, my own and his,
encrusting us."
            The dream flushed on her still
addresses him through her without a sound:
"The time will come when your time comes;
the role meant for you slamming shut,
none of your wit, your artful dodgings,
able to hide you then, each thing you do
at last will prove effective, like a lion
grinding through your side."
                        As moonlight
brims the fog, he hears, in books lined up
around them, richly scored, a honey pouring
through the words, the language passing
speakers, too imperious for words.

Paradis Perdu

To cram one's mouth with other men
and hear the rattling of their spoons
in speech, to order wine that in the foam,
the evanescing of their oaths,
a hairy hand reach forth, cocksure
that apples, did they ripen into talk
of that maledicted day, would mutter so . . .

I

In a capital, for centuries
in fickle words itself,
yet new to us, we walked
the narrow, furtive streets
incognito as gods. To be
the middle of a world

    unseen,
        unheard!
                Winter
full-blown in the wake
of nuns, gamins scurry in
and out, all secrets shared
in lingua franca of the wind,
rubbing up the naked trees.

Through the limbs we go
into a prickly privacy
and out to lovers bedded
in the park, rehearsing
April, fruit, and lark,
those by whom the story's

told: pupil Héloïse,
Blanche, the Lily Queen,
burning Joan, all passing
—a *bon jour, bon jour!*—
through the Arc de Triomphe
as Paris and his lady did.

Paradis Perdu

I I

And cosy as a pair
of clover-snuggled katydids,
we ate choice meals, drank
fervid wines, consorted with
a siren music * and, the gods
no more divine, made love

that incredible first week . . .
then the days fell dumb;
we rambled in a crumbling
tunnel of the endless length
of all the backward ages
of our ignorance: hoary

gullets cackling winds
for words, the winds blew
through each thing, blew
things back to a time
before their names; acts,
untaming, turned on us

till even the moon,
piling up its gritty banks
in our back room, was X.
O the stumbling icy miles
like Sanskrit swarming
under our noses. We were,

I I I

there in Paris (our mouths
frozen crocks, mirror
stuck—odd faces staring
back—much like the dandy
on the wall, ever near
and ever near, yet never

* A cabaret, celebrating in a series of acts famous books of poetry—*Les Fleurs du Mal, E. A. Poë, Alcools, etc.,* climaxed its show with an extravaganza, a Gallic version of *Paradise Lost.*

touching his love), the inside-
out of the Puritans—unhappy
farfetched comparison!
For there in a strange land,
horizons red, flamboyant
red, the fowl flying

bedizens only temptation
said, our forefathers
hoarded antique breath.
Believe! Red men, the dead
of winter, prophets, fuming,
come alive . . . terror-

nested, huddled one
against another like poor
blackbirds carrying through
the Great Frost, honoring
their losses, they survived.
Still the Word came down

and broke like flaky
crumbs east winds puffed
into turkeys ruffling, full-
mouthed plums. The twistings
hived the movements, good
morning, of God
                    cocking
      His green thumb.
                    And O
the crowing under the rose-
bush: somehow children
in that creaky hothouse
under the long, stiff noses
got themselves composed . . .

This it is to mumble other men,
to wander through their lands and times
naming that you've never seen or done.
Yet spot the boats at rotted wharves,
unloading crates at night? Squint
for all you're worth: smuggled goods
from barbarous interiors hove into sight!

Clothes Maketh the Man

(to be read aloud awkwardly)

How hard it is, we say,
how very hard. Clearly no one can say
these cluttered lines and make them
stride or make them stay. No actress
in the land—the best have tried—
can find a pattern or a rhythm
in our day's befuddled monologue.

Concede, I say, a role to test the mettle
of a Bernhardt, who, wigged, without a leg
and in a ragged voice could—so they say—
strike any rock-like audience to tears,
this with only the alphabet.
                    Maybe,
you say, maybe. But then the alphabet
by Racine, no less.
                    And I am depressed.
Ah me, I am depressed to think how we,
with many more outspoken words, submit
to mumblings, silence, only answer
fitting our despair.
                    How hard it is,
we say, how very hard, to find ourselves
stuck in such muck.
                    Oh well, I say,
maybe when we haven't understood
each other long enough, that muck will
harden into a stuff that we can carve.

Already Goya knew the sharp rebuff
of nakedness. With nothing between
he almost wrung his naked Maja's neck,
as though he'd stuck the head of one girl,
a much beloved, on the body of another
(for less aesthetic uses, say), and they
would not set, not in the daring solvent
of his paints.
                    His Maja draped was
a far different matter. I say, I never

thought I'd prefer a dressed girl to one
undressed. Even for me, I see, it's later
than I guessed.
           So let's go home to bed,
Renée, and dress and dress and dress.

A World to Do

"I busy too," the little boy
said, lost in his book
about a little boy, lost
in his book, with nothing

but a purple crayon
and his wits to get him out.
"Nobody can sit with me,
I have no room.
                    I busy
too. So don't do any noise.
We don't want any noise
right now."
                    He leafs
through once, leafs twice;
the pictures, mixed with windy
sighs, grow dizzy,
                    world
as difficult, high-drifting
as the two-day snow that can
not stop.
                    How will the bushes,
sinking deeper and deeper,
trees and birds, wrapt
up, ever creep
                    out again?
Any minute now the blizzard,
scared and wild, the animals
lost in it—O the fur,

the red-eyed claws, crying
for their home—may burst
into the room. Try words
he's almost learned
                    on them?
He sighs, "I need a man here;
I can't do all this work
alone."
                    And still, as though
intent on reading its own
argument, winter continues
thumbing through itself.

Lizzie Harris

First a rabbit died
and then a crow.
The children knew they had
to go the measured way
of funeral.
But Whimpy
got the rabbit first;
without the creaky comfort
of a hearse he popped it
into kingdom come.

So crow was left to find
its lasting room and board.

The weed-lost graveyard
just behind his house
a likely spot,
the oldest boy picked out
what seemed least occupied
the longest time, a plot
most fitting for a crow.

The name upon its pocky
stone was "Lizzie Harris."

Then banging on a pot
to beat the band, he led
a four-man funeral
to cries of "Good-bye,
Lizzie Harris, good-bye!"
as the youngest, dragging
Lizzie by the neck, brought
up the rear.
But Whimpy,
having sped one parted
guest, stayed home, intent
upon the welcome-mat,
to pay his full respects.

And so, unruffled, Lizzie
found her final nest.

In the Round

Catching yourself, hands lathery
and face ajar, inside the glass,
you wryly smile; watching, you know
you're in for it:
              and in the twinkle
of your eye the horny butting goat
and jutting horny bull, the weasel,
goose bedraggled, and the wren
with greedy bill go flashing by;
there too, recoiled as from the shadow
of itself in a teetering pool, claws
contracted to one cry, the spider
crouches in its den.
              What gusto
can it be that blows its violence
through a locust's violin, mad summer
burnishing in such midge mouths?

These the routine heroes, poised,
in resolution black as bulls,
deadlocked like a din of warriors
grappling centaurs—prizes near:
a heifer nibbling grass; the rouged
and gossamer girl, nothing diaphanous
as the fearful hope that flits,
a fire's touch, inside her breath,
each prize forgotten—on a vase.

One wonders how the clay withstands
not only time, but what its hands,
great hearts, command from one another,
art and earth, the audience amazed.

Still, though clay crack, necks
break, twitchy as a cock, they stand,
engrossed and going on, a Bach
of a beetle, strutting like a yokel,
nightlong at its tongs and bones.

Studying French

some thirty years too late
(the rhythms do declare themselves,
the glints, through clumsy clouds,
through stiff-as-frozen clods,
the flowers in their revery),

I, who love our English words
and loll in them against
the several terror and the cold
like any little furry animal
grown cocky in his hole, begin

to understand past supple words
the language you and I grope
toward and, reaching, wander in
among the periods of doubt,
those long, benumbing nights

when ice caps seem to travel
us at their own stately speed
and fury like a moony beast,
a speechless, glacier-capable,
goes poking its rough tongue,

so searching, into the crevices,
the weaknesses, of everything.
For one long given over
to another tongue this French
is much too hard. It makes me

doubt myself, my easy hold
on everything, and everything.
I who debonairly strolled
(I rallied them, I twitted them
with double-talk) among my words

like one among his animals,
once wild, but now their strength,
their rippling colors, blazoned
on him, can smell once more
the threatening smolder, smoke

behind them, open fields so fine
for pouncings and hot blood,
the void in flower we go out
to meet, hand clutched in hand,
as it ransacks us for its tutoyer.

White Elephants

Alone except for one bowlegged, bounding
cur whose yipping scored the frozen world,
that afternoon we tracked the neighbor grounds,
two people and a dog in a sprawled estate.

The snow before and after, trees black
above it as below, had molded to the dips
and curvings of the ground. Winds too like drifts
folded round the stubble sticking through.
Beyond, the Catskills, blue under blue-honed sky,
humped, recumbent days on days forsaken.

Following the road-bend to the coach house,
we sidled through its doors; there considered
its first inhabitants—their shiny flanks
and tails, their whinnyings and oaten smells—
could they be seen in oaken panelings,
hoofs clattering still upon the stony floor.

Out of it, we skirted the old mansion,
these several years fitfully alive, lurched
to one side for the weather's shifty weight,
its corniced cherubim and cedars, carved
in cedar, mostly shed.
                        The formal gardens
wholly formal now, their fountain billowed,
snowbird struggling in its ice-jagged flight,
the Hudson just below had banked, a moonlight,
freezing while it fell, one rigor mortis.

As if fearing those the storm must satisfy
(the stone-pale woman in the alcove, arms
set round two children, and a dog beside,
caught in his friskiness as in their spell),
we went no nearer.
                        But winds struck us, fluster
at the pane of flakes off rubbing boughs.
Or was it blur of frantic beckonings,
now less than thistledown upon the blast,
a curtain flickering the moonlit-shoulder-
shadowed waltzes, glimpses of the Danube,
as from a time that closed with the passing
of the last great lady of the house?

Yet never closed:
                        cracks pried by children
and damp cellar kin, relentless for their chance,
the house shook, shook out its occupants
to quake again with merriment of those
for the first time enjoying total tenancy.

And O what marrying was there, what free-
for-all in mirror, spider, paired-off drapes;
the letters, scattered in a corner, wound up
with ants and wasps, fern's ramifying mind.

The seed in itself after its own kind,
in each smuggled the deeds (stowed away
below as in the rafters' crevices
bats, dragons, pigweed) that grew the Garden
beyond itself, flowered above the Flood:

crimes, failures, flowering too, the first root
must have journeyed through to this, the cluster
it would become, too heavy for the tribe,
smoky over purple as of some sly episode,
a rainbow tangled glistening in its foliage.

And still the rickety mansion stood; the little
dog, yipping round and round, snuffling out
huge footprints, lolloped over the curving lawns
till the mountains swayed, a graceful, trunk-
entwining, cloud-behowdahed two by two.

The outgrounds rallying, the stallions that
once galloped here, cows nodding in their stalls,
the bugs and mice tucked in their cranny darks
like jewels gleaming in a mummied tomb,
all seemed to fly to a single joyous yoke.

And clouds for twilight flushed with riches.
Days on days swept in a rush, at once
the dirty snow went bright, those first tracks up
and down the dips and curvings of the air,
brown shoots off like till-now-drowsing crows,
the flake-doves off, no perch for their feet
beyond the stubble waking in their beaks.

Into Summer

Some days ago, to stop the leaping
weeds, on both sides of the path
workmen scorched these fields.
A short time after, as he passed
the charcoal-velvety, zigzag tracks,
he smelt the strange blend of the
burnt and the growing.
               But now,
just over the black, something flags,
green flicked here and there,
but mostly a transparent papery
brown, like stubborn ghosts caught
in the fire and yet come through,
nodding as though to say, "This is
as much as we can do."
               And he who
tried to pierce the classroom tedium,
to move his students to a grove,
a clearing where the green remains,
recalls some struggled into words,
then fallen back, eyes flickering
a second as though caught with sun.

And they, like one's best hopes
and feelings, singed yet wrangling
through, knowing nothing but the need
to go on, into summer?
               Soon,
of their own greed and by the tangle
of numbers, the weeds will do
what the greasy fire was meant to.

But now each must heed the music
mumbling in him—in some crazy way,
on top of the brown, green sticks out,
and a whitish, tiny kind of flower—
that strange blend of the burnt
and the growing.

The Web

for Hannah Arendt

High summer's sheen upon all things
that dust is glazed and I am lost
within the florid scene, I think
of someone stitched into a complex
tapestry; and sitting in a niche—
five iridescent crows a crown
about her head, held there no doubt
by thread run through their feet,
but held as well, or so it seems,
by what she does and what she sings—
she stitches too,
          as one should sing,
absorbed by what she hears, so sing
the more, her glance, entwining
in her work, lit up, that radiance,
high summer's sheen, be visible
and piling in a telltale foam
from her shy skill, that all things
eagerly like stars around the moon
attain their story, listen to it,
from her lip and hand, her settled
will; and still, as she is nested
in her craft, like dolphins leaped
above their element, she spins.

Ah, let this be a lasting omen:
the world a moment takes its blessing
from the sleight of hand of woman,
and by our passion held in common,
as we when we were young, our limbs
air-borne, bore leaves and ballads
of the birds, the clouds and storms
and all the world beside mere flower-
ing of our singled sigh;
              thought
nothing of the skulking, not yet
lowering gloom such opulence must
shed; nor thought a wind, until now
banked or spent among our breath
with our consent, a gleaming shade

in our design, would, blowing,
blast the web—torn also by the tatter
crows, fled far beyond their thread-
bare wings—and, last, its instruments.

Two for Heinrich Bleucher

A Satyr's Hide

I

In smoky light the students gawk
at plumage reeled off from their lips
as the speaker, groping, breaks
through words into some other air.

But one, apart, till now squinting
through the fumes he tries to fan
with a heavy lilac cluster, jeers:
"I am not difficult enough, not
like these by apathy alluring him.

He thinks persuasion can convert
them into peers, their dust at last
alive as though, bestirred, the gods
were laboring within.
                        And see
the grown-up men he hobnobs with,
artists fuddled as their paints,
perverts, crackpots, moldy peddlers
of moldier ideas.
                        Nobility
and truth gleaned from shallow swamps!"

I I

To see the divine matters, the stars that,
foiled by some events and fouled by others—
wars and trials and deaths—serenely shine . . .

one, old, bald, mottled, with a flattened beak,
bulbous as a growth under a toadstool,
in dress a bumpkin, barefoot in some kind
of fit ("not the sign of contemplation?"),
and in the middle of battle, one-legged, day-
long standing like a crane.
                                    Or, chortling away,
joining ragged kids at hopscotch ("who's
to say wisdom itself, shirt bunched round
its spindly shanks, was not skipping too?");

one with striplings, especially the handsome,
in any wretched tavern, rattling up his heels
the whole night through, relentless, prodding them
("beyond themselves, in chase perhaps of some-
thing only glimpsed, that last ferocious joy").

And then, cock crowing, nothing more to do
than watch the boats bustling at the wharves,
the bales and slaves ("spices like nodding winds
aroused, with distant names and places puffed
from sails. For him Athens was travel enough:
do not the stars each night arrive, the gods,
if incognito?").
                        One unfit for public office,
jester, gibing, bitter toward his superiors,
in court and out, using a lingo, slops
from gutters still fresh on it, that flays alive.

Spellbinder too, throwing those who dare to hear
into confusion and dismay as though
to say their lives were nothing but a slave's
("for the many follies over which they, failing
to see through, toil, turmoil themselves"),
so making it impossible for them
to go on as they were.
                              A man to be trusted?
Little more than the lover he played along with,
drunk ("who ever saw him, wine unmixed,
goblet on goblet flashing like his wit,
inebriate past the intoxication
of ideas?"), in very drunkenness
("of love") proclaiming him a grotesque, Silenus,
preceptor of mad Dionysus.
                                    ("Remember

what those curious, carved figures stowed:
a muskiness deep-wooded, weathered leaves
keep, frolickings among the fauns and dryads,
deities at their numerous delights.")

That favorite pupil, crowned with violets,
bright ribbons dangling, wayward under splendor
like a fire, sprung full-panoplied
from the master's head and thigh ("full-panoplied,
as he himself admitted, had he heeded
that sage reclaiming him to his best nature
he forever fled"), with other young bloods
launched on matters so divine, might tread
down Athens, shiny pebble in his reeling.

("Might indeed: sealed off as he was,
his beauty dazzling, only havoc fed him,
deadly respite from his golden curse.
But the other realized without the State
and the lovely haven, sovereign polis,
of its language he'd be worse than dead.")

The old one—imagine it, death just ahead,
eternity approaching ("a sense of time
for everything")—amused himself by taking
for the first time in his life to verse-making
and the flute ("a Paean to Apollo")
and fables, appropriately, out of Aesop!

A satyr play ("the true philosophy");
so cast him, judged by some the loftiest crag
in cloud-capped—temples like clouds; roads, markets,
rumbling with beauty—fastidious Athens.

"Never forget he did not have that hide
for nothing; shaggy capering, its goat-dance,
rooted him wherever, the course he followed
on the flute.
       Risk it was no doubt, a star
standing out in the open, confidently
twirling about itself, risk or that real thing
sometimes called folly, notes laureling his head;
yet earthiness and the mystery therefrom
never left him a moment:
               divine matters."

I I I

The lilac spray, plucked from one
peak of late spring, resilient still
as the words move through it, seems
to tingle in his hand.
         A deep lilac
breath, the speech in it the air
for ancient voices, rising, rousing
coupled shapes, he sees what man
might be,
         man finding out his place
within the frieze, a marble, braiding
heroes, gods, and satyrs, creatures
confident in flight.
         And in the drift
of words he lets the cluster sway,
its top clump heaviest for buds
closest together,
         still unopened
as though the life in the lilac
had surged through this stem
and on the way, tarrying,
         burst
into flower, then sped to the top,
but cut off before it could gather,
hung there,
         nubbly grapes or the plume
of a boy smitten in his first encounter.
Purpler they than the lavender open.
Yet the words soaring, he half expects
these last buds to respond.
         But death
always more on them, like lids that,
nearly lifted, now certainly would
not, he watches the lilac following
the laws, the scent gradually waning,
the head drooping.
         And when the speaker
stops, that one apart offers it to him:
"If you will take it; I have had it
this hour. The gift, you told me once,
depends on the receiver."
         On the receiver,
but also on the giver who,

in that delicious hunger of giving—
the last, the loveliest, loftiest love
of all, the light and scent of a self-
rewarding joy—gives with no notion
of reply.

The Wine-Skin Foot

> *Loose not the wine-skin foot, thou chief of men,*
> *Until to Athens thou art come again.*
> —Oracle of Delphi

I

The wine-skin foot?
Well as one can he hides it, hid it most
when the land where he first found it
turned into a howling wilderness.

A growing wolf howl, steady twister, blew
through Berlin into Paris. And he saw it—
tyranny, what he loved crushed by the treason
of the state, at last full-blown, bloody—
countless death to stay.
                    (Did not his gentle
friend, to save his son from bestial-
ity and worse, kill him?) Words and deeds
there were, the gods, sacred freedom, dance
and song to smuggle out.
                    The Delphi in him
urging him on, four times over by choice
a fugitive, barefoot through mud and rocks,
the flinty cold of more than half of Europe,
living on wild berries, roots dug up,
raptures of the hunted:
                    in certain seasons
thrilling as ever the pain inside his bones.

Cast on this shore, the language of his youth
much like the rubble of the world he fled
and foreign phrases, stubborn on the tongue
as new terrains to sinews aging, futile
also, once again he tries through speech
the marketplace and the arena use
to reach the latest young.   161

II

Exchange goes on, a subtle flow-
ing in and out of lilac breath,
exchange a dialog as though
someone were feeding, feeding
were thus fed:
                    the well-assorted
voices in his voice that rage
with lilac, grape, the open sea,
as it rolls up, the secrets
of one's life lovely on its crest:

and morning like that beacon
grating fury first ignited,
morning flung from crag to crag,
grown lucid in the wrangling wills:

bow-twang and lyre-, speedy passage
to the spires of snow-glimmer-
ing Parnassus and the summits
over it of stars, the dark
a shadow of what avid thought?

and still the light upon his words
as day, plunging, gladly lingers
in the wings of sportive birds,
the lady's owl-eyed, leafy gazing.

III

Wherever you go will be a polis.

But where is Athens, once that city
in the clouds? Now nameless rubble
most of it, many times nameless—
lilac, asphodel and poppy
famous through its cracks and stubble—

ruins in the wind of what
mad whirling, monstrous with delight,
rushed by, a passion beyond purpose,
hope, too fierce for shape, Athens
pebble shiny in its reeling,

pillars fallen as their gods,
then raised again to fall again
for Vandals, Turks, Venetians, Franks,
the Romans, its own restless will
and a hundred moods of tameless time:

like an enormous cicada shell
of some now-far catastrophe,
the crumbling Parthenon.
                              Strange
that as one stands in it—
                              a dancing
in and out with civil light,
those airy massive girls, that eagle
lit on solid wind—
                    and gazes
through its broken skeleton
the town below should look so whole,
so radiant.
                    And here, the dusk
wine-spilt on the hills, the stars
as they leaned on these pillars once,
near for the centuries ago
they first began, in twinkling airs
repeat their haunting names again.

I V

A pebble in the mouth of one
whose tongue rolls round, a pebble-sound-
ing plumbless fathoms, fames of time.
And it rolls round, metropolis
and temples, traffic rumbling beauty,
clouds resounding, tides:
                              the wine-
skin foot, released, leaps forth,
capricious as a satyr, dulcet
drunkenness where, mouth to mouth
gods and men combining,
                              Athens—
rooted as the strophes of the stars
within the wine-sack of the grape,
like dawn swept down on us through leaf
and flake, the lilac's sudden rippling—
purls through lips and shaping hands.

On Stuffing a Goose

*(after overhearing some students
talk knowingly of D. H. Lawrence)*

Is this fame then and what it is to be
really alive, to go on living after flesh,
having failed, has been officially
hauled away?

                To cast a moment's spell
upon some distant man and girl, a feeling
of familiarity in a gust of fragrance
in a summer's night,

                      of loneliness
made roomier as they recall his anguish,
as though flesh alone, one time and place,
one wife, a single set

                      of friends
were too confining and that life must be
let out to mine its basic cadence finally
in our pondering of it,

                      free of any
obligation save the pleasure that we take
in it. . . . My father was a great hand
at stuffing geese.

                  In the cellar dark
he'd keep one penned. Knees grappling it,
he'd ram a special mash with dippers
of water down its throat.

                    In time
that crate began to bulge; past waddling,
goose managed only belchy squawks.
We knew it ready.

                  Somewhere in all this
I have a sense of what it is to be really
alive. Somewhere in the celebration
of that goose,

                  throned on a shiny
platter, for its mellow crackling skin
a jovial martyr, piping savors of a life
fulfilled,

                our heart's gladness
in the occasion of picking the juicy meat
from the sides and the bones, in that
and remembering the sense abides.

Ruins for These Times

I

To hell with holy relics,
sniffing like some mangy dog
after old, dead scents (saints?),
those that went this way before
and went. More shambling about
in abandoned, clammy churches
and I abjure all religion,
even my own!
    It's much too late
to heft a Yorick skull and, ear
to it as to a surf-mad shell,
hold forth foul breath to breath
on man's estate.
    What's more
I, plundered, plundering,
out of these forty odd bumbling
years have heaped up spoils
with their own kinds of spells
compelling enough:
      a father
who keeps coming apart however
I try to patch him together
again. Old age too much for him,
the slowly being picked to pieces
as a boy with a fly, he hopped
a spunky horse and left
change gaping in the dust.
    Mother
too who would not watch herself
turn into blind and stinking
stone, took things into her own
hands, finished a rotten job
with a rush.

II

    But lest I seem
too personal, I'd like to cite

the grand, efficient, ruin-making
fashion of our time.
                    This earth,
a star, brave and portly once,
now like a chimney belches
filthiest smoke, fallout
of roasting human meat the air
we breathe;
                    the ember-eyes
of millions I have never seen
(yet relatives the more for this,
stand-ins for the role
I missed by sheerest accident)
flare up within my dream's
effective dark.
                    O let Odysseus,
Hamlet, and their sparkling
ilk grope after; here's
a chaos ought to satisfy
the genius in them.

                    I I I

                    Let them.
What's the mess of Europe,
late or antique, great or antic,
to the likes of me?
                    Pottering
about in my own cluttered memory,
I turn up, still in full career,
my grandfather, muscles sprung
from dragging packs through miles
of factories;
                    a grandmother
who bore, conscripted lifelong
to the total war of hunger
and a strange new world,
three families on her back
and then outwore them all
as she outwore her ailments,
one enough to fell a warrior;

that friend whose breath shaped
songs desperately debonair
out of our snarling dog-eat-dog
accomplishments.

I V

There too
I poke out bits, still standing,
from my wrecks, begun in fervor,
aspiration, joy:
those passages
through which the morning strode,
enlightened in its retinue,
choke on the plaster falling,
raspy stenches, refuse of lives
trapped in them.
Is the building
lust for ruin so strong in those gone
before that I and mine are nothing
but a story added, foundation
for new ruins?
The prospect
that seemed the way to heaven
glimmers mainly with the promise
of a final storm, a monument
of luminous bones to gratify
most dogged fates.
Our own.

An Opening Field

for Stefan Hirsch

To mind and not to mind,
to be exposed, open
(like a barn, its rafters
and its walls collapsing,
and the summer, prying
through the gaps, rolled
among unbinding mows,
its tumbled light so sifted
in the strawy rifts), to mind
and not to mind,
                    ignoring death
and yet awaiting it, like one
long played on that new airs
recall his sense of being,
open so that wasps may enter,
throbbing like a central nerve,
wasps and the many moods
the summer's given to,
simmering from one bed
as it wakens to the next. . .

you see your painter friend,
once buoyant to the world,
now broken by the flogging
blows his gentleness
exposed him to: through love,
no less than the world's
indifference, these strike.
And as he, dragged along
by his big dog on their daily
latenoon walk, draws near,

you ask, "Where are you
going?" At first he fails
to notice you, looks about
as though a voice he cannot
see were calling him. Then,
like one returned from some
far land, he peers at you.

"Geh kotzen," he replies.
"But first I've got to find
someone with shiny shoes."

"That's dangerous," you warn.
"Add to the mess already here,
and we'll be over our heads
in it." He nods. Then gazing
up through the cleft
in the trees to the field
beyond: "How fine it is!
No matter what we do
or say, it still goes on
the way it has to, lovely."

The field, light full,
as though the sun delayed,
among the border-sloping
trees and in and out
the solitary trees, has
slowly mellowed, a meeting—
as from its own accumulating—
of mild and generous,
intensely calm (a master's
fitting) glances.
            And he,
who has minded too much
and, overwhelmed—memories
at him troubling still—
stumbles into things,
simplicity lighting up
his face, breaks into smiles:
that bottom purity, blowing
ever more strongly, greets
the world from which it's come.

The Visit

Paris, Winter

To paint without a model,
shun all visits so that what one wants
to do cannot be interrupted or distracted,
as though the many strokes were someone
drawing near, the putting down of a land-
scape that cannot be till it composes
itself like a woman combing her hair,
touching up her face, arranging her shawl.

And then the lover, straining
at himself as at the distance that
intervenes, appears. The evening begins . . .

the evening began early, often shortly
after morning (which, plunged sputtering
down the well, bucketed back again
in a clatter of pots, the cries and smells
mixed in the courtyard, burst against
the walleyed window), in our scabby room
near the Luxembourg . . .
               the rain
would soon be lowering its boulevards
and fountains, upstart there to launch toy
boats with furry boys and grandpapas
marauding golden coasts of smudgy Africa

till noon, bustling up beside the hedges,
in its shadows light upon the couples,
restive as a clutch of pigeons, flapping
out a crackly sky, full speech, around them . . .

you and I feel bare; our English dangling
like any bottomless pitcher over there
or what one might try to say to a world
absolutely deaf (and yet, we think,
if only we talk loud enough . . .), we huddle
in our room.
             Still this so-wintry page
looks English back at me as much as French.
And while you shiver in the crumpled bed,

I try by rubbing words to rummage out
a fire, at least one smoky morning ember,
a bird-mumbling.
           I have, you know, learned
how to paint without a model, how to risk
no visits, many times O long ago.

I I
New York, Spring

To paint without a model,
shun all visits so that what one wants
to do cannot be interrupted or distracted,
as though the many strokes were someone
drawing near . . .
           and so the evening begins.

Once more the stage is set, the properties
of night, so thick with wall in wall in wall
and bending to the page the stars are muffled
like the reassuring common faces
of the day.
         And yet open there, no help,
no passwords, nothing but my need, the some-
one drawing near, deftly as a woman
touching up her eyes with brush-strokes
that apprentice to their purpose light,
my look, the rain's legerdemain
                (I feel,
I hear the tubers stirring, birds far off,
but soon to come, combing out in flocks
fat, multifoliate summer),
             open so
that in these lines what, taunting, passes
daily haunts and shapes, exultant
through the nimbus of a name cast off,
nakedly appear.
           "Terror is not French,"
Rimbaud said. Nor is it rustlings, siren,
savage, of the bush, a bug's argot,
the strange, lost mutterings of tribes
long dead.
         Yet who shall say by way of beds,
lumpy for a passing horde of bodies,

the mirror with its making mouths (nacreous
cries submerged in it, the flesh still greedy
in the far-receding waves, moon giddy
as it dips in sherry, eyes), what does
get said.
     Three apples, shriveled in this bowl,
nattering away: that cocky runt of a maple
at the window, blathering its scrawny
head off, after country matters still:
the rain running in and out its own
Spenserian exercises, blueprint of
a wordy April working one small bush,
these speak themselves so plainly no one
has to listen.
     But what about the whispers
from next door, the mixed-up rush of murmurs
in me, much too intimate to hear?

"A marching on the floor above,
below, those in cellars, attics,
boarded over, shoot forth nothing
but taut glances as they wait,
the days one dark, for who knows
whom, echoing through sleep,
their hearts the thud of shovels,
earth, slapped into new-dug holes."

Night's turned into a sealed-in cave, one wall
in wall in wall, a grave sodded with graves,
sky underground.
     And sitting in this room,
of rooms in rooms in rooms a Chinese box,
with loneliness so honeycombed, disaster
you desire, shearing through the walls.
Inside this city, going up, collapsing,
how can these words, burrowed into, save?

Do we not brush the roaches basking here,
the lordly rats, the corpses heaped, bloody
whimperings?
     Listen. Familiar names,
the breathing hived, lost tribes, sound up again.

The ungainsayable honey-breath of spring,
your silvered glance, as cool and penetrating
as the rain, bursts through the dust to light
on me, stirring birds and tubers, towing
multifoliate, fat summers.
                              Faces,
haloed in their touching innocence,
the reassuring common faces of the day,
whatever sweat and weariness, repeat
through crow's-feet indefatigable hope,
the child they keep, the child they keep on
being, shining more and more for every crease,
so bless this life, the thing I try to say.

        I I I
        Cambridge, Mass., Summer

To paint without a model,
as though the many strokes were someone
drawing near . . .
                    and so the evening begins . . .

the evening began early, often shortly
after . . . no, I know that will not do
(what's Paris or New York to the backwood likes
of me, from tribes remembered best for kitchen
middens), not that setting, not its tense,
not all the cries and smells.
                              Though they a moment
might have bellied out that someone's breath,
as flotsam helps to ruffle up a flood,
they were, especially to French as skilled
as mine, to English gathered up from birds
and trees,
            (and anyway perched now in Cambridge,
Mass., for all their clapped-together, clapboard
churches, as much my state as the Puritans':
the garbage, spewing out of cans, in steamy
stench—how different this from Paris or
New York?—an Indian chief, headdressed by flies,
remarking it no more, no less, than if
in Paradise, droning their own mass),

too self-engrossed.
                              The someone drawing near,
under cover of this clatter, by the cast,
the grandpapas, the boated, puffy boys,
already in their play halfway to America,
or by the traffic, hippies in the Square,

(somewhere, it is true, along that well,
in one room or another—the shades drawn,
still a deeply piercing smell seeps out—
beside the bureau and a foundering bed,
the chairs, awry as with a gale, one guise
of him appears and, eyes glimmering
among the tears, the cries, is happily,
absorbedly at work)
                              reflected in that
rain, each fountain spouting him, the birches
too, and fireworks—the rifles cocked,
it's always Fourth of July—the couples quarry
in the bushes,
                    slipped away.
                              (Outside,
a hullabaloo: machinery, shouts.

Before our door a main, clogged with debris
yesterday's hurricane swept in, has burst.
The pleated water rowing the street, as though
the sea at last had found some one small vent,
I think of all the showers, noon and evening
thirsts, the Mayflower, the Pinta, flapping
sail-loud sheets and shirts on lines, washing
down the drain.
                    By now the giant crane—
a man with a white flower at one ear,
a skinny boy beside him, its quick brain—
has eaten out a crater in the street,
and four six-footers, heads where my knee is,
with cries and thigh-high boots are sloshing
through the glossy mud.
                              A flurry of kids
like flotsam tossed up on the little flood
eddies shrilly at the curb.

One tries
his homemade paper boat along the gutter;
at home indeed, it merrily bobs as though
days out on the high seas.)
Again that someone
slips away.
And climbing the creaky stairs
to our third floor, behind the barricades
of traffic, outcries, mad towns crashing by,
you fiddling in a corner, more and more
at home in Bach,
like a cave dweller,
squatting in that old familiar smell,
his damp flint hunting fire, company
he loves so well the hulking, aerial shapes
he daubs on crooked stones,
or that later one
who lay long months in clammy dark, heaven
flaking in his eyes,
I huddle in our room,
waiting for the words, struck countless times,
to open, let the genie, burnt-match-black
and hot with incense, treasure, out: let me,
Eden-deep and sweeping-past-desire, in.

Or if not that, for a time at least
I, through these hungry words which struggle
to invoke a something beyond speech,
am spared that final visit, its one cap-
ping stroke.

I V
Annandale-on-Hudson, Autumn
(the voices burrowed in me . . .)

Anywhere they happen:
in this learned light now, ripening
through autumn, as though the mellowing
earth had finally imprinted itself,
a gloss, upon the quiet air,

as on the straw-in-amber-
bright pine-needles, matting the little

footbridge: anywhere they start up,
transported from a many-placed,
a many-timed remoteness,

breathing out a young
Egyptian morning, like the Nile brimmed
for its glittering rigs that seem
to bear it, there, surprising
as a passage in an old,

familiar book, frequently
reviewed, yet stranger now. Unfolding
in my flesh, incognito, they travel,
waiting for me, feted in a look,
a phrase—this butterfly,

an eyelid long forgotten:
sunbeams, cleaving the dovetailed
trees, the laughter of my desert-wander-
ing friend and, far behind him,
in him, those who dared

the Red Sea and a desert
also for their dreaming of a land
sweet milk and honey—speeding, waiting,
to speed me farther on my course,
sufficiently looked after.

V

                     "But that's,"
she said, "more farfetched yet. The scene
you sketched, electric in its promises
and threats, you haven't used. Instead you
introduce another scene, another, still another,
topping that.
              Whatever happened to the woman
shivering in bed? Was she the one who
worshiped at her mirror? Or that lover,
smart in terror and delight? The evening
too they might have reveled in?
                           Gone,
all gone, and scarcely touched upon. And you
impressed with palming off a lot of garbled

copies of a lost original; no doubt
a fake at that!"
                        Don't be so sure. That woman
may be you, and you the more she changes,
changing, always more the same, like the face
one finally comes to.
                        Out of all that squalor
piled on squalor—superior to ancient
cities built on cities—I would show
that scene and in its very shiftings
                                    fresh
as a new flower, proved, improved perhaps,
in each transplanting, unbetrayed by thought
or what it has been through, just like a mirror,
polished by the world of pictures flitting
in it, bountiful for its own sake.

The scene, well traveled, is unfolding, crisp
as ever, crystal parks and dapper, swift-
paced avenues, the traffic civil, movements
of a woman, weaving through our steel
and stone and glass, mirror-fluent, rain. . .

    and then the lover, straining
    at himself as at the distance that
    intervenes, appears . . .

From The Last Day and the First
   (1968)

The Last Day and the First

The stocky woman at the door,
with her young daughter "Linda" looking
down, as she pulls out several copies
of *The Watchtower* from her canvas bag,
in a heavy German accent asks me:
"Have you ever thought that these
may be the last days of the world?"

And to my nodding "Yes, I have,"
she and the delicate, blonde girl
without a further word, turning tail,
sheepishly walk away.
                        And I feel
for them, as for us all, this world
in what may be its last days.
And yet this day itself is full
of unbelief, that or marvelously
convincing ignorance.
                        Its young light
O so tentative, those first steps
as of a beginning dance (snowdrops
have already started up, and crocuses
we heard about last night the teller's
children quickly trampled in play)

make it hard not to believe that we are
teetering on creation's brink all over
again. And I almost thrill with fear
to think of what will soon be asked
of us, of you and me;
                        am I at least
not a little old now (like the world)
to be trembling on the edge
of nakedness, a love, as Stendhal
knew it, "as people love for the first
time at nineteen and in Italy"?

Ah well, until I have to crawl
on hands and knees and then can crawl
no more, so may it every Italian-
returning season be, ever the last
day of this world about to burst
and ever for blossoming the first.

Caliban Remembers

I

                            Might
have gone with them. Might. To be—
I heard their scheming—a strange fish,
seasick on land, lurching in shadows,
a monster they, tormenting, make.
No one for me. Not my master's kind
with perfumes stinking, auks at courting.
Nor to me true friends those two
I fell in with.
                       Oh fell in with,
a horse-pond for our pains, and over
ears, scum sticking to, thick scum.

"Putrid fish," all jeered at me.
As if, from king on down, they did
not take their fishy turn in the sea.
As in the way they reached this shore.

On such a day—moons marching by
my marking time—sat I out here,
sat, shading me, beneath this cliff.
The sea, one blinding wave, bulged round.
The sun had soaked deep into it,
into each bush, each tree. Had soaked
into these rocks until they shook
with light.
               There—I fished then too—
a great wind suddenly blowing up,
foam in its mouth, a bloody shriek,
that boat.
             Again and again surf broke
on it. Yet sparkling everywhere,
a blaze that, sizzling, blazed the more,
boat, gliding over this cove's jag rocks,
rode in.
           By then, for lightning's rifts,
one wave hot after me the sea,
I scuttled off, got me to
my cave's dark cleft and, glad at last
to have it, hid.
             My rod dangles,

once more sways the waters, swelling
from the line. New shadows risen,
noises I hear past what such brooding
high-noon brings. Hummings out of the sea
and the air, out of the woods?
                              Long tides
ago, I remember, hardly remember,
there were others. Low voices, rough,
could find me out, prod me, please.
No wasp's bite sharper, whirring through,
no grape-burst sweeter. Vague at best
now, like that name he'd knot to me.

Yet things I have belonged to them.
This gown, a giant ringdove's rainbow-
downy hood, I lounge in, tatters
and all, once my master at his magic
needs must wear, with his rod fishing
outlandish cries, their creatures in them,
from air and sea.
                      Lurked among books
he left. At times, efts in heaped leaves
as out of sleep, they pop. Yet as I
bend they fade, day after day
farther away.
                    But next to my hand
this pebble, blinked at me, a trinket
it might have been, dropped that time
I stumbled on her dreaming here,
dazzled by her still, as her glass,
cast off, raised to the face, a look
flashing, says she's, passing, teasing,
by behind me.
                      Chalk-faced, hair
sleeked down, no otter better, stalked
behind her, basking in her light,
so darking me who saw her first,
that Ferdinand.
                      How push back
this crinkle badgers brow?
                                    Witch she,
not my poor mother, I tweaked as ever,
as a jay its secretest feather.
And most, blood at the heart hopping,
dare I speak out her name.

                  Sometimes
taste still—remembering bubbles—gust
of that liquor. Cloud-casked surely,
music fermented. Those two bidding me
drink, one gulp, and no more goading
for me. God I, the sky my gliding,
earth, everything in it my subject,
far below.
           Now, if ever they were,
gone. Even my sleep, only rarely
whispering in it, slips free of them.

From the thicket, peeping, watched
the long ship I helped stow fruit, fish,
water aboard sweep out and silently,
its sails confused with clouds, folding,
unfolding, melt as though the wind,
seeing them go, blew merrily.

At first I also, kicking up heels,
scattered round their garments, linens,
books. At first. But after—how find
again that whole belonging mine
before they came?—and worst those days
when I, a smoke, fume through my hands,
loneliness whelms me.
               Had I only
his book's good company, that company
it kept waiting, perfect, on him,
humble the world, I'd lord it truly.

My rod, sproutng though it did
from the staff he thought forever buried
and I plucked it, swish as it will
to rouse the breezes, rustle the sea,
fares forth no revelries like his,
nor no revelations neither.

Times I'd welcome the old, heavy
chores, his orders at roughest irk,
echoed in cramps, nips, pinches,
hedgehogs packed and inchmeal wedging
through me.
            Times they rack me still,
those pokes, side-stitches (feared at first—

my shivers mounted—he'd returned;
aches he had, all kinds, fit
for each part of the body, aches
he must have stuffed in hollow branches
sealed with pitch, then like the noises
from his pipe, at will puffed out);
and shapes they do inside the dark,
torching me that I slubber in bogs,
on mad bushes burr me, furzes clawing.
But now not meant for me, no ape-
mouthing sprites behind them to mock,
not anger, only themselves.
                              Themselves
those plumes awag at the water's edge,
draggled through mire, flood, yet dry,
a play straight out of the spume?
                              Not those
from the ship again, untouched, a miracle,
unless the shine they sport be sea's
(my master bragged he kept them so),
but tailing one another, great bugs.

Well, whatever comes pleases me,
my state on the isle. Its flocks and herds,
its slyest creatures, these, as I pluck
for hides, food, feathers, tribute
also in their squawky cowering,
scrape to me King. Tame too
as they never were for those. Long days
I loll, ruler and subjects the same.

Even so things I learned, some,
nag at me still, names that, shimmering,
as I would clamp jaws to, dissolve.
And the faces glimmered out at me
from bush and sky, tide-riding shapes.

Came on her in this very cove,
swimming still on her, whiter, rounder
than a wave, open to the sun.
Then I understood his daily command:
"Stand upright, stand!" Upright I was,
knew at last what he meant by "Be
a man." Saw she was gone there, torn

out by the roots. Wish in sudden,
flushed kindness, pity, give her mine,
all.
    But tiptoed, manhood in hand,
to surprise her, completed while she slept,
as by magic—was it our fires,
crossing, drew him?—scepter quivering,
upright, he appears. Eyes blazed
on me, cares, it seems, nothing
I have learned my lesson, quick
to obey.
        Fear he had I'd fish
his pond? Oh no, not fish it, stock it!
Who else was there to do her turn,
so save the day for the likes of me,
and him as well, on the island?
Not all his magic, age, can angle
new foundlings, me more, out of air.
Even now loss wrings me.
           Still his words,
crackling, strike me everywhere stony,
yet shaking too. One frown farther
I had been done.

    I I

        But hear that hiss.
A rumbling scrabble, skin atwitch,
the sea would speak?
          Lo! the rod
grows taut, throbs, humming, in my hands.

There, dripping, spluttering thick sighs,
bobs a swollen, slippery thing.
Some odd, mad fish I've caught!

Clutch it.
      A book!
         Alive again:
inside its blotched pages, seasick,
for all the sights, blood-chilling worlds,
it's gulped, words, through fingers slither-
ing minnows, hop.

Mixed in its spells now,
nymphs once cropped, nymphs and urchins,
romping, couple, splotched purple swirling.

Clouds my master called this world,
clouds and dreams (a sorcerer then,
a stronger, over him, mouthing things,
wording us, thus puffed into being,
browsing on our aches and rages?).

Such waking cloud this book's become.
Reading before, its gnat-words fidgety,
not hard enough!
        Yet some, tails flouncing
as if plunged into the sea, beswamped
by smudgy ink, I know again.

Put ear to page. Hear something.
Grumbling steady, far off collecting.
His voice, is it, penned in the words?

That voice—like it no other sound—
which, first stroking, then grown gruff,
kept its kindness for this book
he turned to more and more, the rough
of it all that was left and there
to abuse me.
        Master he may have been,
yet could do nothing without me. Not,
unless I, fetching sticks, patched fire,
rouse his magic, its high-flown tricks.
Whatever his flights, had to return
to this island, his cell, me.
Never could, whatever his flights,
go back to his country till they came
with that ship.
        I alone propped him, kept
as earth does sky, else dropped in the sea.

Why then should I not use it also?
Shake me out music, that brave host,
showering praises, presents isle-heaped:
luscious fruits flung from the trees;

liquors clouds, cask-big, split,
pour down, thirsty for my tongue;
fish pied flying in out of waves
as the sea itself, glistening, bows,
then at my feet stows dutiful ships,
with treasure crammed as palm-tall hives,
their honeycombs oozing.
                                    Maybe can,
why not, raise one fair as she,
a dozen, sea-blooms, wreathing her,
bent on one thing only, hooked,
dolphin-sleek, dished in the sun,
one thing: pleasing me.
                                    Cloudy as sky,
bow-taut, is growing, better begin.
Drape the robes about me, so.
Wagging the staff, half crouch, half stiff,
nose raised as if snuffling scents,
the music working under things.

Now find the place in the book.
                                    Here,
the lines most faded. Head nodding
right, then left, both eyes rolling,
till body drops away.
                                    (Never knew
I spied on him mumbo-jumboing,
then jutting ear as if he thought
to hear answer. Was there something,
mutters, say the air's bright crest,
aflutter, speaking, speaking I
now seem to be hearing out of these
drowsy trees?)
                                    Oh, could he see
me now, his lessons like his scepter
clutched, the earth, the sea, the cloud-
packed sky about to wake, how pleased
he'd have to be.
                                    I can, mouth plumped,
almost repeat that rounded phrase
finished off in a hiss.
                                    Lo, now, lo!
Even as I say it, darkness hedges,
crowding out of the sea.

               Beware!
A lightning crashes, fire's scribble
scratchy down sky; and that oak, sky-high,
falls at my feet.
             One twig closer
and I had been—homage truly!—ever
crowned.
            Wake that squall again?
Watching him manage it, hearing
out of it bellows, no beasts madder,
demons not (suppose more loosed
than he could handle?), shuddered me
through.
            There, high on squall's ruff,
an osprey its spray, a cormorant beaking,
in the distance riding, gay as a porpoise,
the ship bobs that took them off!

Desire that: my master back,
she, the others, firewood, fast rooted
where I dumped it, ache in my bones,
the play—I ever cast for monster,
slave, with real blows in it, hurting
words—to be played over and over?

Oh no. Now that his book's mine,
my lackeys they.
             Ah the sweet tasks
I would conjure for them as—standing,
upright, rigid, by, they glare,
if cast down, deadly looks—I lie
in my flower-puffed bed, she, flower
among flowers, by me, mistress
to my least worded, far-fetched whim.

And him I bid bring turtle eggs,
struggle through fanged briers for berries,
prickles too of bees he must snatch
choicest honeysacks from.
             The others,
husked of rapiers, ruffs, fine airs,
down on all fours, the beasts they are,
cuff them, kick. Out of their yelping,
as master's pipe could ply a storm,
pluck music.

One bears me a bowl
brims rose water, petals swimming;
and dabbling hands, on another I wipe.
Then order these pour the good wine
down throat. Or "Scratch the regal back
with porcupine." Wanting the palace
his book shows, "Scoop out that fen.
Put rocks over there. There. And there."
And, put, not liking it, "Put back
again."
But as they, drooping, sigh,
their struts and frets, wildfire plots,
gone out, would I not let them be,
him most, most haggard for these labors
far beyond his years, and he, first,
landing on this shore, enjoying
for a time what he found here, most kind?
As I enjoyed, a time, the silks,
the warmth, the tunes he (she more) soothed
against me.
Best in that moment when,
as now, shadows deepen the wood.
Then, he piping, I sprawled by,
the notes bubbling, moonlight dewy
on them, as in her eyes, already
gleaming secrets of caves, sea-kept,
she sang. And winds and waves, chins set
in their hands, the stars, leant down, peering
ever harder as darkness ripened,
also sang. One radiant sound,
the earth and sky involved in it,
soaked into me, I shook with light.

So he, sitting over me, listened,
I at fishing not more still.
Points at things, making fish mouths,
stranger noises. And a mote
baiting my eye, a mayfly twirling,
whole day, if tiny, on midnoon,
prods with "Mind, mind!" till at last,
no salmon swifter thrashing waters,
flipped above the spray, the word,
words loosed, stream from my mouth.

Joy in him then, love like my own.
Eager to show me this thing, that.
His books spread out before me, shared,
I learn to pin their swart bugs down.

A book, it seems, for everything,
for things that cannot be and never
could. Had one even showing me
and in it called "Caliban"
because I fed, not less gladly
than on ants, on men. How could I,
no man being here? And think
of eating those, washed up, rotten,
worse than flotsam, on this shore!
To them alone such name belongs
who would, not cold, not hungry, kill.
(The name I had I never told,
with mother buried who gave it me.)

But best of all that warbling book,
as on a cloud inscribed, about clouds.
The world so graved, growing, changes,
one thing into another, like a cloud,
its women turning, as the pages
do, into a tree, a brook,
a song. Who would have thought their looks,
their voices, now only a windy leaf,
a rivulet, the hearer's tears
start forth, the world seen newly
in their light.
                        But am not I,
not merely stone, such changeling too?
So she, in one day sped from childhood
stalk-thin, gawky, into woman.
What I became she could not see
but only heard, as I would sigh,
the same old shaggy husk of me,
as that god, changed, so the book said,
into a bull for love, must bellow.

His books I browsed on. All but one.
No matter how I yearned, heaven
it loomed, mocking, over my head.

And that the book I saw him lost
in, sitting by the fire, listening
to its gossip, mingled with the jiggly
words, his stare outglaring embers.
That tongue, so good at wagging, flogging,
little about him then but as it
jogs off on its own. And the eye
that easily caught me out, no eye
for me, a thing that never was.

Mornings too, quick to me earth,
the berries restless in their plot,
the sky as well, I knew it time
to tend the day. But he shut away
as though, beyond those pages marked,
no light, no joy, can bloom.
              Damned be
such book when world in lark enough,
in filbert and in plum, cries out
that I become a winged hearing,
lapping tongue, and those the ground-
work eyes and hands abound them in,
my feelings, ripened as they ripe.

Let him be buried in his glimmering
dark while I sprawl in the sun,
in busy, slow pleasure running hot
fingers over me. Or, plunging,
lounge inside the thicket, tickled
by the shade, webs buzzing, leaf-mold
rotting on mold, a wood-bug sometimes
gulped with a berry.
            Long hours on
and into the night within my fingers,
under my lids, the daylight tingles,
tingle too along my dreams
those sozzled smells, the fruits as when
I munched on them.
            And he, after,
the fire gone out? Grey, ash-grey.

Yet that one book, even as I have it,
is it better than the world, telling
where winds are woven, snows, sundowns,

showing them being made, and played
out as its owner bids?
                    Some god
must have bestowed it on my master,
else dropped it—as later he did—
lying open, wind-leafed, wind-sighing,
like this earth, and my master found it.

Time and place forgot, he wandered
in it, blissfully bound by soundings
he could make.
                    So on this island
all seasons at once or, as he wished,
seasons from strange countries,
mountains in his cell and light
as clouds, tall mountains flaming round
the embers, goddesses too and sprites—
the rites of them.
                    But then he saw—
perhaps the days between the spells,
their willingness to work, grew longer,
harder, or he woke, ash-grey—
what empty dream he'd snared him in,
learned the lesson I had always known:
with that book to give himself, to dive
into the thrilling waters, chilled
at times, hard buffeting, this world,
this life is?
                    No, angrier he grew,
his words mocking him. Angrier,
words like blows.
                    Never knew,
I, finding words he did not know,
like new, hidden nests could show him,
eggs speckled with writing brighter
than his book's, sly birds, the topmost
sky still breathing from their wings,
in their songs still.
                    Then he might
have, once more trusting me, entrusted
the isle, as mate his daughter.
                    Instead
that feathery, ribboned thing! May he,
filched my place with the logs, her fancy

also, drown this time for good,
a delicate food lining fish bellies,
sweet between my royal teeth
(Caliban called, Caliban be).
Then, who knows, she might, seeing
him at last so much in me,
me like the more.
     Or, better, let him,
soaked enough, grown scaly through
and through, yanked out, Caliban me.
If he, pale sprout, could supplant me,
why I not him? Three times as much
as his dragged, staggering, poor armful,
he a king's son, I can haul.

Our names with their three syllables,
two mountains humping a crouched "i"—
Cal-i-ban and Ferd-i-nand,
Ferdinand and Caliban
(somewhere in between Miranda)—
like enough so that the mouth
which shaped out his with loving breath,
a trill the birds would stop to hear,
to mine could be as kissing-kind?
Ah, well, would she ever have—
how could she—loved a thing like me?

Why, instead of all that work,
those lessons, slow, dull, scratchy,
did my master, worlds at hand,
not turn me presto into prince?
Sea, fire, sky he managed
featly; but I too much for him,
an earth magic alone could never change?

Never, as he sought to stuff me
with his learning, asked he me
my thought, my feeling. All I was
was wrong, to change. All he wished
was aping, my face wrought to look,
a mirror, more and more like his.

III

The book in hand, past teaching now.
Try the last words.
                    That grating stink!
Up it dredges from grottos, bogs,
sunk under the sea.
                    And swelling out,
choking the air, one racketing cry.

He's back, overseeing me, making me
do what I do? Or Setebos
with his accursed crew, sneaked in
at last and most to devil me—
who else is left to feed their hate?—
for being driven off?
                    A crack
as though the earth is splitting!
                              Out there,
lit, the ocean spouts. One monstrous
fish?
      No, upright, like a mighty
man in flashing robes and roars—
would I could give this book to him!—
I see it, see his city, so he
called it, climbing the skies, its spires,
cloud-piled, the gardens multiplied
with gilded fountains, songs torch-lit,
and women, each a little bower,
while far below dark fires rage,
the swamp on which such city's built.

Like torrents crashing over a crag,
aimed, writing its zigzag, a lightning
dashes over me.
                Now crumbles,
tumbling, drags the outermost rim
of the isle with it!
                    My doing? Have done
no lone thing yet brings me one crumb
of joy; no singing—only this howling,
sky clipt open, trolls my name.

What if, the salt marsh flushed and pounced
on me, I move the moon, the sea

rushed over the isle, I among mollusks
down there, for sharks a crunchy music?

Ass enough that time I dreamed
I could, with those two clumsy sots,
set me free, be king. Master
I called one, god, licking his foot,
and he, for all the sack in him,
not mire good enough to cake
my master's boot. And I believed
he'd bottled moonshine, music, himself,
the moon's own man, dropped with them!

Oh lessoned I am. Off with the gown.
Break the wand. Before this book,
more than ever my master did,
rules over me, ruins entirely,
drown it again. Never wanted it
in the first place.
    So let it sink.
Dissolved into the restlessly paging
(seems to be reading it), gurgling sea,
the nymphs and dolphins schooled by it,
it may, sea-changed, sigh out its message.
As now.
   Whatever his tempest brought
about, this one washes me clean
of them, blundering on their tottery
two feet (upright they pride themselves
on being!), in broad daylight bethicketed,
wilder than night. And all the time
plotting.
   Then why so foolish
as to toss his power away and, naked,
return to a world bustling with men,
his brother, my silly crew, repeated
a thousand, thousand times over? Expose,
as well as himself, his dear daughter
to infections, plagues, far past the work
of scummy ponds!
    Devils they said
haunting this island. No least devil
till they arrived. Not all the toads
and frogs this island spawns could quell
the viper in them. Devils he sailed

away with, devils, waiting, hordes,
to dog him all his life's last days.
Think of a world, an island like this,
swarmed with them, their schemings, brawls!

Winds blow over me, the crooning
night air, free now, full of nothing
but its own breath, serenades
the locusts chirr, scents of the sea
and this my island, twining with
what stars are pouring.
                 Yet, not burrs
snarled tighter in the hair, they cling,
that manyed voice, as in a sea-
shell, ebbing, wailing, far inside
into my ear.
            Fingers remember
the bowl they brought, his hand on it,
hers, the water gushed forth, sparkling,
laughter, worlds. I polishing,
how it gleamed out pleasure, over-
wrought with my face, fitting in
beside hers, his.
             Its carvings music
swelling to the eye, the finger,
from the pipe the piper on it
raises who is blowing out
the rounded, cloud-big, smoky sky,
I enter it, the little landscape
centered in thick trees a wind
in fragrant waves is wreathing, wreathing
me, shapes watching.
            Him I see,
see her approaching. Eyes smart,
fingers tingle, taught sly snaggings
of silk, as eyes are caught by her
skirt rustling, the drop of her lids
a deafening tide in the blood till I,
battered as by that liquor's gust,
for the flooding over me drown.

Oh no, not that again, not me
gone in the dark of too much light.
Not bowls, nor touching words, to push
me out of me.

           There, smash bowl
to the earth, the dust it after all
is. And through its shattered pieces,
him and her, those others scattered,
I tramp free, free as the air.

Not lost, all ebbed away as water,
precious wines words keep as casks,
for that he would have taught?
                      Too high,
he rose, reached past earth, while I
slumped, an earth, below.
                 At last
as he gave up me, gave up spells,
mind changed, chose man, the life
that all men lead, a magic, dream
more than enough?
            Preferred the bowl
as much at breaking, robes faded
and faces, dyings, their plots too,
their hates.
           And most that momentary,
everlasting human touch—to touch
Miranda's hand again! A queen now,
joy of children throning her
as they, shrill, ruckle round her knees?
And he, does he live still, sometimes,
head shaking, bent in some forgotten
corner over an old book,
muttering maybe "Caliban"?—
the fearful, wide-open risk of it,
touch that runs like lightning through,
feeling, as men feel, as men call it
real.
     No matter how I squat,
leaves thick and dark mixing, dark
from inside owl wings, bat's screechy
darting, my cave sealed off, I stick out,
prickly, listening.
           How I long
to hear once more those me-completing
voices. Come back, would cast me
at their feet. And yet . . . alone, alone
as he must be, loathing, pitying, loving.

A Letter from the Pygmies

Dear Whoever-You-Are-That-You-Are,

Whatever chance this has of reaching You,
I write to bring You up to date.

I cannot, little as I join them
in their skills at hunting,
undertake Your tigers. Rarely
do Your lofty auks invite me
to the confabs of their aeries.
Pastimes Leviathan delights in
never has he offered to share
with me; never has he proffered
island back or cove-snug belly.

Still there is the cat Hoppy
who, whatever our blandishments,
as he cannot drop his creaturehood,
claws flying his pleasure, takes me
some good distance into Your creation;
dew starlit on his fur, the fields
wherein Your wonders grow he smells of.
And when, unblinkingly, he fixes me
as though he were upon the scent

of rabbit, mouse, or other friend,
I know the instantaneous delight
of terror. So elation finds me
in the chickadee that bobs
upon our thrashing window-bush,
skullcap awry like any plucky Jew's,
a Job in synagogue of ashes, cries;
as Hoppy bats the pane, it never
budges from our fat-packed rind.

In short, though there's a scheme
afoot to blow Your ark and all in it
to smithereens, to pitch a cloudy,
climbing tower will convert the earth
into one tomb, I know by feelings
craning, preening, deep inside
the ark's still riding, riding high.

So from time to time, what time remains,
I'll do my best to keep in touch with You.

Faithfully Yours,
Theodore

Robes of the Gods

for Stefan Hirsch, 1899–1964
(after his painting *Robes of the Gods*)

As the wind discovers itself
through fields of thistle, buckwheat,
stalky ragweed, like a carefree boy, blowing
his whistle out of a seed, split,
so the gods use us.
                    This painting,
garments racked on a line like gaudy,
hung-up slabs of beef, knows this: the gods,
a hum throughout, dress up in brave
and bloody carcasses.
                    Still, sly
as they are, loving to lie low, showing
off—a few of us their special finery—when
it suits them, they put on the mob
for daily wear:
                jeans, worsteds,
uniforms. But changes they propose here
too, from shrill mad children, newly dipped,
skipping in and out, designs-not-yet,
to sots, hags, beggars,
                        patches
stitched into a motley. And the fitting
wardrobe inbetween, when, stript to nothing
but a skein, hooks-&-eyes the network
of taut veins,
                lovers set off Mars
and Venus, wrapt in one another's arms;
like a battlefield, in the rough and tumble
of a naked bed, the lightning flashes
then, rain shuddering.
                        Attached
to reels we cannot see, impulsive robes
which, brooding, breed, we feel the tugging:
moods our own, yet struggled through
us, rugged, violent.
                    And strange,
affecting wills that much as not resent,
and would resist, the powers investing them,

resent with horror greedy blotches
and the rips
   the body must sustain
that very moment wills are all knit up
to forward them. By Jove, by God, by bowels
and wounds that Jesus bound him in,
what is this
   most outrageous dress,
this breath that we spin out, on which
we're spun, the blundering flesh and blood
by which we, living, die, that must
at last be thrown
   away with us?
Yet at times, although we seem cast
offs, for days past counting dumped into
a closet crammed with odds-&-ends,
something wakes
   as though we, nod-
ding, snapped us onto a satyr passing;
in a steadfast wind, like hides I once saw
drying, golden-airy, in a Pisan sun,
he takes us up.
   Even as gods, riot-
hearted, drag us, muck their highway,
into bedlam, its engrossing frolics enough
to crack our seams, exultancy bursts
forth that's nameless,
   whole, inexplicable.
And as they shine through us, like rags,
like blubbered stuff a fire, donning,
flaunts, we shine; through tears
and blood we, whirling, shine.

The Ultimate Antientropy *

"Unity is plural and at minimum two."
                    —R. Buckminster Fuller

Whether one paints five Helens
after some much experienced woman
or develops one, his beau ideal,
from the five, most lovely, untouched
virgins of Crotona (such Cicero's
account of Zeuxis' purist practice)
or laboriously patches her together
cheek by jowl out of all the women
he has shuffled through, is not
their end the same?
                    So even he
who will not let the name of Helen,
of woman for that matter, be attached
to what he splotches on the canvas,
refusing to be tamed by recognition—
for he claims he paints a painting,
not a landscape, apples, females—
deems he's plucked from out his head-
long brain and brush a universal
as it is a most unique,
                              concrete
past any momentary model. And though
we may wish to celebrate the fleeting
or applaud the theory as it lords it
over its bleak and boring product,
Zeus, we recall, laid all (this every
time) his eggs in one small basket;
the consequence, in the most famous
case, was a Helen who inherited
her papa's quality
                    most jovial:
being so promiscuous, so radiant-
ly loose, that we have hardly seen
the last of her. The sparks her eyes
shot forth are seeds that will not die.

* According to Norbert Wiener and R. Buckminster Fuller, "Man is the ultimate antientropy." And woman, is she ulti-mater?

203

Men far flung still warm their hands,
their hearts, and more at the thought
of her as at the Troy the flint
of flesh against the tinder of a god
produced.
      Helen, it seems, is more
herself the more she's reproduced.

The Life of . . .

for Bill and Dorothy

I

"So there we were stuck
in Alassio all that rotten winter
in a rented house, no one around
but puffed-up Germans, and nothing
to read beyond a pair I can't abide,
Boswell and Johnson, the latter worse
than his crony.
                    And nothing to do
but struggle on through that wretched
Life of . . . How I loathed it!"

I I

"Ah, my friend," I say, "that's what,
    more or less, it always comes to,
        one book to a customer.

Storms clattering through their lines,
    some, if they've the time for it,
wonder how they'll ever learn to follow,
    let alone unravel, their chaotic plot.

Others, it's true, are luckier:
    richer text, with pictures, colored,
every second page and gilt-edged, bound
    in buckram that's the latest rage.

But each of us, like it or not,
    is stuck in his own Alassio, waiting
        there, flopped open.'"

I I I

                "Actually,"
my friend's wife now breaks in, "after
the first two summer months, after
the Germans left, the flashy decorations
nailed up on the shops for them
pulled down,
           and the Italians
gradually appearing, rotten winter
and all, we grew to love the town,
admit it.
             Why, whatever the weather's
ludicrous fits, just our garden alone,
with its crazy, tangled, nonstop blooming—
    roses, geraniums, and the rest—
through shattered bottles, cans, and every
kind of litter.
            Or those narrow, dark,
malarial streets at the end of which,
on our long walks, the sea greeted us
like a blaze burst through a tunnel.

And that's not all. Have you forgotten
the forlorn little fishing-fleet going out
each night as we went to bed and, at dawn,
returning as we woke,
                threw open
the shutters, and watched behind it
a red heaped up on the creamy water,
the sun rising, as though, towed
in, part of the catch?
            And a bit later
too, once we learned our way around,
the mountain that we loved to climb,
looming over the town and high enough
with its paths twisting to the top
so that one seemed to see—
                a new day
previewed there, just as it was forging
forth—eye to eye with the moon."

The Life of . . . (Cont.)

for Irma

(the poem is speaking)

"Since, after one quick look,
another friend of yours dared say,
'This poem seems to need some resolution,'
I, a kind of Party of the Fourth Part,
stand up to insist
            the poem is
satisfactory. Some lines—the eyewash
about a new day, etc.—are a little hard
to swallow. But at least you resisted
gab of chariots,
            Apollo and his
nags chafing at the bit and all that.
Even if you couldn't as ever, withstand

your blather about books. What's more,
one whiff of Germans
            and off
you go like an old horse to a blaze.
OK, don't blow up. I know you deserve
some praise (living through so much
revision, I had almost forgot)

for blotting verses in Part II
after 'each . . . flopped open.' Lines
about people like books, suddenly hurled
across the room, 'with dozens pulped
or fed into a roaring fire
            that . . .
at last the words all crackle.' Sure
the title fits, just right with its dots,
neat X's marking the uncertain spot,
for those millions
            razed in smoke.
In any case, I am here to offer exegesis:
like the trio in the poem depending on
one another as their talk composes
it or, ever stuck
            in their high-
wire act and in the hazy air of new-

comers to the show, the pair your friend
abhors, you stand on them (so Renée
and you twirl
          through space
with no rope, no net, and least of all
trapeze beyond each other). As I now do,
the latest overlooker, telling you
how much you supervise
               the rest.
And it continues, like the shuffling pages
of the sea that in every different light
(as by the lights of him who looks)
look differently."

Mount Washington

> At Mount Washington, in Tuckerman's
> Ravine, Thoreau had a bad fall. . . . As he
> was . . . getting up . . . he saw for the first
> time . . . the Arnica mollis.
> —Emerson's "Thoreau"

Insert 942 of the poet who views
and reviews his work from summer's *aperçu.*
The day had been a day, a genius,
to study out in intimate detail
the earth's sweet, airy plenitude of June,
itself exactly mirrored in that multiple
response.

And now, night-lidded, day's so many
ages beguile themselves among their dreams
as dateless snows are adding lofty stories
to Mount Washington,
      the one—"highest
in the NE United States, real quality
for skiing"--friends are urging him, afraid
of heights, to climb.
      Had he not crept on hands
and knees—from childhood up: the thorny bluffs
his gang explored—along La Scala's gallery
while Godunov, mid-career, appointed
like the candelabra, lit in its own pride,
giddied him the more?
      Afraid and, as
a guidebook later told him, rightly so:
"The first effect of standing on the summit
of Mt. Washington is a bewildering
of the senses at the extent and lawlessness
of the spectacle. It is as though we were
looking upon a chaos. The land is tossed
into a tempest."
      Inching through the Alps
by train, he felt them, churning, scramble him,
yet in their uttermost wildness with a logic
of their own, serene for very fervency.

But he has now lived long enough to know
he need not awe himself with icy heights.

Wherever he may be, a full-fledged storm
spreading anonymity, and he is lost.
Or sometimes caught flatfooted on most daily-
seeming ground, the stars at midnight striding
that low street, and there abruptly stirs
a vertigo good as the proudest peak's.

A flower, basking in itself as in sunlight,
let its perch be pinnacle or ditch,
plucked, can instantly unlock the pit,
sprung up, impassioned, slavering, of Dis,
sky plummeting as by that tiny ledge
the body is.
                    And so, his pages crawling
with revisions, queries to himself,
and with his doodles, intricate way stations,
he tries to find a certainty inside
against such dreadful falls.
                    Nor, as he views
his work, is he averse to plying tales
of other travelers who climbed this way.
Kindred especially as they had spent
their lives striving to map the hazardous course,
map often nothing more than accurate
report of perils, loss, and being lost,
scale map in color of catastrophe,
and yet because they had been here a light,
provisions cached in sudden crevices
along the slope.

INSERT 942

                    In New Hampshire, crisp
despite mosquito-fretting notions of July,
a full moon close as any fellow New Englander,
the crickets choral in their book of airs
as though a grassy hymnal hummed itself,
the poet thumbs *Ein Bildungsbuch für Kinder*
that his host had brought from Hitler Germany.
The first of its kind, put out in 1796
by a friend of Goethe. A most serious magazine
with tidy drawings of the matter-of-fact
wonders of the world
                    (the sometime text below

now in bookish German and French, now also
in an English never heard on Anglo-
Saxon land or sea).
                    Fish ripple through
    his fingers, swum in their own radiance
    as in the foamy shoals flipped pages make,
    names flickering,
            "mackerel, pickerel, perch."

The poet, squinting, cocks his ear. Might he
not overhear, among the moonlit murmurings
his window frames—the lake, moon-piled, impatient
mica mountain, brimmed into the mirror
by his side—these piebald things?
                    And so
he is entranced as flowers seem to leaf
and, sniffing, laugh through him:
                    nonchalance
    in roses, frizzled manes. But others crinkled
    as—not to be told from—crinolines.
    One roisterous, all ruddy nose, for drinking
    its own wine.
            Narcissi, self-absorbed.
    And then a twinkling edelweiss atop
    its precipice, as though these pages heaped
    them up to mount it that it supervise.

    Much like that bird of paradise that preens
    as it goes teetering through painted eyes,
    a fan conquetting.
                    With great moths set off
    like sunsets, mazy dreams, a map each one
    of the Babylon informing summer
                    glancings
of this night, a someone blinded as he
looks, gets mixed up in.
                    And choice volcanoes
    about to wake, bouquets most artfully
    arranged.
            There, bigger, huffier than the rest,
    "Vesuvius," with people by, watching
    from low balconies.
                    Several bending,
        robes a burnt sienna,

                              especially
        now they blend with the poet's studious shadow
             (few pleasures like the looking down on mountains
             happily in hand.
                         So only as mists,
             roomy as clouds, had cribbed him had he dared
             to scale storm-battered Snowdon.
                                        With the ease
             of dreams the mists like curtains parting, scapes
             dissolving into scapes, some cows float by,
             sudden pastel vistas, autumn clearings,
             prim as album scenes, the leaves compiling
             light upon each other:
                                   see that intrepid
             mountaineer, S. T. C., but on the top of Skiddaw,
             in the vales of Quantock, best in one of many
             paper-drifted, frost-at-midnight rooms,
             hot on the tracks of Hegel, Schlegel, Schelling,
             Fichte, all in turn after the edel-
             weiss, and not in a cloud-cuckoo-talking,
             smoke-baroque salon),
                              New Hampshire and
        the poet intent on this High German view
             (perhaps the eyes look up that once set here,
             the scenes, asleep as at the mirror's bottom)
        of a medieval dusk,
                              toward others, backed
             by hairpin arches, churches fly-eyed, blinking
             on devotions, assignations, plots too sly
             for any prying,
                              strollers in the wool
             of ripened peach and pollen, volubly browsing
             in a homespun moonlight, someone strumming
             a pandora,
                         as Vesuvius, twitching
             in its slumbers, sputtering, snores along.

        Meantime, roused in a lower corner—
                                             the poet
        thinks he sees their busy, black-cowled buzzing,
        this highlighted by the gnat that perches
        next to them, a more than life-sized, gem-
        like angel, stunned by what they're at—
                                             flushed

on them the luscious vines they, tending, trample,
and their sheep, well-fleeced, two monks exhort
a woman, sketchily got up, a touch
too rosy if offhand.

        And cheek by jowl
the mightily scowling "Giant of Ecuador,"
decked out as noble savages should be.
Swashbuckled, ruffed,

          the spitting image he
of George—so wigged and snuffed as—Washington
crossing a replica (the artist's version,
a watercolor scooped from out the Neckar)
of the Delaware.

        Foot on the prow
as though, for all the cakes and floes beside him
like a glacier's brow, his hand is eloquent-
ly drawn to plant the Stars and Stripes Forever
on Mt. Washington.

        There, hard on the General's heels,
those fabulous louts, half Indian, half cow-
boy, trooping in.

        And blurring with the poplars
(the paper, peering through, as though it were
brown twilight's air and of a forest too,
confused with whatever woods were meant;
nor can this moment's moon make clear how many
voices since, how many tramping feet,
have sounded through.

        The poet thinks he senses
their retreating and can draw them back
as he divines the future already marching)
   as they did for Burgoyne and his Hessians
until they fall on them, lined up, a whooping,
bloody fall, the red coats redder, deepened
in the sun as by the flash of guns
and powder horns.

        Across the page more apes:
the four above seem reasonably real;
the fifth however—

        some inbetween, a sport,
flaunting its cocksure tail much like a fur-
below and drooping, gold-red locks that look
a German spoof at newest *haute couture*
(did not Marquis de Lafayette inject

a Gallic note into the coonskin war?)—
"shows itself plainly through the long, thin
& almost horn-shap'd nose from other apes."

The poet knows attention must be paid
even to the unlikely likes of such
as to that daedal kin as well—their amours,
Weltschmerz, rituals, cuisine—that can
not be unless aired in our words:
                              call them
atoms, gnomes, or what you will, the Great
Migration teeming through our dreams, the thicker
they swarm the more invisible they grow,
much like snowflakes confounded in one snow.

So, in reverse, that starry race, the farther
off they are, sped to us from a world—
a book?—that's gone, the homelier they glow.

        Like these "colibri" or hummingbirds whose hover
        held, the wink of snows, dusk wading trees,
        circumfoliates plumage.
                          Particularly one,
            "the Tree-creeper, ivygreen, with a flacat'd,
            trifurcat'd bill."
                    In its quiver moonlight
is shaking loose (only a leaf or two
between such slippery seasons)
                          the Russian Winter
        of 1776 or thereabouts that flocks
        like flakes from pages otherwise brown:
        sports "of the most belov'd divertissements"
        of the Slavic people, viz:

                "Fig. I,
            The Mountain of Ice,
        wooden scaffolds, about 18 yards high,
        one side a wooden slopeness, cover'd
        with pieces of ice, & sprinkl'd with water,
        on which the lovers, being always numerous,
        or seat'd on little sledges, or standing
        on skates, with such violence slide down
        that they continue gliding, & for many
        miles,"

        far as the poet's fancy, savoring
this ice, no sherbet sweeter topping autumn
fruits—
        he too, despite his hating heights,
has clambered hand in hand with a companion
up a glassy mountainside, blood tingling,
eyes bedazzled with a noble white
        (who knows whose gazing lightens over them,
        its breath ignited, buoyant, in their breath,
        that crags once more become hot gamboling,
        so paced by them, the Jungfrau passionate),
and then, sledge or skates or no, swooped down—
darts out
        "on the snowy way prepar'd below.

    Such artificial icy mountains are
every year in the carnival's week with loving
care construct'd at St. Petersbourg
[in Peter the Great's glacial Sommergarten
Mars & Venus long ago deferr'd
to the Cossack snowpair, sparkling as long days
& nights they twirl out capers]
                  on or near
the Newa."
        Now the poet, certain he
can hear the grapplings, happy first as games,
children tumbling round and round in drifts,
sees lovers' volleys, mixed with others, graved
along the groaning ice of lakes, the years
enrolled in riots, massacres.
            And still,
like all the stars in revolution gleaming,
fires rollicksome puffed cheek to cheek,
flakes, confetti whirling, dress most savage
winds in furs, the rivers, famines, prinked
out so, stark degradations.
            There, just below
the Mountain of Ice, snow huffing like a samovar,
are swaddled folk, selling refreshments,
"a mead of sugar & pepper, to be drunk
with or without milk, & Russian gingerbread."

Is this the spot, the poet wonders, ponder-
ing his page, this point, its dotted line,
to plunk the snow, lugged from childhood up,

that makes the world a mountaintop, a lunar
sight, immutable?
             As then, no less,
     when through him, like a native shivering
     in his tent, a fever roamed that little room,
     its wallflowers, wild through the glaze, maze
     quite practical for his hallucinations,
     good enough to grace the proudest crag.

This the spot to press the child's first flakes,
memories embalmed in them, the rose
of Chartres not more crystal-clear, or what
a tapestry sought to capture in its spinning:

faces spinning, kindergarten faces,
pouring out to storm him in the playground,
chalky teachers packed within a word,
loves opening like furtive, scribbled notes,
one face among the rest a flowering
that time can only intensify—
                 the dead,
     his mother, harried spirit, freed at last
     into the winds; his father, bolted past
     the failures of the flesh in one swift hurtling
     by horse; and his dear friend, a poet, veteran
     mountaineer at least ten years ahead
     it made good sense to follow.
                 (Had the heights
         not sprung up, loving and at once available,
         inside his gaze, blue lookings from the snow,
         the piercing sky, as mountains blaze, dawn molten
         down the sides, that time their lives, their vague
         if urgent, lovely fates, loomed over them,
         awaiting their triumphal climb?
                         So they,
         breathing in their hopes, airs of the much
         loved great, longed for their earthly paradise
         on a forked peak, floating with the stars.

Yet paradise was almost theirs in knowing
those, compact of wing and song, also
depend on them, the moment's topmost mount,
for being as for exaltation.
                 This
     in the city man has built and restlessly

rebuilds, adding lofty stories to,
nomad as the most desperate heart could wish,
a windswept Alp tossed on itself they wandered
day and night, admiring its spired
citadels, its frosty lights,
　　　　　　　　the range
spread out far below that he must shoulder
even as it, dizzying, props him.)
And follow though his friend, having danced
out on a precipice much like a sparkling
rapier's edge, plunged into an avalanche
and now, two decades dead, grows light—
between the pages of this basic book
no one will open, ever find, past mining
itself in some all-giving flower:
　　　　　　　　voices
ice has locked, climbed out, climb over it
in crocus, lilac, columbine, and clear
the cry the hyacinth remarks.
　　　　　　In front,
as the plate has it, by a line of stands,
a fur-hatted, fat, mustachioed vendor,
having already tasted of his wares,
wildly, a nine-day-wonder astride the world,
gesticulates.
　　　　　One cocky edelweiss,
these snows its fathomings—
　　　　　　　　like an Alpine climber
perching on a stock, the poet stalking
via pen onto the slippery hillock
of his creased and tracked-up manuscript,
then out into the air where eagles loiter,
stars in undress, much at home—
　　　　　　　　looks down,
a summer's *aperçu.*
　　　　　　And so the poet
sees that we, whatever crag or ditch
we stand upon, by craft of gaiety,
by feeling's cubits, top earth with itself,
its latest blossoming.
　　　　　"Through this," cries edel-
weiss, the daylight haloed round it, stars
nearby, "the nights yearslong, the storms and wars
the world at winter hardly seems sufficient
for, my unique taste has brewed, brewed me
my single honey-home!"　　　**217**

Far Out, Far In

I

What we go out for
we often do not know,
though some are lucky
thinking that they do,

like those priests
in their white cassocks
diving into the canals
of Venice after the cross,

or those explorers
plunged, perverse enough,
through swamps and jungles,
most at home when lost,

and those luckiest
of all perhaps, gone out
simply for the pleasure—
limbs set, mind—of going,

as from this beach
a stand of grown pines
closes in, protected past
that by a mountain range.

II

On stilt-like poles
nets, dangling, shimmer
in the wind coral-crimson,
minnow-golden, seaweed-

green—in the fish
one wishes to lure one
must anticipate varieties
of taste; nearby glass

knobs for floaters
that craze the sunlight;
also mats adazzle with
fish laid out to dry;

and boats in whose
high-pooped shade men,
women and children sort
the day's many-sided catch.

I I I

But now, newspapers
spread out on the ground,
rainbow awnings strung
up from the trees,

the picnic, a festival
of swimming, begins;
food taken, some half
awash in the frothy surf,

a few, up to their chins,
go through the motions
of swimming, their arms
a lazy mimic of the waves.

I V

But there, far out,
near the bigger, seagoing
fishing-boats at anchor,
one ambitious swimmer

shows off her skill.
Hair flashing as the sun
catches, already low,
on arms as on the water,

fish dart to her
and as if excited by her
presence, her performance—
no less than their habit

at this hour—frolic,
in pairs, sometimes
in schools that seem one
rainbowed curve, leap high

V

above her. Then
even as the day goes
down, sinking somewhere,
a molten treasure

at the bottom
of the sea, the swimmer,
done with swimming,
by some artful strokes,

sure of herself
as of her course, returns
to shore. Whatever she
was after, as she stands,

dripping yet serene,
a last reflection, on
the sand, she has, for
a time at least, found it.

V I

So, night glinting
round in mottled waves,
two, swum far out, far in,
through one another's arms,

desire briefly routed,
drift upon the moon-
lit current before sleep.
And as the mind goes out,

exploring memories,
sensations like deposits
in the veins, the far-
out, lively places where

the body's lain, elations
gather, sun and wind
and water freshened, able
so, intrepid, to remain.

A Sow's Ear

And for our time
a mushroom cloud to temple all
in rapt devotion, like Elijah
in a whirlwind, heaven bound?

I

Talk about killing. In a life,
translated into chickens, how many
chickens? Enough to stock each coop
in Princeton for at least three seconds,
a tick maybe of all New Jersey.

As for cows, how many cows?
A herd to shepherd the assorted grass,
the mooing too, Nebraska requires
on a fine, sunny day.
                    And sheep
with frisky lambs abounding as they
crisply turn upon the spit. Fish also,
and like the others first dressed up,
sizzling out in luscious smells,
then hurtled
            over the flashing water-
fall of your teeth, your gullet gulping,
down the canal. All of it, churning,
turned into one small body.

I I

                    Body
of you, one and only heaven I have,
would have, no angel in its snowy down
of warbling wings more comely or so
gifted to enhouse and ease me.
                    So you
rightly think your skin the paper
walls the world, whatever its twirling,
you the room

in which its mysteries,
sweet and juicy, are unfurled, spleen,
guts, and reveries of a violence
converts the violence into song.

I I I

So it was when towns out as on holiday,
rags shoulder to shoulder with jewels
and furry robes scenting every step,
dragged whole forests along,
      haled
in mountains, dug up by their roots,
a sow's ear soothed to hear—its melody—
the grating of the axle-trees,
      the body
of Notre Dame rumbling in the carts,
the forges ringing, belching spark-
lit smoke that thickened as it mixed
with savory fumes.
     Mettlesome men,
hammering themselves into slim bronze,
their hearts by way of eyes emblazoning
mosaics of glass, reared generation-
glutted piles, crag-lofty sculpture
   with the lava living in it.

I V

Call it killing, loving.
So now, standing in this wilful ark,
hanging as from a starkest cliff,
I feel the heaven-high, dark
carvings come alive.

V

Outside and in
we are assailed. Fingers surging,
loins convulse, as that ark
does with the cataract
of all ensealed along the walls
they stanchion, burly, battered words.

The cliff beginning to wheel,
we, rushed on by its windy rocks,
are caught among a roaring
tide, processional:
not only saints
and martyrs once more jigging
as they bask inside
their fire, lighting up
the gargoyles and the animals,

but loitering in archways,
whores, painted as any stained-
glass window, beggars on stumps, slumped
drunks, the building glaring
as it rumbles at itself.

A Midsummer Nightmare

It is the waking . . .

Maybe now it's come to this,
a tale patched out of countless tales
some idiot is blabbering, remote
as it can be from its original.

Backed by glossy deer, their glazed
looks fixed into the woods or on those
plastered others, idolized creatures
in her more or less real frontyard,
Bessie, loose at every seam, flaps by.

We might as well admit that we
at last have come to this—the core
of high-toned stories, of curvetting
lords and ladies, sleek and furred
and fit as cats
            ("cats nothing, rather
flittery tilts of gnats and midges,
courting sun")—
              the stink, the boredom,
nameless under the moment's gilt,
their Maytime-buzzing fame.
                      Are we
not proud to think ourselves the first
to see hell's plenty in a furnished room,
in Helen's charms the flyblown brow
of Egypt, germs at seethe beteeming
her blood's Nile?
               ("We sound, in me
no less than thee, the very base-
string of humility.")
                  Yet still
the race by its ground sense commands
respect enough to make me say—

and if already mutants, they will find
their necessary lingo, fables, place:
no less impressive than the virgin
and the unicorn disporting, Bessie
queens it among her fabled animals—

whatever setting and ragged, green cast
its roles must put up with, the play
goes on.
        Inside the obscene clatter
local voices, silences
colloquial, like little lolling
waves in wallowing storms, hold forth
as ever: cricket, river, mountain-
lofty trees.
        ("You think there is
no havoc here, no looking after
rights, good cheer, of catastrophe?
This giant tribe that troops, so grave,
soft-footed ants like shapes embossed
on urns, with their heroic dead
are laden down.")
        Perhaps the time's
come round once more for trotting out
that greybeard of a musical,
"The Battle with the Centaurs," sung
by an Athenian eunuch to the harp.

Old horseplay never long suppressed—
Cretan, Trojan, or the jovial god
flopped, rutting, into slubbered goose—
those shaggy beats, black leather
jacketeers, half man, half roaring
motor, now break up the wedding,
the barely held decorum.
        We'll none
of that? No lout, a hempen, playing
Prince, and no falsetto fumbling
at the strings?
        O let the muses,
thrice three muses, appropriately
mumbling in a row, dumbfounded,
mow at the birth of poesy
in those unlabored in the brain.

Brief though their toil, their fame,
may be, some ten words, ten days, long,
in all the work not one word apt,
the roles forgot before the play begins,
and still I have respect enough.

The will—whether the Will of Avon
or the fouled Passaic—is still here.
Muddy the mouth? An ass's frowsy head?
A centaur's cleft and clumsy hoof?
The yearning that is love still blunders
into loveliness.

This Grey Age

Had I known it then, really known,
before I began this wretched scribbling
(my dear friend, older in the business,
even as he was about to leave the stage
forever, did his best to warn me;
but how, caught up in that dream, fame
and its glamor, could I understand him?),
known how deadly the lines of passion,
clutching at the throat, would be,

I would most certainly have scorned
all this desperate fiddle, this dressing
up my feelings, I all absorbed, in high-
falutin craft. One fumbles away at first,
scarcely aware of the price he has,
in effort as in fevered pain, to pay.

But now the act is done. Instead
of gags and jugglery, glib cleverness
that hogs the stage a moment, this grey
age like Rome, bored with mere sideshows,
wooden daggers, bags of spouting
pig-blood, cries out for the real thing—
that the actor, falling in earnest, die.

When passion is the play, play,
alas, is over, and the one who long
had sought the spotlight, in it at last,
finds to his astonishment that he's
not mouthing art, the phrases he's put
through their measured paces a thousand,
thousand times, but the fatal, final lines
of earth itself, life, destiny unbudgeable.

Wunsch-zettel

By Lake Winnepesaukee, New Hampshire, 1950

Oh, no, it is not hard to be alone
the whole year through. Though I at times almost
forget the sound of voices, laughter, alone,
in any true sense, I am not.
               The seasons
visit; memories. If well attended to,
new crops they bear, surprises like a shoot
that, overnight left out in dew, bursts forth.
Solitudes ripen, silence, from these mighty
days over my woods and waters browsing.

There, you see, behind the house, my mountains
watching, sensitive to every whim
of light; on the other side, the mountain quick-
ening my lake; and, far beyond, the Alps.
To share their presence you think one needs to be
with them?
          I have the good, long winters here
when snows, big at this window, fill, as though—
just like our skiing days—high over my head
they loom, the Jungfrau's summit reached. Great climbers
too we were, my husband a champion,
you know. Then down, earth rushing to embrace,
the body air that through me morning flies.

And made of eyes, peering into this room,
the woods look round, as through my working hours
stride little life and large. They know no fear,
the birds and squirrels, the rabbits and the moles.
Some noons, horns sparkling in a sparkling day,
four deer. Bowered among the parent antlers,
the young frisk so the lawn and the bay window,
like a sunbeam flashing, seem to leap.

But come, let us go upstairs; for there
the study is, an even better view.
My staircase knight a little startles you?
A creaky ancestor who guards me from night's
mares. Oh I a sprightly ghost would welcome,
but ghosts at best, alas, homebodies are,
by waves unsettled.
                      227

The carpet came with me.
In its deep quiet one walks as in a park,
and straight into the past unrolling, ever
by me those I love.   This is my room.
Hushed, no? A den with moss and rushes lined.
So you see, sitting here, free as I am
to my work, my memories, maybe I—
your visit's kindness I do appreciate—
can make you understand not I from every-
one am lost.   That top shelf bulged with books?
The garden books I've turned my days into,
best telling how, how long, for this I've striven:
in each mind a garden to be implanted,
with fruits for others, blessed community.

This edelweiss pressed—between the brown leaves
of childhood's *Wilhelm Tell* I keep it—smell
it please.   You catch the windy mountain scent
still clinging to it? My leaving this house
it recalls for me, my leaving the first time
Europe to visit again.   To Switzerland
I went, for six weeks in a tiny village:
the world's lost young, war's handiwork, as in one
proving bed transplanted. Yes, others there were,
villages of children American money
built.   Quite so: Pestalozzi named,
after the great teacher.   Why did I go?
Because of all my work on me they called,
as you do now, gardening to teach them.
Children, think of it, Polish, Russian, Greek,
from everywhere poured in. Looking up to me,
one their hunger made them.   No, no lectures.
For such a group, children and teachers
as well, speaking many languages,
what could I prepare?   So then the moment
I used, out of both sleeves whatever magic

I could summon. Nature, I told them, can be
trusted. Though how they, plucked from the wreck
of Europe, could trust to trust me I do not know.

Starved looks, the Greek children most, fixed on me;
haunting it was. Expression, you know, by eyes
one tells, the upper part of the lid. But those
had saucer eyes, at least as round below,
in each disaster heaped, huge emptiness.
And then on next year's wheat to bid them live!

There in Switzerland those wintry weeks
I stayed, high in an attic, peaked its roof
among peaks, a cot, a chest hand-carved, one candle
giving light.
                    By candle I love to work.
To sit near it, before you the night, the whole
great night at once around you, faces leaning,
flowers, to the light. Then all we are,
the selves of dream and wake, together flare.

By candle—in Germany for darkness all we
dared—my third book I wrote. A night unbroken
composing it. In itself joy, though for it
waking hours and my daughters suffered.
No father there to comfort or amuse.
Books and buds so pressed their only out-
of-doors, and I striving to dam the darkening
tide of shouting voices, dim the growing
clack of marching feet.
                              Midnight knew
no stop. That May the first a fever-glisten
as of sun gliding up and down massed guns,
droves of relatives and friends—my grand-
mother's "To a new world go. Forget!"—
in vans boxed away.
                          Our one companion,
constant and reliable, terror,
in that long, unbroken night we fled.

Yes, time has passed, much time like heavy earth
turned up and piled upon that time.
                                          So then,
and in that children's village, living so,
round us nothing but their needs and the good-

natured elements, soon signs of change
like crocus tips from frozen clods peeped through.

Here, that time's first harvest let me show you.
As European young ones used to, for me
a Wunsch-zettel they drew, a Christmas wishing-
list. And think of it, not one of them
had ever seen a garden. Drawings these
of dream desires, flowers they would plant.
All this and this just one week's industry.
These French drawings, such bushy frolic greens,
such candy reds, are best, yes?
                                        Already
I had reached them? Emptiness still crowding
their eyes, in their hands earth began
again.
         To see them watching their hands, skills,
hard won, surprised in colors and shapes surprised,
like petals spread to cup the sun that molds them.

These—a little cramped and pedantic, no?—
the British children, with no sense of gardens.

Gardens you thought deep-rooted in the English?
Not in these, in London mostly raised,
cockney, the underground their home.
                                              Themselves
deemed better than others.
                                    At the Christmas party
with hymns and games, the Britishers, as if
by signal, their caps sideways, rushing in,
started to push the Polish from the room:
"No place you have, none here!"
                                        What did I do?
To disgrace their fists with words I was not slow.
Then futile I knew. Beside my grown-up shame
how should they feel shame?
                                    Still the faith
my father had in language as in nature,
had in me, prevailed. Words must reach
them.
         As such words at last reached me.

Till three no single word I said. My mother
worried, but my father, smiling, said,
"That child only when she can put her words
in perfect sentences will speak." And tied
a tinkling goat-bell round my neck.
                           What other
namings needed I? Clear voices they were,
the animals, wings, petalings, voices
like the sun in heather loud.
                      Each day,
that goat-bell playing out its watery notes,
I took him to our flower-beds to show
each fragrant task the seedlings were performing.

Then, dew still wet, fists clenched as though inside
a seed the world I bore, to him I came
and, opening, to show the sod I clutched:
"An affection for our fertile earth, dear father,
I have always cherished, and will." Amazed
he was, as much as you, and pleased. Later
he learned my sentence had been read to me.
Still that to memorize I chose, no other.

For words, as they first blossomed in our breath
from picture books, soon wound into my life.
Already cuttings I tried to keep in beds
of pages to look at when the winter came,
though, turning to, I found that while I slept
they, wind calling them, had slipped away.

Stories too, striding through our endless days,
round the garden echoed that the birds
over their chirpings seemed to nod. For her words—
our aunt, loved before the rest—bent over
us, turned all into a fable, the daily
far and lofty, the lofty near, like stately
gowns by ploughs and geese and hayricks twirling.

Even now, as I glance at my curving
path, out of some grand tale jogging here
it seems, with sweeping chestnut plumes like knights
and ladies cantering.
                   A dream it is,
mere revery. For little here can imitate

our first house.
                    Oh, yes, fine enough this one is.
The past I've done my best to reproduce.
But how compare it with that other's court,
dense orderly rows of chestnut, or the pool
carved curly dolphin flanked?
                    Then I was twelve.
With boys the garden rang, with games and stilts.
At dinner on a poplar we hung hawthorn wreaths,
shaggy colts to wait for us.
                    To wait!
Like laughter all galloped away. In the dark I woke,
many trembling nights, as though the dark had sickened.
Not all my tears could warm or comfort it,
not though those tears, like bread crumbs waking
in the moonlight, sought to take me back.

Still even now my aunt, and near the fire-
place, in the standing mirror that I keep
by me, appears: the first terrible time
a grown-up cried.
                    Festive her visits had been,
her wildfire haunting me. Always with flowers
she came that her face, whenever thought of,
loomed a flower among flowers.
                    But see, she stands—
far in winter it is—with her back to the fire,
hands thrust away as though their touch she hates,
this body that into joy betrayed her, pride
struggling, my mother turned to console her.
And down her velvet cheeks the tears, spiky
with the fire, stream.
                    "I cry," she cries—
the gates in my first garden clanging shut—
"because crying, as women ever have,
is all I can, as though the ones I mourn
from those long gone were little different.
Oh not to Him I cry but that the world
can do without them as though they'd never been."
Without them: her son drowned on an outing,
and just some months before her husband found,
slumped by his manuscript, his hand fixed round
its "finis."
                    I could only blame those two
for carelessness to wish those tears on her.

The heartless ways of boys! Men too I saw.
The new wound started up the old, her son
not even killed, as schoolfriends soon would be,
in numbers, we then thought, past tears' accounting.

Nor those more easily wiped out, as we
one summer day might douse a hornets' nest
and listen to the crackling. Our friends,
whole streets, whole neighborhoods, all rumbled off,
in smoke a moment tracing the wind's design.

And though her husband's dying and her son's
were terrible, I could not know, no more
than she, how comforting they would become.
For theirs not deaths to tear apart the house,
the garden, and the world.
                              Still vastly opening,
deepening, the flowers stood. I sought them
as if the days, the years, in them might ripen.

At sixteen to those much older I taught a garden
class. People shook their heads: "Of such
a noble line and happiest when grubbing
in dirt!" And looked at me as though they thought
out of my fingertips the weeds must sprout.
At eighteen my first garden book I wrote.
Behind me five now, five paper greeneries.

And they go on. In them the games still race;
like giraffes the stilts lean over ivied walls.

How carefree once we were, carefree with brook
and sky and bird, the covered bridge, with boys
and girls, skipping across into the meadow
where the loaded wagons creak with summer.

One after another every window shut.
After such as these, my grandmother,
my father, and my aunt, such radiance
put out, what other light could I look to?

You are right. The dearest faces stay:
the little ones, themselves like candles lit,
the air around me wafting their warm breath.

Hardly surprising then I worked with children.
But how one touches them one must take care
lest like powdery flower, butterfly,
the cool blue flame, the fragile breath, be smudged.

Though many scoff, what community beyond
mere place and time such efforts mean I know.
Community: Comenius first and then
a host untold, monks in their monasteries,
Rousseau, and even Goethe, by me toiled,
the rain and sun so bending, no less busy
with me frog and bug.
                          Note that brown drawing
over my desk. Dated 1840 it is.
Precious itself, far more for what it shows:
Friedrich Froebel's venturous first gardens,
in the village of Blankenburg in Thuringia,
with little children playing, tending the beds.
And in the background can you glimpse the steeple
and the housetops overseeing them?
At once Herr Froebel would implant in them
the sense of being a part of the community.

His lovely word, *Kindergarten,* shines.
But his hopes for it, his work? The rose's breath
often in my beds divined his love.
Him and the others, my gardening's choice wreath,
my father at last, and my husband, by my side.

My husband, eyes on some far distance fixed—
glinting in them the loftiest, fresh snows—
my hyacinths shaken by his swift passing,
strides toward the mountains.
                          Always he
must go beyond the last peak others dared.
Oh I can understand the need, to plant
a flag, my flowers, and to stand in a place
where no one else has stood, as I my feelings
first, then in a spot least promising,
those children, say.
                          How well I can remember
earliest winter dawns, the first wind, sprung
as from my sleep, on it a mist, the pond's
calm breath; and there in its pane, sheet-thin,

as with night's starry back besilvered, first
I was to see myself, the only one,
even as the sun sucked up that pane,
my look, my breath into the air. Oh well
I understand.
           After that day I never
skied again. That day as ever water
I heated in a great pot over a bramble
fire. Returning, pride—his dip among
far crevasses ice-cold—flushed on him still,
into the hot water, and singing out,
he'd plunge.
           The water cools, then turns
to ice. In it no face but frozen crags—
my tears, wherever I looked.
                  Moments that mountain
thawed. Through its briny flood a prow
would jut, grating on new shores.
               New shores
that wait upon the olive branch restored.
Wherever dark earth is in time I know
flowering can be. In those small villages
again already Froebel was, you might
say, flowering. In no easy way be sure.
Yet overnight pinched faces seemed to lift.

Yes, quickly in the village such circulating
with the fragrant things taught everyone
good cheer. Strength also, what hands can breed.
A humbleness before the mysteries,
nature at its workings past our reach.
But not alone great lightnings, flooded storms.
The smallest, wood-deep bud, only by shades
and butterflies attended, the light hidden
in it already dreaming, loveliness-
to-be, from blossoming is not held back.

And patience that instructs not every weed—
some for the flowers keeping water—to be
plucked. Faith too, as after furious hail,
nature calming, a bed can be scooped up,
replanted, healed.
           One night the Polish beds,
and more completely than a storm could do it,
were torn up. Complain or cry they did not;

235

only the faces, of a calm inconsolable,
turned from me. And still again I tried.

At night, after we saw how over us stars
prevail, in darkness best, stories I told them
of famous men, their trials and mighty triumphs
through such trials, read to them from books
savory as the worlds they, born of, bore,
more piercing not the taste of the sassafras-root.

From that an easy step it was to move
to gardening in other countries, ranging
from the Zuider Zee, Salt River Valley,
far back as the Hanging Gardens of Babylon,
the Pharoahs and before. At last to Eden,
the Great Grandsire, nodding through the rest.

So human beings in their aspirations
stay alive. Not only in books and stars
do men engrave their names, but artfully
in earth's perennial habits.
                              Think of having
in your garden flowering—as those children
did—at home, to time indifferent,
the proud Narcissi: Horace, John Evelyn,
Sir Watkins' Crew, Franciska Drake, Lord Wellington,
and all the other gallants, ladies, full-
blown in one bed, on every passing breeze
to one another passing messages.

More definite than we, these flourishers,
in better than belief enrobed. Attended
to, new buds they bear, surprises that,
just overnight in dew left out, burst forth.

But at our nodding sleek weeds overwhelm,
the lusts, the greeds, the savagery of marching
men to tramp down all our choicest crops.
In the middle of the night so Germany
became, a world around us madly crackling.

Out of harm I saved these: my children's piano,
their earliest lessons, father's music-stand,
the mollusks gleaming on the table, bent

to their own song, stronger than iron cities.
But, like sea-rocks imperturbable,
their siren voices always sounding stranger.
Not long my children valued them, the lessons,
the piano, as though, one with the mollusks,
muttering still that lost intolerable world.

And so it goes. In German my youngest writes
to me; though a young lady now, her German
grows, grows daily, worse. Amusing the errors
from English creeping in. This to explain
the few letters she sends.
      No, I do not mind.
With me the little girl she was it keeps
alive, as in this glass her still I spy.
But spy her less as more and more my girls
depart, as though they, growing, women now,
and living in a different climate, soil,
were growing away from me.
        It may be so;
our first flight may have set the course.
Part of that early world they seem to be,
a world like ripped-up paper dropped behind,
like bread crumbs scattered many a bird pecked up
long before my girls could grow enough—
have memories that would, in one place, house
their senses that they knew, whatever other
lands they went to, a security
within themselves.
     Well, maybe later some
reassurance they will find—quite so,
like those children in the village—landmarks,
in my books, a home.
      Meantime? I wait
and, welcoming whenever they return,
study the glass.
     No, not my crystal ball.
But in it sudden surfacings; and sometimes
too, when I look out this window, amazed
I am, as though a stained figure had leaped
into a painting, strange and yet belonging,
the way one shade a scene can rearrange.
Or on the brightest page a shadow strays.

Ah, well the summers thrive, great golden days
enhiving all, on woods and waters browsing.

Then, when the world seems a triumphant blaze,
the fanfare of some lavish conqueror,
a loosening sets in, a letting go.
Each day a leaf strews at its tree's foot
till leaves in sighing companies speck sky.

And soon, the winds a blinded swirling like one
lost, the snows months-long as though a wilder-
ness to cross.   And yet each flake a footprint—
his who sought to climb to the end of snows?
So lost, their end he may have shared, to melt
into the skies.   The summers through him—
the gaze of—once more rise, a hyacinth,
as this one on my desk, with his last cry
contracted down it in a crooked streak.

But how can I release, as out of books
this sprig of edelweiss, the loved ones, spelled
in leaf and reed and flower? Say how much
can one preserve or smuggle through in leaves,
stamped with all one's love and grief, cuttings
kept against the cold?
                    Never to come
again, not though I plant and tend ten thousand,
thousand hyacinths, upon small growing
things spill all my care.
                    Why, one could slash
through all of them and still not reach the dear
ones they are living on.
                    You may be right.
By being themselves and nothing but themselves,
to our outlandish deeds impervious,
the hyacinths, the deer, the hills, the rivers
make, and cleanly, our lives possible.

What would it be if all our looks of anguish
clogged the rushing waters, all our cries,
resounding in each wind, shook mountains,
clambered till forever they darken skies?

Five years ago in Germany once more
I visited, an old schoolfriend most ill.
The hospital, a huge new metal block,
in rubble stood. At her window I saw,
and all alone, a tree.
         Instantly
by the bole's slant as by the twist of branches
spilling shadows over the wall, I knew:
the limb on which our wreaths we used to hang.

After some fifty years all that remains
of my first garden. The fine, spacious court
now one bristle of geometric lines,
like those black ledgers father used to keep,
figures—garden too, he, smiling, said—
I could not follow.
         No, I'll not go back,
not though your asking me to carry on
my work, dear to me as it is, appeals.
Froebel would understand, and Goethe more,
seeing what they had striven for so lost,
Germany, the whole of Europe, changed.
Of refugees, uprooted ones, alas,
there is no end. Nor place to hide the grief.
The birds' sweet cries ensnarled with other cries,
that soil for countless overturnings, burials
on burials, too spent new crops to bear.

Here? Nothing so close, so tangled with
beginnings, nor yet with ends so glutted.

New gardens? During the War far as my lake
land I plotted. But the War itself engrossed me.
And after I gave over, let nature take
its own set course. Plants only in the house.
As much as I can tend.
         But now, the sun
descending, to my favorite part of the day
we come. Above the lake twilight, gathering,
brims, the mountains as at birth.
         How good
of you to say from out the children's drawings
heaven's colors flow.

                    Over the mountains
the woods have crept, and like the dusk they sweep
to cover scars. And let them sweep.
                           No, no,
I'll not go back lest scars, discovering
new strength, like hungry mouths ask more of me
than I can bear.
               One never knows, I know,
from what surprising source, this hyacinth, say,
deep cradled in its petals, sorrow springs,
wayward as our joys.
                 One night—if night
it could be called, for the late summer sun
had been so strong a thicket of shade it had
heaped up and brought in after-dark a rush
of voices, wings, loud wagglings round a candle—
at my door a sudden clattering.
                        There,
as out of earth, ice-bolted earth, pawed free,
forelegs uprearing, mouth enfrothed, a horse.

Maned with midday blossoms, is it winter,
dark, denied and roused from its stiff bed
of snows on snows, my childhood mount, chafing
on this moment's peak for being lost,
now for me at thawing come?

From The World Before Us *(1970)*

Pleasure, Pleasure

And watching Hoppy curled up
in my lap, the way he goes
purring under my hand into sleep,
this watching is a pleasure.

A pleasure too Renée
in the next room practicing
the violin, going over the same
tracks again and again, trying

the notes like doors
to stores more and more open
for business, like stars lighting
up some Persian night asleep

under the skin of day.
Is a pleasure and a pleasure
this friend and that, a light
of one color and another,

not only to read
by as the world takes shape,
the sea rolled over like Hoppy
in a rapture of churning,

but a light
that is also the thing lit,
the world in its juicy, joyous
particulars. And outside the day

in each leaf now
is lighting, each leaf by its own
lights, maple first, then sumac,
inspired but responding

as it must. Already
the year is more than half way
here, to be followed by snow,
at first hesitant midair,

going up and then,
to go farther, down in a very
ecstasy of windy cold. Pleasure,
pleasure and the darkest light.

The Heir Apparent

My father's ripped pants,
my grandfather's bulging shoes.
Get used to the patch that covers
the seat of one, his knees
stuffed out with prayers and a kind
of crawling, tight, tight, on a proud man.

And bundle the toes
for those miles of walking
factory floors that turn the world
into one tiny spot with girls
at machines like machines until
his satchels, bursting, spouted trinkets,

ribbons to prank
a country fair. And hair
spun out of the web of my mother,
hair like a nest hatching eggs
of her anger igniting each other,
a desert ensuring the eggs' eggs' future.

And plying them all,
bright threads on a loom,
playing them out, then pulling
them taut and, having bitten
off frayed ends, knotting them in,
my grandmother who never admitted America;

she lived in it
as she had lived in Warsaw
and traveled over the dizzy sea:
a few familiar rooms, jammed
with bodies lurched against each other,
only she swept good space among.

I jostled by these
and the many nameless, my walk
a bit cramped for the bunioned shoes,
the baggy knees, the hair full of snarls,
but my grandmother tidying up, serving
cups of hot tea. With lemon.

"Yes, But . . ."

for WCW again

There he was—having spent
the night with us, the first
time away from home alone,
terribly frail for another stroke,
his dreams still shaking him—
his fame steadily leaping ahead,

and he complaining to me,
struggling just to be somebody,
expecting me to comfort him!

Manfully, if with a bitter sense
of injustice, I did my best:
"Why, Bill, you've left a good
green swath of writing behind you."

And he, in a low voice,
most mournfully, "Yes, but
is it poetry?"
              That years ago.
Only now I begin to understand
the doubts necessary to one
always open, always desperate
(his work's honesty, spontaneity—
work nothing, life—depended
on it),
          one too so given
over to the moment, so lover-
faithfully serving it,
he could remember or belief
in little else.
           (Some months
later Frost would visit,
older, sturdy as an ancient oak,
unlike Williams, who could not read
to the end of a verse,
              intoning
his poems well over an hour

with tremendous relish, then
standing on his solid stumps
another hour batting it out
with students,
                    no doubts shaking
him and few new leaves breaking
out of him.)
                    And only now,
the years, the doubts accumulating,
can I be grateful to Bill
for his uncertainty,
                    can I lean
on it, lean more than on all
his accomplishments, those greeny
asphodel triumphs.

The Youngest Son

Cast out among your impatient,
scornful elders, the oldest a scholar
hunched over his books in several languages
before you learned to say "Sorry";

the second quick, clever,
finding your clumsiness like dirt
all over your body; and your many sisters,
grim, raw, willed like jealous men.

With your wiry little father
always a smouldering fire, a single
word enough to flare him forth, exacting
instantaneous obedience from his stiff brood,

treating you like some mistake
his wife unforgivably had made. Soon
you learned the skills of skulking, stealing,
hiding. Knuckled words, blows

aimed at one's weaknesses,
mold one as well as any other lesson.
You became, perfect, exactly what they said
you were: a cheat, a thief, a liar.

And yet they found you
useful for the minor, dingy chores.
You brought in water and wood, swept floors,
carried messages, often those

most revealing since they
hardly cared about your knowing.
Maybe it was then you started, broom in hand
and shears, some flowers, of a Sunday

to take care of the family
plot, tending graves of brothers
and sisters who had barely lived, some dying
many years before your birth.

Then, grown-up, you went
about your business, from one job
and trouble to another, your second brother
bailing you out exasperatedly,

the whole family meeting
to recount your failures or, worse,
to sit over you in hourslong, noisy silence.
Still no matter how far

you wandered you could not
let them go. And reluctantly they
grew used to your dependence, the weakness
natural to such a ne'er-do-well.

Now age has come upon them.
The oldest, more stooped than ever,
recognizes no one. Only you can reach him,
feed him; only you are there

below his books. And one
by one they turn to you, efficient—
for the arts you've learned—in the larger,
necessary chores. You, the cheat,

the thief, the liar,
come of age at last. The training
they were all so set on giving you now works
splendidly. And you move among them.

Having been a child of trouble
all your life, you take the family over.

The Last Letters,

whether they be followed
by what we call a natural death
or suicide, tend to be the most engrossing,

a kind of undressing
so complete nothing else possibly compares.
Leant closer, squinting at the lines,

we have the sense that
we are drawing near to something
ultimate: whatever the force of the occasion,

and the affectations,
not to say disingenuousness, death may induce,
a man, precisely as he turns

his back on what
he has been thirty years or seventy, is bound
to tell the truth. And turns his back

on the future also.
Not all its promises can make him wait;
what he's in for, he now sees, can only worsen,

deprivation, emptiness,
worst if he's been happy. And even if nothing
more than nothing should ensue,

the void ("he took his dog
for its evening walk, then shot
his brains out" or "she set out her rare plant

to catch the rain,
made several phone calls, downed
an overdose of pills"), something must crackle

over that last broken line,
something, we cannot help feeling,
from the other side of that life even as it is

being consumed,
even as it consumes itself forever
in its own private flame, now breaking loose,

like some great moth
throwing itself into the fire
which is itself to enlarge it, but lost to it

in the very moment of having.
And most of all if it is someone who has been
a master. As we say, a great gift,

gifts he finally admits
no help to him, a burden rather.
And, much worse than that, a terrible taunting.

As if to say we as well,
whatever admiration we may have felt for him,
did not find his gifts enough.
                              Not till now.

A Certain Village

Once in late summer,
the road already deep in twilight,
mixing colors with some straggly
wildflowers, I came to a village
I did not know was there
                              until
I stepped into its narrow street.
Admiring the prim, white houses
nestled among their veteran,
lofty trees,
                    I found myself in
a tiny square with a little dawdl-
ing fountain and a rickety tower,
its owlish clock absentmindedly
counting minutes now and then.

And in the fountain the face
of morning seemed to linger as
though searching. The air was fresh,
breathing out the fragrances
of a recent shower.
                          I luxuriated
in my senses, like meeting
unexpectedly a pack of friends
years and years unthought of, laden
with all kinds of gifts.
                                Then
as I stopped to knock at the door
of a house that had seemed occupied
with happy noises, a silence
fell on it,
                  the light went out—
and was it instant eyes like flakes,
ten thousand, thousand flakes,
and all unknowing, flurried
round me?
                  Wherever I turned
I was met by the unmistakable
accusation, "Stranger!" I, who had,
I thought, begun here and who now
required lodgings
                          for the night,
was denied and from the start.

From Fireweeds *(1976)*

Ten Little Rembrandts

There, with ten Rembrandts
or so, he slumped in the corner
like a sloppy janitor, an ex-sexton
in a corner of heaven, one eye opening
to say with a sigh as the bustle
flutters by him, "God again!"

So you speak with uneasy,
loving regret of Paris: "I do love it
but never feel comfortable in it.
And this time I gave it ten days.
But then the Parisians don't seem
much at home in it either.

The Louvre with its ages on ages
of dust, rooms empty, and the room
with ten little Rembrandts, and that
crumpled old guard snoring away
in one corner! Well, I flew back
home soon after, and almost at once

the whole trip, the cities,
their people, pictures, plays
became little more than a jumble
of names. But I assure myself
that each did something, is doing now,
and will go on doing. Who knows."

So you remind me of another
brooding on the Brooklyn lectures,
one in particular of a famous writer,
she heard in her youth: "A Russ
he must have been, enflamed
about the havoc that had plagued

his world, its scars long
after visible, about the dead
there seemed not earth, not mind
and time, enough to bury. But I can't
remember anything any more. No, not
the speaker's name or even some

one quirk he may have had.
But I keep hoping that all that
got into me and is working still."
All that, like ten little Rembrandts
hard at work, in the mighty space
of our forgetting exerting wily wills.

Your Father's Sunday Baths

What you remember best
about him, your father,
was his smell. Always,
despite the nasty little
black cigars forever puffing
billows round him, he smelled
nice and clean.
                    No wonder.
On Sundays, dressing up in
his best robe, he'd spend most
of the day taking hot baths,
even though your mother was
a great traveler and it was
hard on her.
                    The rest
of the day he'd read
the dictionary. But how
important he was, his razor,
his razor strop hanging there
in the bathroom, to you
four girls.
                    You'd go in
after he was done, the whole
bathroom swimming, lost
in smoke. And now you think
of him, a full-dress admiral
in the flagship, smoke
its standard,
                    leading
a mighty fleet on a Sunday
up the Amazon or the Zambezi,
repeating words unheard of
he had read that morning.
And your mother thought
he was a stay-at-home!
                    Years
later there they hang, so many
sweet-smelling outfits, one
for each trip, of the kind
he would take that day, hang
in the closet, his smoke-
plumed Sunday baths.

Off to Patagonia

for Pili

Say it's an important event like this:
a famous foreign dignitary about to arrive
or the government planning an excursion,
a messenger announcing it or a newspaper
dispatch (by now a rumor should do,
a clouding over of the day), and those
under suspicion without a sigh pack a bag,
kiss the family good-bye and for the duration
take themselves off to prison.

It had become a way of life.
But that's the way life was in Spain.
And no doubt countless other lands as well.
When you were a schoolgirl you had this mad
highschool Latin professor who, arranging
the class in two straight rows, kept
the rear section of the classroom clear.
And if anyone of you failed to answer
as he liked, pointing imperiously

to that demarked, empty zone,
he said: "Off to Patagonia with you!"
The Latin you had learned? Forget it!
But you did master something: grammar,
punctuation, syntax of a basic sort that,
whether you realize it or not, now stands
you in good stead. The time, standard
Spanish time, comes when it comes,
and then—for less than a word,

an imperceptible lurch in the day,
you and your life suddenly grown thin—
it says: "Off to Patagonia with you!"
And you, packing a bag, kiss the family
good-bye and for the duration disappear
into that prison, promptly clanking
shut. And there you wait patiently,
stern as the treatment is, doing your best
to remember that, so far, you have returned.

Snow Job

"It's my nerves," Mother used to say.
"I'm just a bundle of nerves."
And now I'm on that circuit too.
At last she's getting her message through.

Like that panic of late crazy flakes
shooting every which way, each one,
it seems, set off by its own private wind,
yet in their utmost reel converged on me.

My gifted student put it rather better:
"Feel? I feel like a man with a BB gun,
Apaches, hundreds of them, screaming
down on me."
                    Or those artists chasing
after every snowflake-darting stroke
(their work, in all its zigzags does it
chart-like repeat their heartbeats?):
pointillist, impressionist, depressionist,
a kind of pointless joke?
                    But I
no less go out to meet the monster
deep inside with a paper shield, a vision
that's bifocal, and a year's supply
of ballpoint pens.
                    Nearby reinforcements,
poised in their ambush, nestled cheek
by jowl, my shock troops—aspirin, Alka
Seltzer. (Such allies Mother left me!)

No wonder increasingly (the latest news
redhot in the belly, each cell hard
at work) I see what shook Lucretius:
to wit, atoms in unceasing, civil war.
Or the local life—the reeking garbage
heaped, the muggings, rapes, collisions
also, on the churning streets—of our star.

Ah well, if winter's here, the hardest
lump of it, can spring be far behind?
Soon on this zany stitchwork, so bemired,
you will find a rash of leaflets, puffy
buds, birds shrieking their fool heads
off: nerves bejangling on a giant lyre.

In Defense of Dull Times

I

The recent past, its crop of poems,
did they seem dull for having little
to do with you?
                    Perhaps you both
went at it absentmindedly as though
you were, together, a duty to perform,
a mild, established habit like old
married couples.
                    Well, that too
is a reality of sorts, the vagueness,
the going about it routinely as one
breaks an egg or turns the spigot on.

Meantime, the mind roams out,
grazing in a field at best half known,
mingling with figures so preoccupied
they hardly tell themselves apart
from the mist rising out of whitish
grass.
          Or maybe lying on a cliff
that seems miles high, the sky above—
though close beside you on your rock—
one rumpled cloud, plumped over a sea,
its set of frizzled waves doing
the same thing over and over again
that they look standing still.
                              And there
mid-sea flotillas like matchsticks—
dolphins? seagulls hovered?—sailing,
sailing, never moving.
                          And that steady
drone, almost like the air itself,
a sighing, where does it come from?

Going nowhere this way, being somewhere
in between, ensures a kind of ease,
the minor success, of not insisting,
of not pressing down upon oneself
as on one's words, hoping to catch them

unawares or to oblige them, half agape,
to snatch at certain forbidden things,
sizzlings they had not thought
they dared.   This music rambles on,
heard by no one, least of all itself.
Thus, like a shifting cloud providing
space, it makes the story possible:
the fire can eventually declare itself.

I I

Imagine, if your dawdling allow, a time,
anonymous mostly, mostly well forgotten—
grazing in a field half known, mingling
with figures, grand yet so preoccupied
they hardly tell themselves apart
from the mist rising out of whitish
grass—that time before the princeling
met his match (Troy also) in the guise
(she cloud-wise led him on) of Helen.

> All the brush it takes,
> beyond the mighty, crashing
> trees, the slow, dry, tangled,
> whitish stuff, to make
> a conflagration!

I I I

And so there are those times,
calm on the surface, to most men dull,
when someone slumps like a thing, stared
out of countenance by his idiot-whey-
faced paper, or another, cross-legged,
turned to stone, looking out into space,
the sky, the past's, his nebulous own.

"Studious peace," the "exuberance"
(or is it the "exultancy"?) of nostalgia.
These occur when they do mainly to give
altercations, wars, the sudden eruptions

of the blood, the knife slashing air
like a meteor, or in the ambitious mind
a fixed yet raging star, the opportunity
to be once more.

      I V

           One would, enhancing
all his idleness, dress the very body
of the sea, sprawling, salty Neptune,
in the puffed velures his vowels spin,
break ships upon his speaking's rock
that their spices make a breathing
Arabia of the waves.
           But no eloquence
can long costume that testy codger.
Any more than it can tether fire, guy
lust in its gravity.
           Venus, also rising,
unexpected and unbidden, on the crest
of contemplation, wresting the scepter
and the pride of place from hoary power
by the power, naked, blindness-making,
of her beauty.
           Another, hating the daily,
yearned to thrust himself into the middle
of disaster, haunts demons frequent,
into mystery.
           So he sat above himself
like some brooding spell, a trapdoor
glad to welcome any cataclysm, tigers
packed, jackals, monkeys snarling
just beneath his skin. And was that,
firecrackers popping, imps?
           His words
may not have won a single apparition,
yet they conjured him.
           And, watching,
others were so smitten too. Felt mammoth
creatures never met before in flesh.
Out of his ardor, flagrancy if need be,
he made realities—as knives can fix
two opposites—a metaphor by coupling
one familiar with the mysterious.

First grazing in a field half known,
mingling with figures so preoccupied
they hardly tell themselves apart
from the mist rising out of whitish
grass, the sheep one casually tends.
Not till they turn, insistent, on him.

V

Helen call it in its beauty,
    belling all the devils
        out of hell
and belling deities as well,
    elate to wallow in debris,

    a delicate, small link
knits up the myriad contrarieties,
the countless, plodding moments
        earlier:
        an oafish husband,
        lout for lover, slow,
    dry, tangled, whitish stuff,
sufficient—she the first spark
of the holocaust—to set it off.

The city spouting towers
    high above its towers,
        faces crackle, cries
of love and hate, offsetting her.

Another and Another and . . .

. . . to go on living after all.—Odysseus

Even the liveliest of us had
to regale himself with farfetched
lives he had not lived, spontaneous
roles, spun out with plots, inspired
complications, accidents, seafaring,
like the spumy wonders that his wife
aggrandized daily from her hands.

It must have refreshed him
for a moment to shed his briny,
pounded body, habits of a lifetime,
tugging always, nagging at him,
like the gods, fate he must follow,
for its daily due, allowing never
one digression from its course.

But given the space, a new
world waiting—charged though
it might be with trials, dangers—
of a stranger's eyes and ears,
stage like no other to frisk on,
apt for any fantastical performance,
he could assume a mask, that role
lighter than feathers with wings

working them: a name, names
made of breath alone, and deeds
to stroll in like a god, the same
daring, the same freedom. And those
eyes, sparkling their amazement,
mounted snowy peaks upon his words,
composed—those ears—a music balmy
round him birds might loll in,

glad to add, to drown in,
their own most luxuriant songs.
For a moment, far past all that he
had done, was yet in ways unknown
to him to do, he was free to wander

the way—lighthearted, true—of his
own wish, to do the things he was
not meant to. And by feigning so,

his acting another and another and . . . ,
he became that much more himself.

The Storeroom

I

So many things
at her—day after day those madly blooming
things, crammed into tiny, rocky Ithaca,
a bare exposure in the sun—no wonder
the storeroom's twilit cool entices her.

Where else, long years of yearning worked,
close-figured, into yarn, the suitors crowding,
more and more suspicious, round her loom?

And there, the ruses, every hard choice, shed,
absorbed as if by her dream-riddled sleep,
she stands.
At first the shapes seem satisfied
to keep the dark. But glimmers of them gather,
and in huddled companies, then one
by one they press toward her:
an axhead,
scythes, lump bronze, lump gold,
piled under, earth and earth's
before the race began,
restoring
her to a time the mind was not yet
here to trouble, time itself
of small account,
and to a time
washed, fired, over both of them,
but lovely-slow, the world not yet
intruding.
Hung next to the scythes,
his longbow, shadowed as if by
offshoots at their feathery, light-
shafted darting.
In the corner
just below, bow's echoing, a lyre
leant, slack with its music
drowsing.
And beyond them, sagged
from sweat-black, ragged thongs,
his cuirass.
Her fingers carefully
trace dents in it. At once, air heaving,
uneven throbbings thrill her fingertips.

I I

Like bugs flying, beams flit around her.
Strayed through slits, attracted to each self-
lit thing, what are they if not his goddess
never blinking?
　　　　　There, as though the grey-
eyed sea had fixed its gaze, Athene stands,
her favorite beside her.
　　　　　And her glance,
igniting his, strikes studded bucklers,
spears racked up.
　　　　　Instantly the room
one ricochet, he's plunged into the clash,
yet stayed by each thing in its sovereignty.

The glare too strong, his wife looks away
to a deep-bellied crater.
　　　　　The country glow
it basks in, brimming like a wine, pours
over on a polished chest.
　　　　　Opening it,
she fondles tunics she had woven, thinner
than dried onion skins; a shining, long
collected in the dark, erupts,
　　　　　　　　sly movements
of a body like a soft breeze in them still.

And shadows step, diaphanous and supple,
forth.
　　　Step too as from the man-sized urn
a flock in flight encircles, and wildflowers,
whirling over dryads, satyrs, beaten
that they seem to cry, their bodies writhing,
rapture.
　　　　Startled by her glance,
　　　　the urn revolves each daedal
　　　　side:
　　　　　　fat summer preening
　　　　first; then swiftly turning
　　　　colors; paling
　　　　　　　　into rigid
　　　　winter, mounds like eyesight
　　　　banked,

              night underscoring
      as it threatens, by it death
      pitch-bright.

   I I I

             But there, just outside,
the land he, never letting go, is blind to
till the goddess hail him down to earth.

New crops rotted on old, the vineyards
slumped within a drunken buzz, the suitors
swarm, retainers and the women servants
waiting on their appetites.
              Once luminous,
each dawn delighting like a bright-eyed child
to gawk among the loveliness, rooms now
one trough awash with swill.
              And by the house's
gaping doors his sheep and cattle mired
down except as they are turning, turning
on a spit.
          The trees, their untrimmed limbs
a flotsam many seasons, steep in leaves
like someone lazily drifting.
              Drifting
geese and drowsing drakes, but often flurried
into squawky storms by wild curs, sure
to rend him should he return.
              Only one
old hound slumps peacefully. Long worlds ago
gold fleece to morning.
             A party hurrying
by, aimed at the shimmering grove, the horns,
the hallooings hovered over, much as August
breezes fail to rouse the dog.
             But then,
like that beggar dumped on steaming dung,
sunk in a dream, a sting abruptly at it
out of streaming afternoon—
               is it a sparkle
from some leaf-and-shadow-speckled chase,
a boar's tusk slashing in, or merely one
of its abundant kin, the sizzling fleas?—
it recollects:

at once love's piercing blow
shatters its tough heart.
　　　　　　　And weeping bitterly
among the gnarled, hard-bearing pear and fig,
his father, like that beggar beaked by suffering,
its whole flock which, nestled in him, spawns.

The son, a sapling, hardly grown enough
to master his estate, so let the arrow,
pacing its ravenous covey, loose.

　I V

　　　　　　　　　　　Best of all,
his wife, loving the old man for the memories,
the miseries, they share, as for his own
which, though unknown to her, reverberate.

She, catching in her son's eye glimpses,
always nearer, of her husband, the wonder
which their mingling with the goddess flared
inside the hidden room, devises schemes
to save their world.
　　　　　　　The hidden room?
　　Entering, she remarked a spider
　　neatly fasten filaments from bow
　　to lyre, chinked light gliding
　　on those lines,
　　　　　　　then link them
　　to the massive double doorpost,
　　though the door, each time
　　swung open, broke the web.

Never making, even if she could, her work
too finished lest the goddess, much offended,
end her world, but keeping death, the suitors,
dangled at arm's length.
　　　　　　　Kept them,
　　like the captive figures
　　flitted in the tapestry, alive.
　　　　　　　　　　She
this day, though squabbling as before filled
the house, resorting to her own becornered
yet commodious storeroom:

       weaving;
              then,
night come, a revelry swept up, unraveling
the fabric rippled on her warp.
          Just so
   from moon's collaborating loom
   the nymphs play out—diversely dyed
   and buoyed with dappled creatures,
   ripened to the West Wind's breath—
   the sea.
         Beguiled—by weeping,
   sighs?—to interrupt their sport,
   they jostle round her whirring work
   and gape, their shadows purpling
   the thrum, at her elaborate design.

   V

                The web
daily spreads the fabulous tales she's drunk
from suppliant lips, inspired by their need,
by gods greedy for such nectared songs,
drunk also from the mouth, mellifluous
and terrifying, of her dreams:
                steeds,
   hard tugging at the stitches
   to run in harness with the coursers
   of the sun, a slowly galloping,
   one summer day:
          and rumbled
   in (the clacking of her loom?),
   the lumbersome horse, turning
   into thread which draws it forth,

   forth armored men, the ten years
   blazing out,
         redoubtable deities
   emblazoned, for the immortality
   their moment blossoms no less
   glorious than the blown May
   fly,
      to swansdown women
   shying from her shuttle as
   from centaurs:

         strewn wreckage
when the day's light settles—
bits of limbs, a jetsam glance—
as if smoky Troy:
         then crises
quaking in the woof, each sea-
and landscape of his peril, rocks
sticking out, tide-sucking monsters,
silky trap a minor spirit spins.

Gladly she snaps threads.
         But such exploits,
though every night nipped with the sun,
next day transformed as in the myths, for all
the life rammed into them still magnifying.

V I

His wife who angles him upon her shining
line to haul him back—sometimes how he,
dragging, hangs on it, on her, the power
of her loneliness—from out that years-
bereaving, sea-and-wind-reeled tangle.

This shuttling, ceaseless, must chart out
his zigzag course; and stumbled on the clue
through her own maze, she carefully tracks him,
secreted in it, figure slow to show himself.

Must, as it keeps his crested helmet bobbing,
like his masted ship, above its element.

She, kindred to those spinsters never tired,
spider-canny, leaving just so much
each night, the narrow lifeline quivered
through her hands, for him to cling to.

    (And yet see how simple,
    blank even, though the sharpest
    needle guide it, each stitch
    seems to be;
         a stitch snarls:
    is it a sortie, far off going on,
    a battle waged and lost, his death?)

Strings, and heartstrings, twanging at his tug,
how can she hold him fast, that slippery one
a thousand twistings?
                                    Her breath snags;
a stitch drops. Has he let go?
                                    O, no,
not he, cliff-clinger, and most masterly
as castaway, afflictions gaping round him
in his craft.
                    But still those ominous rifts
(recesses where, becalmed, and variously
bedded, he might recover in, might dis-
appear, so loved, forever?) moments when
she fails to find him under her fingers,
in her thoughts, her fears,
                                    forgettings.

VII

Without him near, completing her, she feels
as much remote from home, confusion all
her once familiar things. Confusion all.

O for a time the giant space he'd filled,
his clamor claiming it, his urgent needs,
so emptied, pleased her; she could roam in it,
inviting, tasting, portions till now hidden
of herself.
                    But soon the emptiness spoke out,
increasingly, as emptiness. For there
where his dear body used to be jag-ends
of her own.
                    Hot tears crash over her,
tears would sweep him home, but these she fears—
his enemy so strengthened—must confound him
more, hurl him against some rock-ribbed coast.

(And yet within its dish the water winks:
morning, perched once, singing, on the crag-
like shoulder?)
                    So his name repeated, sputtered
like a torch, should lighten every furtive nook,
but sighed, its syllables, to her dank pillow,
crumbles into air, winds rushing through

(a gust of voices,
          riotous,
               the scamper,
ruffling moonlight).
               Someone brings a strap
wrenched off in battle, insisting it belonged
to him, bloodstains of course pure Trojan.

Another with a flourish proffers, tarnished
for the bearer's scratchy gutturals—
yet her breath can burnish it—a scrap
of speech he hoarded from some far assembly:
breaking through like sunlit surf, patched
with mist, that loved voice, thundrous still.

And showering its words on them, parched
listeners enrapt, an April spray when kindly;
raging, flakes like fiery shafts sure-aimed.

Flakes, fiery now, but blown by many a gust,
confusion all, a witless storm: each thing,
the most familiar, drifts, roost for such
forgetting.

V I I I

          But does she not at times,
as if, having tied a knot into that web
to hold it (so hold him), absentmindedly
drift too?
          For even she, days dawdling,
must admit sun's blandishments, a bubbling
pipe, or else an air that springs, surprising,
from her lips to waken in her aimless
gaiety.
          So, darkness near—the loom
bulked silent, empty, capable of all—
putting her hearing out, her sight a scarlet
thread stiff in it, she, adrift on fragrant
sheets, sails not so swift, is dozing off.

          From out the night-pressed summer
fields, sighs mixed with hissing
locusts and the husky breezes

rubbing stalks, all the madly
blooming things rush in on her.

At once the salty god—her blood
his wade—his hatred ever at tide
for him she loves, churns round.

His tempests swarming through
her breath, the headboard satyrs,
dryads (suitors, maids?), entwining,
whip into a fury.
              Like a ship
assailed, her body quaking, she grips fast
the rooted olive-post he shaped.
                    Must she
forever play, the restless moon at work,
fidelity, a statue's role? Attend that knot,
her breath's dead center?
                    Wanting, much as he,
to be enmeshed (much like that godly duo,
naked in the net of their own, however
let-loose, farfetched weaving, and the net
her art would settle on them).

I X

                        Adrift,
distracted—
          much as he by the wine-
dark, huffing sea, by the exotic
sites, diverisons there, awaiting
him, and, raced ahead, clamorous
to greet him, fame;
               one appetite
waylaying him, another, blown
several times past home, his breath
the gust outstrips all, driving him
earthward—
             suitors, lusty eyes to dress
her shimmering in.
               She in little having
what that Helen needed armies of,
a city's ruin, to highlight—that flush
on her she feigns her own!—her loveliness.

X

And yet how speak of her as one distracted?
For, unlike that other, she, housekeeping
her whole lot, can ill afford to play
the prodigal. Forget the prudent lessons
he had taught her?
                    So many years, not growing
younger, less sure daily he'll return,
spurn them, the choicest of the islands?
Or spurn the here and now, the meant to be
lived, whatever shape it happens to take?

Rather wait and see who might emerge.
No certainty that, given time, some one
of them will not become a man—fledglings
hardly older than their son, shell sticking
to them still, can any spread wings yet?—
like him.
          (And what use eagles, lions,
          prowling on some foreign shore,
          or maggots' rapturous song? Better
          a lout, this ancient beggar even,
          travel stinking on him, blessings
          of survival.)
                    Let notes be sent each suitor,
promises by private messenger,
a bait priming their hopes to win
the gifts they think, once having wed,
to recover many times over.
                    Had he but seen
her craft at work, fluttering in and out,
inspired, on that loom!

X I

                    A sleight.
                    Can they,
appetites blinding them, egregious longings
that have helped her cunning dupe them,
dear, goose-fattened enemy, who unwittingly
had bade this be, the seamy warp essential
to her tapestry, spy him
                    emerging,

slowly and yet clearly as in her ever-
lasting dream?
     (The glinting intermittent
in the rain, as on her tears, is it
his buckler, look?
      A glinting
bunched into a hand on hers;
or merely the first warm touch—
she reaches, reaches, cannot touch—
of dawn, her own hand stretched
before, not yet reclaimed?

Her fingers, nimble at the loom,
the dark, to summon up the instant—
honey spurt that stings—fit man
of him, responsive to each whim,
her dream no less than day outwits.)

There she stands, a goosegirl tending her
flock, winsome however they compare
with Leda's swan, just waddled from the pond.

And as she throws them grain, delighting
in their greediness, an eagle, thing
of iron, fire, arrows down to scatter them
among her hot, moist sighs like thawing snow.

A hard thing, hard, to be long bound to, bound
yet driven.
    Most as he is iron.

  X I I

        Iron though
that, fired to the utmost, can be loving,
tender.
    And when he takes light—light!—
hold of her, under those extended talons
dove most godly, no, most human, tender,
to embrace her into flying clouds
cannot compete with.
      And in a half-drowse—
O that it would come to that again!—
side by side, after the wine she has set

out for him, in the firelight watching,
like a drama nearly forgotten, fitful
snatches from their lives.
           There catching
on the flames' far side a glimpse of those
not yet, and of that one straining, as he
used to in her tapestry, to overhear,
so weave into, their story.
              Thus they might
live on, their exploits magnifying still,
in minds of men to be.
            (He wandering
from town to town, dust coating him,
encountering tribes so far inland
they have no sense of ships, oar-
winged, his grappling with the sea;

then boredom, lotus-eaters, sprawled
in it, more passive than those he long
ago had met,
             vast desert kingdoms
churning out mirages, making Scylla
and Charybdis mangy pets;
                men so far
inland his words can hardly pierce.
Yet by its bitterness summoning,
to his surprise, the best in him,
even if ignored.
            But not entirely.
For he would make his way to solitary,
hungry shores, through solitary,
hungry men, from Ireland to Russia,
sail dazzling, homecome, in some
hidden inlets of America.)
             Forgotten,
the occasions he, and she no less, have spent
most of their lives on?
           Never forgotten,
however she forgive.
           So much of him,
the glamorous stranger, to be uncovered,
so much to step forth from the shadows,
supple, diaphanous, she will not judge,
not till she's heard the complicated story
out from his own lips.

XIII

             And yet can she,
her look coupling with his, endure the battle-
like blaze, the ricochet:
               a thousand eyes
of men and monsters glanced from him, the grey-
eyed goddess, summoned by his gesture, women
also plucked, a nosegay;
             in his hand,
soft yet fierce, the ram he gripped, and striplings
doomed;
           Troy's flames, and Helen's, flickering
in his look, as through his voice the sirens
singing;
            that so tangy sprig which kept
a sorceress humble, loving, near as now,
sometimes swirling out within his breath
her wayward scent.
           As starting up again,
the joyous grapple; and at once, snuffling,
beasts between them, the rank sweat, a marsh's
under-musk, soaking their pelts, behind it
ocean's biting souse.
           Compare a Circe's
airs, keyed to the silken score
upon her loom and mingled out
in cedar smoke, in smoky thyme,
a fragrance binding every sense,
with his wife's customary chores?

Like one commanding a storm-
struck ship—or ship becalmed,
with a ragged, mutinous crew
its storms, stuck on this rocky
isle, the madly blooming things
threatening to run amok—
               plenty
here for her to lift voice to,
but hardly such in silken, soothing
harmonies.
           Yet had she, like that
charmer after all, not changed
the suitors—bound by few things
only, their designs on her,

ambitious to devour his estate—
into fat, rooting pigs, geese fat
for slaughter?
                Forgive that Circe.
Forgive also—grateful to—those nymphs
and goddesses, the women whose great love,
collaborating, helped to keep him, keep
him, hale, for her.
                Recesses they were
where he recovered in. And most of all
as he, emerging headfirst, feature for feature—
his eye seeking hers, seeking him—
from out her hand, shies off her daytime doing.

XIV

For suffering the bitter weather of his wars,
the battering sea, how different he must look,
how like a stranger.
                Why any tattered beggar
might be he. That straggly greybeard, say,
rags bunched on a stick, and many a day
skulked about their grounds.
                Her gaze
fixed on far distance, on an image graved
into her memory, can she take in
this lout by her, the story he'd be telling?

(Any more than he the country he pines for.
No doubt he thinks he can shuck off,
and all at once like rags, the tangled past,
its spells and lulls in their enormous power.)

Fooled before by her unruly eagerness,
snatching at rumors, greeting every stranger,
time, sufficient time, her mind must have.
No lumbered, hollow horse for her, no midnight
storming of her gates.
                Betray her lover, host
to every pleasure, for some beggar, shaking
hand held out, a filthy cloak clutched
round his body, no less foul, and old
enough to play her husband's father?—she
now old enough, lithe, lovely as his mother!

(Yet his travels heavy on him, blessings
of survival, rippled through his arms, how he,
grappling, felled that churl a score years younger.)

Twenty grating years to be so casually
cast aside? For has it not, that mountain
of time, by what they have put into it,
become almost insuperable, precious, hard
and hard, an iron?
                Treat it now mere summer
snow, a drifting mist! Or equally dismiss,
a movable, removable, like their bed,
her steadfastness.
             There, as in her dream,
she stands, never, though the world crash
down upon her, shifting, never yielding.

So much washed away, the rotted crops,
the vineyards slumped, the years nothing
but exploring, slow perfecting, of her grief,
now open herself to these appeals, expecting
a new zeal of her, fresh suffering,
another perilous life?

      X V

                Still he wooingly—
her name, brought home to her upon his lips,
new lit by its renown in all the world—
the gust of him, sprayed from the breakers,
would regale her:
              tale a kin to others
he has told, and like them subtly twined
with truths. For being pinned together
by the brooch she gave on parting, telling.

(Prickly now beneath his cloak,
a jabbing at the heart: the agony
of that hoof-flailing, golden deer,
a golden, snarling dog clamped,
solder, to its haunch.)
              Tale glamorous
as he has been, the tunic, woven of love,
she wrapped around him leaving.

                        Tight-fit,
shiny as an onionskin, to draw her
tears, he sparkling the more for them,
and that way draw her near like women—
droves of them, she gathers—gladly won.

But still she takes her time as he knows how
to do, for waiting's what they have together,
have apart, proved most accomplished in.
Both understand, like stars, tales of such deeds—
the lightning and its thunder laggarding—
require time, time to be heard, be felt.

Had they not learned it at the first
from one another, earth's own seasoned dance,
the measured pace of things completing
themselves,
              from their dear time together,
the great tide washing over them, yet lovely-
slow, as honey, pouring from a vase?

   X V I

Time ripening for the bow, she, lingered
in the dim light, is about to bring it
from the storeroom, hands still warm on it,
with hers his, summoning its past while relishing
the pleasure it will soon, become a swallow-
twangling lyre, loose.
                And revolving it
for wear, worm-borings, while he's been away,
the glamorous stranger, always expected,
all ways surprising, dawn arising headlong
for its travail with the sea.
                   Now gathered—
plummet-time approaching—like that bow,
its long starved arrows, through her skein
that sped them even as it held them back,
the room about to burst, a fired rush,
one ricochet,
           but slowly, slowly . . .

As You Like It

An old master yourself now, Auden,
like that much admired Cavafy and those
older still, in this you were wrong.
                              People
are not indifferent, let alone oblivious,
to the momentary, great scene.
                              No,
like Mrs. Gudgeon, the smart little char
come with our London flat,
                              listening
to the wireless, a most impressive array
of "the best minds"
                    engaged in difficult,
arduous talk, and she intent on it,
to her husband's
                "What're you listening for?
You don't understand a word they say,"
rejoining,
          "O I enjoy it, just the sound
of it, so musical. And anyway I take
from it whatever I like,
                        then make of it,
in my own mind, whatever I will,"
like Mrs. Gudgeon
                  most of us, watching
the moment, some spectacular event,
be it Icarus falling,
                      Cleopatra consorting
with the streets, or the astronauts
cavorting on the moon,
                        bear off those bits
that we can use. This is the greatness
of each creature,
                  the mouse at the Feast
of the Gods, one crumb doing for it
what heaped-up platters cannot do for Them.

Facing the Music

That creature was one thing,
I another. That creature my eyes
kept too close to the ground
to see.
        And yet when he,
my master, least suspected I
was there. One with the scratchy
thickets, part
              darkening
those shadows, as he, passing,
paused to lecture his daughter—
watching her,
            airs packed
round my heart. Or lectured he,
and listened, to that creature,
touching me
          like flutters
in a tree, a puffing prickly to
the skin. I, squatting, learned,
though he was sure
            that I
could not, the astounding story
of that one. If nothing can be
one, the humming
          left of a
gone hummingbird. Ariel he
called it. And calling, Ariel
came: a twig bobbed,
             the light
twittered, the air bulged. Well,
it was one thing to be, as he
enjoyed reminding it,
            long
pegged and howling—like an air
choked in its pipe—in a cleft
oak. But what to be
           like me,
a shaggy trunk, one meant to run
four-footed, happily confused,
among the underbrush?

                         And one
confused indeed as though that
Ariel, stuck in me, howls
yet most musically
                    to get out.
So I raise my head to sing
and howling strikes my ears
instead.
            And yet as I have
heard—myself was it or that one
buzzed round my head?—"Where
the bee sucks there suck I."

News from Avignon

I

A stranger?
     News from Avignon,
it's clear, or from a place, Palmyra,
you have never, not in fancy even,
visited.
     A glance that, staking light
on carpets, chairs, your reproductions,
now selects by its peculiar background—
a Parisian, say, at home in this Picasso
as in Montparnasse, his favorite bistro:
for the sketches scattered, fireworks
of witty drink, no less a lavish maestro—
many a feature in their background
you had hardly noticed.
     (Like flowers
that emit no odor and confess few colors
till you press them. Innocent and yet
beneath the skin pure Persian.)

I I

     Just so
the sun, studying out the vase's scene,
reflecting on the titles of your books,
hazy with gold. One, open, has never been
more boldly read.
     And sauntering along
the dusky lane inside a print, the sun
makes—O its bantering observations,
clever glosses—light of it.
     An instant
thicket overgrows. Oaks lofting perky
leaves, the sun ignites tips, flirting
out like slanted eyes, ignites a drowsy
moon which, though it blinks myopically,
almost confounds the sun.
     Accordingly,
the night, loitering in the distance,

looms there, Nubian, its mysteries
glimmering around it.

       I I I

                    Or the stranger
flinging your window wide, breezes
rearrange the room.
                    You are surprised
by your own things, a garland twining
with the vase's foliage, the carpet's
intricate traceries, its butterflies,
surpassing Venus' doves, and every furry
bird in full formation, swift-winged,
on the wall.
             Like someone startled—
water caught with fishes its own flashes
body—nose hard-pressed against a pane,
the mirror, peering, cranes upon itself.

       I V

Why not? Outside the sun is also well
engaged, the flowers eager to unfold
their latest merchandise, goods smuggled
in last night—from Iran was it, Isfahan?—
that like a honeybee the sun's sucked
in by nectar ripening for it.
                              So gold
the wallpaper keeps, with daylight
lidded all the day, in semi-dark,
set off by birds the garden doubles,
blazes everywhere,
                   as though your room
had suddenly been hurled into a far-
off kingdom—Iran is it, Isfahan?—
the garden in which the world began,
its satraps rallied round to favor you
with your own things, made intimately
strange.
        No wonder even trouble's—
this the point where you, your gloom-
compiled perplexities, come in, attaining

some perspective—having trouble playing
more than second fiddle to the sun's
extravaganza.

      V

      Morning mounted, as one
opalescent, gouty poet said, on afternoon,
how not capitulate to the swart stranger,
quarried out beyond all former seeings,
of yourself?
      Especially as Renée,
dipped into daybreak and your hearing
with her bow, is striking sparks spiccato,
demisemiquavering motes, from Beethoven,
Piano Trio Opus 70, No. 2?
      The news
from Avignon, just now, as in that scene
and on a stunning scale—a very papal
opulence, a revelry out of heaven itself
or out of Rome at least—developing.

Views & Spectacles

It's Greek glasses I want,
that's just what I want,
to see Athens, Ithaca, Parnassus
undaunted by the centuries

the Vandals overran, the Romans
and the Turks, the loving, paint-
removing, professorial Germans,
and in every firefly
                    a spark
that's Troy before, during, after.
And, to be fair, a Persian pair:
if I'm to see
                    what's here
as well as what's been there,
why not—the sea obeying Xerxes,
waves salaaming
                    like trees
which doff their leaves before
the winter's huzza, many horsed—
what might have been?
                    I also
want a pair that focuses French
so that every "cave" I enter
is my favorite haunt.
                    I'm tired
of those so haughty, volubly
gesturing words hissed out
like a snake,
                    ruthlessly
outspoken before my very back,
rebuking my accent for its being
quite obscene.
                    I'm tired
too of impressionism, its gloss
& flair for making the most
(that solid tide
                    in green,
in red, is it flowers, mountains,
heaving haunch?) of what's a
casual least:

why must
every flyspeck in each field
be designated flocks, haystacks,
crows to make it real?
                        And why,
Nana bending, should we have
to see the stains detailed,
alfalfa, clover?
                        But I want
a pair—that's why I have two
eyes; though I'm myopic, I'm not
a dunce Cyclopic,
                        roaring
epithets irrelevant—which spots
at least two times at once
or routs
            the blur & tense
between what's in, what's out;
too often fallen between, I speak
in vain.
            Glasses, reflect!
Be Sanskrit, Eskimo, be ultra-
plain. The latter's surely nearer
bears & snow
            than anything
I know; the former's now engraved
into the open face, the first,
of dawn.
            But finally I must
admit that most of all I want
glasses which, quicker than fists,
eliminate glasses.
                        Certainly not
my nose squashed everlastingly
against the candy windows
of the world
            but of Olympus
a bifocusing, or simply something
godly: to wit, at once to see
and, seeing, be.

Things of the Past

"Your great-grandfather was . . ."

And Mrs. C, our tart old Scots
landlady, with her stomping legs,
four bristles sprouted from her chin-
wart, she who briskly
                          chats away
about Montrose, founder of her clan,
as though she's just now fresh
from tea with him,
                          regards you
incredulously, a bastard gargoyle
off some bastard architecture,
one grown topsy-turvy:
                          "Not to know
your great-grandfather! How do
you live? O you Americans!"
                          She
cannot see what freedom it affords,
your ignorance,
                          a space swept
clear of all the clutter of lives
lived.
          And yet who can dismiss
her words entirely? It burdens too,
this emptiness,
                          pervasive presence
not a room away that, no matter
how you hammer at its wall,
refuses to admit you.
                          As though
you woke and in a place you thought
familiar,
                          then had a sense (what
is it that has been disturbed?)
of one you never met
                          yet somehow
knew—looks echoing among the dusty
pictures:
                          that myopic glass
reflecting, like a sunset lingered
inside trees,

　　　　　a meditative smile:
a breath warm to your cheek,
your brow:
　　　　　the hand (whose?)
moving on your blanket in a gesture
that you fail to recognize

yet know it as you know
the taste through oranges of sun-
light current in them still—

then gone as you began to stir.
And for a moment dawn seems lost
as in a mist, seems wistful

for a feeling it cannot
achieve . . . the sun breaks through,
an instant medleying the leaves.

~After All

Robert Frost, expatiating
on his work, confessed to David Daiches
that if, after the first few lines,
a poem faltered, lost its wits,
grew skittish, he let it go.

So he got no more than the idea
of it out into the open, into another
man's mind (now mine). That way
it was, after all, recorded how,
going out to work
                  in the woods,
he often saw more—the eye freed—
in feather, leaf, and little creature
than going into it with sight
in mind.
         Later, thanking Daiches
for writing about the Latin writers
plainly behind him (a fact most critics
failed to see), Frost explained that he
had started studying Latin
                  long ago
and with a schoolmarm in no way
interested in the poetry but only
the Roman road-like grammar, and he
for the longest time resented her.

But now he saw it may have been
for the best: not a mad beeline
to the honey but laying out the slow,
pedestrian cobbles block by block,
then footing it uphill,
                down, letting
wayside flowers, butterflies, and birds
waft out their fragrant stuff, a crazy
traffic run athwart the wars, the work-
aday, the slogging legionnaires.

An Everlasting Once

I

Your whole life faithfully
you went your way, belonging
to no place, no school, using
your wits to rub out every trace
of influence or imitation.
     Knowing
how browbeating memory can be,
how easily it thrives by shrugging
off the new,
    you kept yourself
to yourself, doing only those few
basic chores needed to survive.
No one knowing you—not even you—
your work took over altogether.

I I

It is as though you, tossing
everything into the fire, kept
the heat and light, kept them
going, like a man in a siege,
besieged a terrible, long winter:

first he gave his furniture,
then his clothes and papers,
one by one his cherished books,
last pieces of the house itself,
inviting snow in, and the wind.

Starvation gnawing at him,
having devoured his close friends,
dead relatives and all his loves,
he hacked a finger off, a toe,
till only a mouth, sealed up
in sighs ice-packed, remained.

I I I

And then, you gone, they found
the work unspeakably your own.
Try as they would, they could not
tame it into names, a scheme,
an explanation.
                        Except for this
they might pretend you had not
lived at all.
                        But that work,
unblinking, brutal almost,
not to be denied, prevented them
from twitting it or calling you
a minor this, that crazy that,
at best a ludicrous eccentric.

They might turn away; they could
not still the whispering fear
your course, despite deflections,
passages long underground, had gone
this way.

I V

                        Daily now that work,
thawing out, grows louder, grows . . .

The Good Grey Poet

Look to your words, old man,
for the original intelligence, the wisdom
buried in them. Know however that it
surfaces when it will. Perfect comrades
words have been, constant like few others
in your loneliness. But they too have a life
and a time of their own. Responding to
the slow, essential music of their natures,
they must go their ways as you go yours.

After so many throes, so many convulsions,
not only a war that threatened to tear
your world to pieces, the world you had
most ambitiously dreamed, all the pieces
of bodies you had seen stacked under a tree,
the maggots working overtime, but deaths
accumulating of those dearest to you,
politics, conviviality, love, the rest
at last exhausted, do you not hear hints
from the vantage point of what you've become?

Your ideal, you wrote a healthy time ago
to guide yourself, was Merlin: "strong
& wise & beautiful at 100 years old."
Strong & wise since "his emotions &c are
complete in himself. . . . He grows, blooms,
like some perfect tree or flower, in Nature,
whether viewed by admiring eyes or in
some wild or wood entirely unknown."

For your liver fattening, the cyst ripening
in your adrenal, the left lung collapsed,
the right perhaps an eighth suitable
for breathing, a big stone rattled round
in your gallbladder (righter than you knew,
you were—and even at the time you wrote,
rock-bottom feelings under you, your poems—
truly incorporating gneiss!), the ball
of string tangled in the gut like a clue
to knit up all contrarieties, you must be
more and more yourself.

Often, leaning
against a ferry rail, the sea your company,
your words beat out a rhythm so continuous
inside your body that you hardly noticed it,
content to let its current carry you along,
wherever it took you your place.
Now
you, who thought—sufficient stores laid in—
that your awareness had already pierced
the distant future, view these phrases
and that rhythm, still pursuing their course,
as any stranger might.
Your doubt does not
surprise. Who can miss the unexpected things
emerged to startle you, even waking shame
and fear?
But then you surely realize
how lucky you are, not only to have them,
these words, striking out on their own,
bearded with faces you scarcely recognize,
refusing to bend to your wishes or regrets,
refusing to acknowledge you in any way,
but to be able to use them—most because
they refuse—to measure that essential music
as it, and at its own sweet pace, moves on
to find the latest version of the truth
in the changes it is making.
Beyond that,
your words work, and work for you, by what
they do to others, bringing you—this
from far-off continents—reports of pleasure,
love, the tender might your poems go on
gathering as they inspire it.
And those,
the first breezy verses informing the winds,
your words in all their youthful innocence,
become so different, yet so much themselves,
like fruits more and more are bearing, bearing
out their father tree.

A Charm against the Toothache

By these windows we perch, tourists
still, in a cuckoo clock, this starred,
three-storied hotel.
        The cabinets here,
filled with random, little things,
porcelain shards, contorted figures,
seem to be exhibiting leftovers
from a flood,
        like the hotel teetering
on a cliff, its rocks at tumbling,
breakers in recoil,
        a halfway house.

Up against it wide open space,
with meadows far below—herds grazing—
gracing the panes, we urchin cherubs,
backs turned to the church-capped heights.

Behind us also, just beyond the road,
the town itself, sprawled uphill
that the sky looks as if it's spilling
over.
        Is the whole town asleep,
napping in its shade-drawn dark?
Or did its people wander off
with the army that once encamped
among the valley's slopes and meadows,
in their fashion tourist too, waiting
for crusades to sweep them off?

Or like us are they sightseeing
in Copenhagen, in Schenectady,
wondering what those stuck in Vézelay
are up to?
        At least oil-trucks
clatter round the bend; brakes jam,
screeching like a cargo of wild animals.
How it flails, that fox tail
from the latest lumbering down.

While the light's still strong enough,
let's start the famous climb.
Famous once, I tell my students,
highway to a star-roofed city;

297

not as now a dead end to the past
abandoned.
                No doubt the villagers,
backs aching as they toted the church
up rock by rock, had reason to adore it.

Restlessness at them, ache
of a tooth that never stops, maybe
for a time at least they shed it
in the churchyard at the top.

What a tourist jumble, this path,
of shops, mouse-holes in the walls,
showing off exotic stuffs—
exotic in Vézelay!—
Indian bags, Parisian skirts
that I'd look Aztec in, and hempen
baskets, belts, from Jerusalem.

No doubt what the earlier pilgrims
must have put up with. Trinkets,
snacks and drinks, phony relics,
clay-baked monkey saints, martyr-
looking truly!
                Bring one back,
puff over it hard as I might,
my students would never see the flame,
only the gritty, crumbling dust.

For the houses crouched along
both sides, gates barred, windows dark,
forbidding backs, I feel no farther
off from home than home itself.

What's home in a world flits by?
Like trying to nestle on a storm-
tossed sea. And we, each one a medley
of cells, atoms in a maelstrom,
performing their St. Vitus dance!

Ah that enviable wife of Bath,
ever more at home the madder
the jig. On permanent pilgrimage,
her body the welcoming Lady Chapel.

No less the Faithful Ones, believing
with their sheep that the grass
beyond their reach was evergreen.
Restlessness—not destination—
also their resented, chosen lot.

But most I envy those in Schenectady
who care to be living nowhere else,
the local Woolworth's gewgaws
their true relics, movie houses,
banks, and bars their heavenly hangouts.

Well, we make do with what we have.

Though we moved from town to town,
my hands recall cracked banisters,
in rain wool smells like snuffling
animals, and I at a mirror, frozen,
drowned in my own pimply stare.
My ragged doll alone gave back
the love that I poured into her.

Beside my sister, twin yet pretty,
out of ribbons palely shining,
I a feather swirling from the wing
of some wild-flying, ice-&-wind-swept,
never-minding thing.
                        And still
those thickets, snarled by vines,
my memories, scratching, clutch at me.

My suety aunts, forever fussing,
pinching me "Sit still!", gabbling,
nibbling, one fatter than the next,
their armchairs squat, stuffed like them,
smelling of mold, I, like our zoo-
crammed tigers, pacing inside a roar.

My parents, also keeping me leashed,
spent their care upon my sister.
It's true, I did rail at her.
How could I watch her disappear
into such stony, yet anguished sleep?

At last they packed me off to school,

a dismal jail. Yet happier
than facing them, mother's chatter,
her ratty neckpiece of a fox,
its beady eye hard fixed on me.
Fox in the attic, fox in the closet,
under my bed, glared from my dreams.
Or father's ever looking away,
eyes pale with miles of empty sky.

Again and again I'd hop a bus
just to be moving, going somewhere.
Safe only while we rolled along,
rain tapping at the pane, or snow,
ghost eyes peering, recognizing.

Dawn, rising, made a rose-
flamed window: sunset: starlight.
Highway we call it; high way it was—
our Notre Dame—to heaven.
                              Meantime,
two by two the passengers slumped;
pews they filled, carved-out figures,
yet flying with me in a private,
feathered revery.
                  And there,
still at last, still in the eye
of the storm, blissfully alone.

Like being transported through twilight . . .
our secondhand Apperson, fancied up
with cutglass vases, ruffled curtains
swaying, zooms along, father driving,
as if straight into a lucid dream.

Clover incense-like wafts round,
honeysuckle, lilac, twining
with the grown-up murmurs. Wheels,
the engine, tuned in on the spheres.

Yet even there in dreams father
stops the car (has the gas run out?),
shoves the door: "You're on your own."

And where, the years sped by, faces,
buildings, cities, flicked away

faster than an eyelid's blink,
am I?
    Still fragments of my first
small town remain, its homespun people
fixed like hacked out, graveyard
statues.
    A smoke drifting off,
I take myself from clouds and brooks,
from every leaf waving farewell.

Like that day on a road somewhere,
a drizzle, with nothing to do
but walk on and on. Never a body
except maybe some bird going
its own way in the darkening sky.
Nobody knew where I was, I not knowing,
the land casual, lopping, as though
absentmindedly dropped, a lazy
man's curved whittlings.
    Till I came
to a barn, the piled hay smelling sweet,
and no one there to fuss or chatter.

I asked to sleep in it.
    Next morning,
waiting at the door, bread and coffee.
A place complete it was. But had,
alas, no longer than passing through.

And circling still, as though hoping
to find that place again, I babble
like the natives, no doubt prompted
by this spot and by that millrace
far below, the women working
near it in the field, like poppies
bobbing under the church's frown,
shadow once countrywide.
    But now
no longer menacing, its portals
yield to our touch.
    Grey light.
Damp, moldy smell. The stone-cold floor.

Look up. See the figures squat,
foursquare on the church's capitals.

Caught they are, fixed by nightmare
faces in some ancient pagan rite.
While doubtless down below the pilgrims,
too poor, too numerous for lodgings,
slept huddled on the stone-cold floor.

High over them and, as at first,
leading the parade, glaring though she
is, and runty, Eve it must be,
root-gnarled with the trees
writhing round her and her mate.

Stark naked like the rock
she issues from, she offers him
an apple rounder than her breast.
Passport to the world?
                                    At core
the worm curls up, knowledge
pitted enough to break the heart.
Their hands touching as they try,
she and he, to cup that apple,
keep it intact from their fear.

After them that must be Noah,
set on a breaker-wrinkled peak,
topping this peak, the Ark by,
a wicker, big, one-windowed basket,
Mrs. Noah looking, bug-eyed, out,
tugged between the yet to come,
the yet to go, the animals,
a ceaseless rustling, just out of sight.

A rustling—the lion loomed above,
and, after it, two elephants,
the pelicans their sculptors never saw—
menageries galore traipsing along
the margins of illuminated texts,
from out of fantasies, nightmares.

A rustling over me! No dream
it was, no fantasy. A body
striding, stalking, something out
of farfetched scenes, he Adam
to my Eve, expecting me to be forever
caged, caged like those couples
handcuffed to their capitals.

Like them I also kept an ark,
crammed with fidgety creatures.
Whatever course I tried to hold,
the voices raucous, bodies jostled.
But at times they chirped a song.

Not like those animals, packed day
on day in one small, stinking box,
ravenous enough to eat each other.

Land once more appeared.
This pile of stones, much stonier
than its builders meant, call it
our Ararat?
        A Rock of Ages
once, sheer eloquence of prophets
towering spilled over it like summer
rain.
      Then hatreds gutted it,
rebellions, envy, pride. Next it
was sold and finally restored,
a monument, a tomb, the spirit flown.

The waters receding, dryness settled
in, dust on dust, what sorry beast
loves snuffling round such husk?
And shall these stones cry out again?

Yet the figures in very homeliness,
with their carvers lost inside the work,
believed their moment monumental.

Static though they are, they move
beside us, granite in our speed
and broken off, forever apart,
parents,
        sister,
            husband,
                aunts,
and I,
      stuck in our more than rock-
carved pews.
           Yes, like this place
haunted those figures' originals were
by every antic image as it scoffs
away: mischief, folly, envy,

lust, the passions in their jeers
gorgons petrifying themselves.

Us too as we gape up at them.

Tail end of their procession,
must we be bearing their wedged rock
that they look back at us?
                       Who's
to say we're not what they have come
to, their lone heaven? One dusk, one cold,
we share with them, one stoniness.

Pretense of standing still!
                     Writhing
stone we are, writhing like them.

So this place is little different
from that grey Schenectady.
Oil slick on both waters, fish
die in crowded shoals. Birds plummet
from their skies; for mercury rots
the air that song once cleared,
sparkling of seraphim as they
repelled the devils. Or so men then
read those heavenly commotions,
savage enough to scourge the earth
and all in it. As we are ready
once again to destroy ourselves.

The beasts in us, arked in sea-
sick feelings, trumpet out the rancors
stifling the hard-pitched body.

No wonder restlessness,
an ache, is all the rage: a fox's tooth,
the snake's, and mother's rampaging.

Still one reassuring thing
I stumbled on from out the Middle Ages,
a charm against the toothache:

    "Walk thrice about the churchyard
      and think not on a foxtail."

Should we try it now, circling
that weed-clogged plot, its graves
on graves many times forsaken?

Rather lean on this low wall,
extremity of Vézelay, vast supervising
of the gradual hills, azured
with distance, the vineyards, the winding
roads that, entered, seem to linger
in mist-shaded patches of the woodland,
alive with swarm after swarm of night-
ingales.
          Even with the trail slimed
over like a slug's, clouds of pollution
left behind by trucks, it's clear
why I prefer that bus, my travels.

The feral smell of gasoline
I've always loved; spilt on earth,
one vibrant stained-glass window
it becomes.
          Ground in its atoms,
fossils racing, bison, reindeer,
as along the rock of hunters crouching
in their smoke-filled caves.
                    After
countless aeons the animals plunging
still, as I rush on in plane
and bus.
          This height speed and travel
enough for you? It does command,
this low wall, the summer's rambling
countryside, we everywhere
at once.
          But look! Down there, a couple
picnicking, what's that tugging
at its leash?
          Looks like a bobcat,
a furry cub? Oh no, it's a white fox
flicking its tail!

The Family

This place, these persons?
Name a conqueror, even a puny one,
paused here to study out its customs,
its fair women, or to take the baths,
his florid ease.
    At one time
or another surely some plague must—
a witches' craze, a war, the painted
Indians whooping it up—have been
at its best here?
     No emperor
idled through, dropping spices,
prizes, blessings, horses rumbling
long years after in snickering tales,
his men in bastard cries.
      Saints
never settled in this place to draw
the heavens near, praises flowering,
and awe, as common as marigolds,
the daisies winking
       cherub fancies.
But my father found it, brought
his hungers and ambitions, Tokay
overflowing, in their gusto angers
amply translated.
     And at table,
heaped with fish and fowl and fruit
he had scoured the countryside for,
a banquet served up piping-hot
with voices chiming in,
       a guest
might startlingly appear, welcome
for his strangeness and the horror
stories he could tell, belling echoes
in the resident blood.
       A living-
room, a bed-, run wild with workings
of small flowers hard to identify.
And put up for the night, Adam
dreaming, Jacob, Moses,
        happy to take
heart, take color, from the family.

The Cure

And what can you appeal to
if you have nothing but this language
to handle your feelings, this rout
altogether Scythian, say?
                    If blares
blow up in you drowning out each tootle,
simultaneously you their puny pipe,
your flesh the jettings?
                    You watch,
cowed by your body's brute enchantment,
truths, chimerae, rousing. Sinking
in this flood of voices,
                    English,
you think, to accommodate such tidings!
But its deficiencies become speech
also, silences a grace,
                    chinks
which let the antediluvian dialects
resound; epochs too—tribes of dialects—
not yet.
                    And you are abounding
in the middle of a medley flouting,
by its bedlam, time itself: an only cure
for the vivid bane, the sometime

curse, of clarity. Nothing
but this English, tatters flapped
around the giant-bodied blast, streamers
that applaud the rapture passing.

See, it sweeps everything
before, mobs speechless, capsized
in this turmoil, satisfied that no voice
lives can sever it from itself.

But then it is, like rain,
a vernacular which nothing can translate
because it refuses to relate, its own
nature all that it relates.

The Library Revisited

"Weiss," a new anthology observes,
"is even able to be quite cheerful
about the burning of the library
at Alexandria."
        A scholarly book
relates that ages long predating Rome
and Alexandria, exemplary though they be,
already had remarked
           the artist's
predicament: competing with the awesome
past. Thus I am positive the latest
of the great
        Cro-Magnon masters,
pondering the Michelangelo among his
predecessors, as he beat his matted brow,
his wooly chest,
        had all he could do
not to haul up his massive boulder club
and finish off that handiwork. O
there they sped,
        the birds and beasts,
forever grandly caught, and only lesser
ones remaining for his careful daubs
to trap.
        According to that book,
in the Eighteenth Century "the thought
was to cross more than one mind
that the burning
        of the Alexandrian
library had its advantages." What would
those minds have said to the clogged-
up libraries today?
        That modern
English anthology alone, accounting
for a hundred years, sports "over 1200
poems by 155 poets."
        In the middle
of our florid fall, blinding in its sun-
beat spell, shall we try saving all
the lovely leaves
        and all the seasoned
tunes these birds, departing, spill?

The Late Train

What's it like?

A horn suddenly jammed
in a car junked years
ago.   An alarm
gone off in a town
that a volcano leveled.

Or, snarling out
in me, a siren that must
belong to a time, a far-
off country
          I have
never known, shrieking
like a jet-black van
lurching
          to the wrecks
it's most successful in:
my countless relatives
minus
          faces, names,
mumbling from flowers,
birds, this windy smoke
clotting up our sky.

Throttled before
they got their word out,
it must break through
some way.
          How satisfy
except to let it go
and listen
          till it runs
its course, father,
mother,
          else a curse
choking itself, choking
him it's locked up in.

Before the Night

One poet tells us
of blinded children beating
at their eyes, perhaps to strike
the sparks from them of light
burnt out.
        And another
is much moved to make a poem
out of a report that H.D.,
having a stroke, fiercely desires
to communicate
               and "strikes her
breast in passionate frustration
when there is no word at her
tongue's tip."
        No word,
no word wherein before one's
heart was gratified, a jetting
out as of a fountain, fire,
lute.
        No word, no sight:
one beats against the wall,
be it blindness, be it flesh,
the body
           turned to stone
against the wish that Lazarus-
like would rise.
           As she, a lovely
poet once, now, at the end
of sight, those children
at the start, haunted by all
the light
           that they were cheated
of, beating, beating, bird-like
thrashing, in their own bones
prisoner.
           A fired, stony gleam
for us who still can see and see
the blinded priestess, writhing,
racked, on her enormous sight.

The Polish Question

for M. L. Rosenthal

I

Suppose your powers such
you finished every poem painter-wise,
the light, its bias, so enduringly
sealed in—regardless of the time
and place the reader pondered it—
exactly as you wanted it to be
on this particular line, on that.

Suppose you gave instructions
at the relevant moment: "Pause here
to drink a glass of icy water so
that in you winter know itself,
you know yourself in winter."

"Honor this empty space (

as the place where what can not be
said, of course the most significant,
is being accorded a total hearing."

Finally "At the dots (. . .) the reader
is expected to think of his beloved
in her most memorable stance,
one so compelling it inspires
fear at storms already storing up,
her radiance, for drove-rich shades
attendant on her, troubling the more."

For is not Poland, Poland
of your grandparents, of terrible
times thereafter, waiting everywhere?

II

By this eye, north of its frowning,
Poland lurks;
                    inside this finger,
sheathing its arrows, in itself

so sensitive to, so lusty of,
the slightest pain,
                    yet also
sheathing silks of a tenderness
that quickly knot—sleight of hand—
into a lash, a noose, a shroud,
Poland, Poland,
                    where the sleeping
cat curls up, a scratchy, burning
bush, the porcelain cup a smashing,
through the cracks of which storm
troopers pour, as through the mouth
most cooing musics curse.
                    That light,
and by this eye, should light, so
buoyantly, impartially, on such
a gross array.
                    As though the sun,
nestled in dung, sees prodigalities
it can perform.

I I I

                    A painting, finished
in the light of Normandy, is bound
to differ from another done
in Burgundy.
                    But a Normandy work,
carted off to Burgundy, how would it
look?
                    Try pondering it in Africa.
Siberia. Or a country which unites
those two. You did say Poland's
waiting everywhere?
                    A Polish winter
lit—each flake a wick that focuses
ice-hearted hell—by tallowed rags
of flesh, by crackling, bloody cries.

And can we, so set off, warm hands,
warm hearts, at this and this and this
artwork for what each one supplies
in its fragility of paradise?

The Theory of Repetition

Well, is it not the virtue of art
that it, somehow surviving, happens again
and again?
          So the shot in the cinema
of the exploding tyrant's house which goes
up in elegant, slow, silky-colored smoke
a dozen times.
          As Hector over and over
and over—their chase as well, like racing
round and round a vase—
                    is had by Achilles,
who would have killed him if he could
a hundred hundred times, but only
in the *Iliad*.
          Each time however
differently if only by the repetition
of the explosions, fatal draggings, gone
before.
          Or thirteen ways of looking—
one's remarking it a second later, thoughts,
new light, and other events intervening—
at a blackbird.
          (Similarly a coward
dies a thousand deaths, yet so perhaps—
unlike the low-nerved, brave man—
lives a thousand lives.)
                    In other words,
as Heraclitus said, You cannot, even
at the seemingly identical place, step
into the same
              movie, love affair,
despair, joy, composition twice.

          I V

Stacks of illustrations
                    (paintings
piled on paintings here, like leaves
from under maple boughs, all mixed
with apple, sycamore),
                    collected

out of Burgundy as out of Normandy,
reflecting on each other,
                lamps
with tawny, skin-taut shades ajar
to ponder them,
             the generations
falling leaves,
a rubbish their pale bodies
raked, anonymous far as the eye
can see, the teeth amassed, shining
in one steady grin,
           a gilt that,
striking, reinforces heaven's gaze.

V

Thick smoke coils up, the shriveled
leaves, the shoveled lives, the sky
one darkening cloud.
          Back those eyes,
those lidless, bloodshot eyes,
into the light.
         In sleep, in wake
your body, like an earth, is quaking,
like the waters, choked with cries . . .

V I

O, no, except for newsreels, books,
dispatches, most of all from dreams,
and the daily anguish of my mother,
ashes wind-strewn nearly twenty years,
I've never been to Poland.
           But often
now I shudder at what the morning
light is likely to reveal.
          Then Emerson
in his benignity chimes in, proposing
we accept "our actual companions
and circumstances, however humble
or odious, as the mystic officials
to whom the universe has delegated
its whole pleasure for us."

At once,
mid-sauntering up his slippery mountain
to the Castle, a later, dapper, Chaplin-
esque explorer of our circumstances
and companions, officials scarcely humble
but to perfection odious, leaps to mind.

VII

Over the phone a good friend asks,
"You know the latest Polish joke?"

Watergate its crux, the next
the hottest thing in transplants.

VIII

Words, words, such deeds words, come
from Poland or America, can do. (Words,
so to speak, felled Jericho.)
　　　　　　　　Another friend
from London, hearing an earlier version
of this poem, says:
　　　　　　　"The one thing I know
about Poland is that I'm responsible
for its bluebells.
　　　　　　　A young translator
called on me and, much admiring my garden,
carried off some shoots,
　　　　　　　　then months later
wrote: 'Do come. Now Dannie Abse bluebells,
and several Dannie Abse poems as well,
are flourishing like natives in Poland.' "

IX

We talked the last of the mild,
rain-grey Christmas afternoon away,
our old-world-courtly host, historian
of science, his vivacious spouse,
the political economist and his wife

in literature, pale for her trials
with remedial English, my wife's
musician brother, she and I.
                                    Discussed
world politics, the desperate plight
of Israel, proposed some of the few
impractical solutions to that as to
the oil question—the Jews, our host
suggested, may have been at their best
diffused—
                    till the economist,
picking up his glass that brimmed
the day's dwindling light, remarked
in a kind of toast, like wine cast
out across the troubled, oil-slick
waters:
            "Our views are all so grim
            this may be the only solution."

Meantime, over the fireplace,
in deference to the painting's glimmer
never lit, the Monet meticulously
observed its delicate changes.

And as the party ended, standing
by the painting, our host, the woman
in English, and I, admiring the infinite
regression its pale, overarching
lavender suggested, a luminous fog
encompassing London Bridge, our host
said, "Yes, it repays study. Sometimes
I can see, far out on the horizon,
vistas usually shrouded."
                                    "What a thing
it is," I said, "this multiple vision,
this never-ending solution. I wonder
if Monet took into account—he must
have—the painting's future when,
as now, this scene, fixing an April
afternoon of 1903, submits to our looks,
the amber wine, the glancings, rainy-
mild, of Christmas, 1974."

X

But suppose
you could, like a painter, nail down,
yet softly with the pointed brush,
your mood's each nuance—
                              "emerald
green": "Pozzuoli red," splattered
like blood against a white backdrop:
and "raw sienna" (or is it "burnt"?):

"Italian earth," that "Naples"
like a lava, though the rapture
be Jurassic rather, Scandinavian,
a racing through the misty meadows,
but meticulously observed and fixed,
a cinematographic shot. What would it
come to?
           Nail it down and nail—
lid stripped away—the eye itself.

Enlarged then till its curdy white
became a screen, design with bloody
slashes like barbed wires marking
the juncture of the thing seen
with the feeling—transfixed
feeling—it released.
                         Ah, will they
ever know what earthquake strokes
you undertook as the tremors began,
a hue and cry, Scandinavian, Polish,
rippling under your hand?
                              Breathless,
you flung yourself out of the room.

Envoy

So, to complete the spectrum,
for the last time instruct the reader:
"Wherever you chance to be, introduce
(and also, whenever, on rereading,
you may feel inclined to interject it
in this poem) a section of your own:

a variation on what the rest
suggests to you or, if you prefer,
a departure, far as its antithesis,
an inspired or deliberate misreading,
a precisest disregarding.
                                    And name it
after the room you are reading it in,
the room and time of its occasion,
you declaiming your spontaneous words
in the special dialect each place is,
letting them echo with—an underscoring
of—this purely local happening."

From Views & Spectacles *(1979)*

The Quarrel

So they hurried to the barn
which only they knew about,
for they had built it together,
the door where they wanted it.

And with never a hitch
they picked out a certain day
early in March, some thirty years
old, not moldier than when

they dropped it, a scrap
of churned-up cloud sticking fast.
They picked it because the day
they were in, hot, scratchy,

hulked there, dumb-eyed,
and they hungered for something
cold, biting even, garnished with
dangers. So, the table set,

they, finding their place,
gladly sat down to the feast
each time new, delicacies heaping
as they ate, more and more

strange guests, guffaws
like wine spattering the room,
the spot a steaming stew of odors
deepening all these years.

Sated, they slumped back.
And they were pleased to say
no more, already relishing dishes
no doubt simmering away.

The Rapture

You came in
and the rooms were empty,
all the breakfast dishes dumped
in the sink, scattered pieces
of bread, the butter melted.

And your heart leaped:
"It's here! The Time
has come. They've gone,
and I, I'm left behind!"

A cry clogged in your throat,
you rushed out of the house
down to the lower garden.
Maybe you could catch
a last glimpse of them
leaving.
      There, admiring—
arrayed in dawn, dew-waded—
early spring, the gnarled
crab apple over its head
in blossoming,
          they stood,
their breath viburnum gusts,
caught in the current
of night, still drifting

downhill, its cooler air
mixed into the warmth
emanating from the earth,
stirred by worms and tubers,
groping their way:
           everywhere
a gentleness, already
tinged by the promise—you,
your cry at last breaking
loose, heaved forth a sigh—
of brooding, savage summer.

Autobiographia Illiteraria

It's the lost, the hidden,
sections of my life, those pages
not yet come to, I keep
looking for.
        So I continue
probing, sniffing, like the cat
Hoppy whirled round and round
on the mat
        he's filled countless
times. And missing it in this
spot and that, a long trail
scored with ruts,
        I think
my missing means it's somewhere
there . . . like the woman who
collects dolls still.
        "Sometimes
I look at them, bangles, satin
sashes, mousy little shoes,
cluttering up the house.
        What
do I do? Rush out and buy a new
one. This Japanese with moveable
arms and legs,
        a swivel-neck;
the Hopi too—the Mud-Head Clown
askew—images Hopi children
can grow used to
        of divinities
who saunter down from the hills
to live with them a certain
portion of the year."
        Still
there is a side to the ubiquitous
familiars I've little inkling
of; still,
        beyond the smell
of myself, a strangeness which
goes out from me far as the world,
far at least as time.

The Aerialist, Paris

dos moi pou sto

I

Having cast your line, you glide
along the morning, dapper promenade.
In the garden cloistered just below
five high-coifed nuns are drifting.
Into their wake schoolchildren spill.

And surges forth, like later spring
surprising March—the upstart daffodils
or maybe sparrows hatched—a moment
out of stubbly things.

I I

          You, hanging
on the least detail, must conjure
with this moment's temper.
             Riffles
first, and lightsome as the air,
barely disturb the dawn-frail hues.
But sniffing out each drowsy odor,
reinforced by all they have unearthed,
they sidle through.

I I I

          You need as well
what you have been, the boy of you
admiring stars, agile over dark,
the fowl, surefooted on the breeze,
from swallow looped to mounting eagle,
hummingbirds self-perched,
             and squirrels
bounced from tree to tree, the spider
spry along its listening line,
dangled, mote in sun, from nothing
but itself.

How these inspired you—
jailed by chalk marks as by the cloak-
room for your playing truant with
the clouds, and by the gloomy parlor
moored in obese chairs—
               to scamper out
the windows onto boughs, your house's
ridgepole, and the ragged bluff
above the river.
           Childhood dreams
of walking water, plummeting skyward—
space your capsule—also sweep you on.

IV

This inspiration swells in you
much like a god, his passion still
involved, his will, in this that he
set going, its detours entangling
as they speed.
           Indeed you cannot
get away. For what you have to do,
the overseer impulse gripping you,
stand here you must, unshaken stand,
attentive like the dawn, dew-cool,
embracing all,
              that city, spread
out, multifarious, at your feet,
yet made by height—sun striking it,
an ember blazed—an instant one,
one heavenly view.

V

                 From chimney pots
smoke, climbing, hovers, fuzzy plants
and ash trees, shedding
              soot, which,
smudging, underscores your spire-
vying stance; the gargoyles glare,
astonished, you like music towering,
a lover's gaze, a lonely, that would
span the world.

                              In courtyards shirts,
puffed up as if with sighs, and sheets,
at their lustiest, like huffy ghosts
jigged on the lines, recover St. Vitus,
by the screams of children soaring,
hard to tell apart
                              from neighbors,
high-flown thrushes, current-clever
offering to nestle in your hair,
also wild geese, their clamberings
as deft, but raucous, wondering what
odd bird you are.

          V I

                              Others under you,
Mondays dusting, scrubbing floors,
make such a hubbub: bobbing featherbeds,
bewarbled as they fly, then quarrels
punctual:
                    and broken sobbings too,
the mad, the dying, at their chores:
on Wednesdays marketing: and Sundays
windows polished,
                              catching glimpses
of you upright in the dawn, at dusk
maybe, serene, if struck by beams
nimbusing you, the chirping kin
a vibrant crown.
                         Most enviable to us
who cannot stand securely anywhere.

          V I I

Yet also something else: the moment,
be it spring surprising spring, urgent
in all things, like a glance opening
the world,
                    as promptly shutting
down, that lumpy clay peers through
the daffodils, and rawest wind sounds

out the thrush's spiraling trill,
its notes fat flakes swirled round.

On top of that, night snapping tight—
wind in wind, snow-hooded, huddled
like an owl, one star alone to tell
how dark dark is—you disappear.

   VIII

                              Still
mud, startled up and needing little
more—or so it seems—than its own
pawky steps, hard on the heels
of winter thawing,
                  stalks each snow-
drop, shoot, to streak aloft the iris,
feather off in swallows, weaving
complex patterns, twined with flutings,
fluttery hats that twirl the garden,
windows, rain-pocked, luminous
to quick reflections.
                  Even stones
let's say—great nuggets goading dawn
to skitter over them as over bug-
fat, scooting cars—the rugged words
a god might yearn to utter.

   IX

                        So you,
a Frenchman, knowing how to navigate
each snag-toothed, all-expressive,
Gallic ripple, briefly grounded,
juggle questions.
                  "Why do it?
Because I love the air up there,
the solitude, and the one sure step—
room for no other—after another."

Taken by the overseer impulse,
do it light-foot as a lion stalking,

vigilant beside you, brother death,
that every doubt, hate, misery's
suspended.
      Rather, pillars they
become, as storms gird air,
a temple migratory,
           you with heavenly
bodies, kindred to the creatures
hove across cave walls, its sparkling
witnesses.
      "The time I spend
down here is merely marking time,
the world at large a jostling prison,
men and women one another's bars.

Fear? I've none. The work's exact.
One learns to balance on a wire
all the things he's been and done."

So you have learned by compact
of your actions' grace, confirming
like the earth your steps keep steady
pace with.

       X

           Domesticities resume.
The flocks nestled by clouds, pillows
heaped on pillows, every window
hoards the steepening light.
           Buoyed
by voices' frothy surfing, ceaseless
sough from cars and buses, you
glide out once more on glassy crags,
blue as a gaze, the frank and bracing
air, everywhere dependable.

Recoveries *(1982)*

Recoveries

Day after day I work. For this I've come,
eager as some medieval pilgrim,
or that ancient wanderer, bent on the past,
the underground, to find his bearings,
worlds spanned, centuries.
            This country's art
I learned from others, first from picture books
in black and white, in tints I thought—thought
till now—precise.
            And yet details of vantage,
which the naked eye must fail—unless
like mine it scale the painting—cameras,
deftly zooming in and out, command.
Pages, strewn about me, flurried so
I, flying, seemed to land upon one site,
another, of a church forever making.

Making here, as high on this scaffolding
I stand.
            The church's shady, tranquil cool,
rejecting summer, takes the traffic's drone
like mutterings of prayer. And yet I feel
the window-filtered morning as it angles
off these ancient stones.
            Inching along,
light singles mica-flakes which keep the sun-
struck sky, reclining on the far-off peaks.
A certain crag composed these walls, still lofty
in its stones, still breathing out the snow-
pure air that cloud-banks once had pinnacled.
The church, battered by its years, remains
a heaven earthed.
            And having reached this fresco,
morning startles at what greets it: embers
glowering, a tiger looms, a burning
bush; that redbreast, lit on its curved rush
of air, with each translucent, tiny bud
a ruddy daybreak.
            Never see-through saints
from him who made the painting, never bodies
little more than twigs pale souls are perched
on to be taking off.
            Whatever stains

accumulate, and cracks, time's handiwork,
God's plenty crowds the fresco still, a passion
for the praise that is exactitude.
And it exacts its niceties, as light
assumes each image easily as a coat
its maker first brushed, fitting—fit anew
for what the sun now does—on this disciple,
brine shone round him, on that brawny saint.

For what the sun and I, studying out
each hint, now do as we collaborate.

But caught upon the painting's jagged cracks,
the morning seems amazed to see the cross-
hatched lines of the sinopia peep through.
A sprite it looks, not yet confined, conformed,
by flesh's reservations.
                              Still the good
red earth that sketch is made of binds us all.

And binds me too, laboring to bring
to light again that pristine moment when,
the master's last paints having barely dried
as now, my brush once more awaking them,
the early worshipers, who stood, stunned,
before the work, confused with what they saw,
for their time being completed it, this church,
its town, its noon completing them.
                                    Their flock
contained those figures standing by to be,
in their red cloaks, accounted for; contained
that shepherd who, his body disappeared,
still blushes to the latest beams.
                                  I too,
the sunlight in its freshness sealing them,
at last have learned by heart the fresco's every
shade and shimmer, each—the fresco, I—
the other's mirror, frame.
                         But sudden glare—
a stray mote bouncing off?—strikes—whose eye?
mine?
       A murmur grows, from out of figures
thronging the fresco's center focuses
into the raspings of a rusty voice.
Having turned, its owner, finger pointing,
pins me. Phrases splutter from his lips.

I

I speak that cannot speak, that have
not uttered words—except to those
few passionate to understand
and able to—since paint lay wet
along my mouth, sun fluttering
upon the stroke as at my breath.

Brushing my mouth moist again,
assume that it must speak to you?
Mirror, framed, indeed! You, squatting
here, add touches that would be
an homage, blessing, to our fresco.

The years of all the centuries,
as dirt collects in sticky stuff,
mix in our paints (and never more
than with that recent mired flood)
till they've become one bulky coat,
its folds too packed to separate
(your skill intends to honor them?),
the guises, the disguises we
have had to don, as He did, pressed
into the dust-and-water mold
a mortal body is.
                    And pressed
until he gushes forth one cry.

The air, the heavens, hardly large
enough to hold that voice's tidings,
they have flooded on. Still sound
through those can hear.

          * * *

                    Crowds earlier,
that, trooping in, had stopped by us,
would press us too. Instead their glances,
stuck fast, thickened time's patina.

You mean to wipe that all away?
Then how not wipe us out as well?

Ever now a swelling flock,
tricked out outlandishly enough
to win eyes more than my worn scene,
as if for some abandoned cause
it little knows, old comfort lost,
shuffles sheepishly round us.

Assured you know, tell me what they,
the generations upon generations
straggling by—our immortality!—
their fitful shadows squalling us
into a dun, expect of us.

But what can they expect who judge
us daubs upon a crumbling wall,
our red the usual hue, scant,
casual, as the things they are?

* * *

Here I've lived. Lived, if you
would call it that, in contemplation
of the figure just beyond,
beyond him, where the fresco breaks,
the shepherd with a lamb slung round
his neck, all faded, flaked.
                    Yet shining
through them, as though interfusing
our whole sky, gaze of the One
the shepherd looks toward fixedly.

O yes, as you can see, He's gone,
gone except as something lingers
in the shepherd's look, in mine,
a kind of echoing.
                    And stationed
in the shadow, lasting—fiercer
than day's gleamings—of that One,
I see.
          For so I must. The vision
seeing is, intrinsic part
like tint indelible this fresco
cannot live without, has been
suffused through all of me.

* * *

But who,
that other One apart, are we?

These, rigid, rapt in prayer, sharing
one look, like nimbuses their Christian
names attached to them, you can
identify: a frieze of saints.

Those too, heroic postures on them,
twined with great events.
And last,
drab as their order's habit, monks,
a parcel of our donors, slipped
into the fresco's bottom hem.
This they requested, hoping to be
hailed into some heavenly nook
where feasts forever wait on them.

I, standing in their midst, apart,
the visible I am, the seen
become the seeing, become the scene.
But someone not to be confined
to names, to local time and place.

All that had gone before, conjoining
with one moment's genius,
here crested out of paints. Those paints,
with fresco's self which must be swift,
by that moment's zest were fixed
into the singlehood of my being
wholly here.

* * *

Even so, new glances
stared at me, new guises I
assume, disguises.
In my own eyes
by things they see, whatever image
shows, I must admit its truth.
Any surface, new light striking,
fancies shapes within itself,

gods and demons, never before
suspected.
        On such common mercy
I depend. Like a blind beggar,
his cup glinting in the sun,
here only when some money jingles
out the value stamped on it.

* * *

I can look to myself as much
as to those slouching in the doorway,
bent on selling trinkets, pamphlets,
picture postcards of the church,
of us diminished and distorted.

Heat on them, as now, those hawkers
droop in sleep, a scraping breath
their thin lifeline.
        The winter griping,
frozen, they become extensions
of the church's statuary.

Aping us, they liven only
when, their candles bought, a flame
is put to them.
        The flame first breathed
in me ignites at likely looks?
Winds incessantly blowing have
looked after that!
        An X I am,
marking this spot, scribbles on a wall.
Initials of a couple knotted
in a strange design which lingers
on though they've long gone, their names,
their meaning lost.
        Lost not at all?
Rather I, prompting viewers
to a greater sense of self
and thereby to a deeper sense
of me, more and more am that
I am?
        Well, be it more or less,
since now your squinting nails you fast

to nothing but this wall, call me
the latest evidence of you,
the evidence such moment comes
to when one claims that he divines
another.

* * *

Yet, joining the rest—
your strokings make it very clear—
you run my fellows here and me
together, even as you suppose
the underdrawing's red, my mantle's
hue, cloaks others wear, the flush
upon the shepherd's cheek and mine
the same.
Deny it? See then what
you make of all the other reds:
that bud burst out into a rose,
that bird flaming across the sky,
the sky our window lets us see,
composing it, now roseate
its sunrise in the stained-glass panes.

All match those highlit splatterings
upon the Christ which prove a man
nailed to his cross can outsoar flight.

Soar most as, hovering like humming-
birds a nectar lures, five cherubs
cup His each drop's sacredness.
And cup through all eternity.

That moment supreme and many others,
different ingredients, a past
unique, have gone, forever gone,
into the forging of each red.

* * *

Ponder it hard as you will,
you cannot track that color down,
its origin, the wealth it packs:
rows heaped on rows, ancestral kings,

all that they did and said, breathless,
just beneath the pigment's skin
waiting (at a touch from you,
a breath!) to blaze again wild days,
the nights, themselves a mine piled up,
smoldering.
     Still you are right.
The red enclosing us, that rose,
bird, Man, and me, however fed,
whatever channels each may take,
such hues admit one lineage,
the good earth binding all.

    * * *

Consider that fresco facing us.
Though it glimmers ghostly now,
departing's shade swept over it,
its several colors seem with ours
dipped from a single pot.
      Yet senior
that the fresco is, its red
accommodating divers rust,
it looks on us as upstarts, friv-
olous intruders, here to strut
flamboyancy.
    Its figures will
not, cannot, see—you notice how
they turn away—that we, a similar
vision pervading both of us,
regardless of our distinct miens,
endure one fate.
    Resentment rather
that we've come to spy on them.
They cannot understand ourselves,
like them, not more than prisoners,
one cold, one dark, our fellow world.

And rancor at our stealing looks
belong to them!

    * * *

Despite their years,
despite the fading settled in,
their red like ours endures.
                    And were
there any look acute enough,
red's strokes, earthquaking still, reveal,
as if the earth should cleave, riches
in that painting as in ours:
ancient days like ingots, kings
in state, their radiance amassing.

Their old dauber, nameless now
as when his task took him by storm,
its lightnings for that moment his,
woke them, white-hot flakes shot forth
to make one heaven-flashing scene.

    * * *

Whatever greater skill he had,
so worked my master, swiftly sketching—
chaos first, its elements
aroused, embattled in his heart—
the world charcoal permits.
                    And then,
charcoal put by, red chalk assumed,
his breath informs that chalk with lines
gone taut for humming out the thrashing
fish they've netted, precious catch,
foreshadowing us.
                    As that old fresco
shows, so God employed the good
red earth that binds us all to fashion
men, His breath sealed in, like song
within a pipe, a clay-pinched, chirping
bird.

    * * *

And yet wind, blowing, wind
that might belong to that first breath,
breaking through my master's breath,
makes knots or sweeps strokes hither, yon.
In fits and starts the work proceeds.

His chalk cannot assuage—its eyes,
still lidded, raking him—the tiger,
raging in its charcoal stripes.
Cannot assuage or shift, a burning's
black, that shrouded one—you see
him there, back turned and yet severe?

Sometimes the chalk runs wild, a squall
there is no banking.
                    Then, his breath
a jagged cloud for churchly cold,
his face, his fingers something like
the hue he's made illustrious,
my master shakes as with an ague,
past what churchly cold can do.

Aspiring it is and dust
engaged, dust waging savage bouts
against itself.
                    Some imp within
the chalk and him lays out—sly shapes
mounted on each stroke—a riot
of alike alluring courses.

            * * *

And more than that stood in the way.
Pored over us, a war of shadows,
monks, our donors, flail the air:
a blast, indeed the churchly cold,
would blow us out—too bold we were,
too live for them—into the dark.

Blow most, goaded by him, grimmest
among them with his cinder face—
be glad you cannot view it now!
He scowling-silent in his scorn
for all adorning save it be
the scant sort which the other wall
proposes.

            * * *

340

Some deem his the form,
back turned, my master charcoaled in.
To never let him be, be seen.
And just, since he in his contempt
refused to countenance the earthly
world he made an irate part
of.
     Others speculate the figure
is that One Whose look—the world
enhanced in its dear warmth—did He
turn round on us, must sear.
                         To you
both seem farfetched? And you suspect
none other than my master stares
into the scene?
                    What he saw fit
to keep concealed I shall not now,
not even if I could, disclose.

          * * *

At last, unable to endure
the things which balk his vision, torn
between his own competing wishes,
claims his patrons would impose,
the price he has to pay,
                         he rushes
off to leave us less than half
made up, a wisp of his bruised will
our own.

          * * *

          Returned (long he must
have stayed away: clad in their frowns
as in their black, many a time
the monks, wrangling here, stomped out),
uneasy truce,
               he scrubs away
those faces, limbs, his chalk too nicely
traced, hands, loose in the big wind
that blows through them.
                    Scene on scene

colliding—a fertility
outrageous sketching cannot keep
up with—the men and women, droves
of, tangled, founder in each other.
Destruction such creation's based
on, one body springing from another,
grinding and devouring as it springs.

Hard times also strike those he'd keep.
A tumult in us as in his blood.
Again and again he jabs at us,
no less the rubbing out, accused
that we, crabbed, proud, perverse,
conceal our virtues, spurn the shapes
we ought to be.

* * *

For all the flexing
of his arm, the furious strokes,
the furious strikings out, the strain
his thews and mind must undergo
against my will, my body's skilled
to try his craft beyond itself.

Locked in a grip he cannot break,
he stares at me. As you do now
for strokes I'd thwart.
Perplexity
plays on his face as if some shadow
of a deed too swift, too bright,
of powers much surpassing those
his earlier paintings had revealed,
teases his gaze. So tires him.

* * *

Now, though he still leans toward me,
his eyes wander.
Distance in them
as a window frames the sky,
the houses, scattered by the hill,
the palace near, with lives in them
like fish in the river run beside.

Dropping the chalk, he hurries out.
And he is gone to what river-driven,
other life? The private time
he gladly spends elsewhere in one
such dwelling or another?

     * * *

               Still
one day, long days gone by like night,
the dust heaped upon our chalk
which swipes have blurred, he dashes in.

A gleam surrounding him, a hum
of warm sounds pulses on his lips.
The monks, here too in knotted bunches,
grumble for the long delay.

But he, impervious to them
as fleas in buzzing self-pursuit,
us too, inside our chalk mere ghosts,
attends to some more taking sight.

     * * *

The monks in twos and threes creep out.
Assistants, summoned, carefully
prepare the scaffolding, the paints,
his brushes cleaned.
           The plasterers
prompt to apply the first day's coat,
at last the time for painting's come.

As he dips brush into the pot,
that brush then poised, a feathered thing,
his eyelids flutter:
            scenes he must
repeatedly sweep through, a bird
seeking its nest, the one secreted
in a shadow-littered wood.

The first stroke aimed, as it's put down
at once the forces of the world
converge.

The fresco headlong, sure
against the hardening, its plaster
like a naked thirsting, sucks
each careful drop.

* * *

There my one eye,
glistening with the paint he plies
as with my first look's fluency,
a spark that sets all April going,
swifter than a bud to sunlight
opens!
Watching, breathless I,
eye strains, unlidded, out to see—
my straining helps and like a lamp,
casting light to see itself,
attracts—my other eye, the shape
my body comes to,
ramifying
from itself, an instant, blazing
tree luxuriant with leaves,
into my lasting pose.

* * *

His hand
a new touch brims (informed with other
touches, blood-warmed, silken skin,
lingeringly musky?)
imparts a depth
of wonder, luster of a depth
of feeling, we could not know before.

* * *

Yet that wonder he's brought back,
even as it spreads a glowing
like his gaze throughout my body,
rampant in the reds and yellows,
terre verte, burnt sienna,
rouses more in me, a jealousy,
swirled fire just beneath the skin.

Still I cannot long resist
this ardency which throbs through him,
his blandishments, his cunning hand,
deny the help that I must give,
that urgency which limns me in.

* * *

Now eye to eye at last, he needing
eyes beyond his own, together
we peer at mastery required
that our eyes by hunger's strength
discover food, the food we are,
he and we each other's creature.

His rending rage as in the tiger,
jubilant with gratitude,
now turning powerfully tender,
smooths wrinkles out of him and me,
uncertainty's crude blemishes.

The day and night of the first day.

* * *

First taste whetted, feast soon follows.
Next day's plaster spread, my master
speedily fills it:
          one taut stroke
the gist of tiger, paw explodes
to haul the panting body after;

swans, won of a single feather,
winged, full-fledged, from his brush,
out of their rufflings float a lake;

and rabbits, bunched, fuzzy smudges,
nibble in and out the edges
of the dew-and-shadow-dabbled
meadow.

* * *

Quicker than a foot
can climb, hillocks he mounts next:
a waterfall, in all its rushing,
upright, spouting still though paints
be crusted, flashing—sunlight spun
into its texture—like a temple;

by a grove which, rifted through
with nervous, blinking leaves and busy
little lives (those crinkles, are
they cricket cries? young lovers nestled
in their passion?), at the vanishing
point does not conceal the hoary
graveyard shaded by dwarf pines.

A look beyond, three towers, shot—
so fast his hand pursues its course—
like arrows greedy for their target:
stonework, sturdier than any
fortress.

* * *

Meantime, to house
the rest, he rears high noon throughout
the fresco; massive building it is,
and yet a buoyant.
Banked round,
the noon is lit—as though that One's
regard still set—on leaves and rocks,
which spurt gold lava-like, on glances
spinning out, on cry-shaped mouths.

Their words reverberate, a riddling
undertone, the way this moment's
sunbeams swim, within the paints,
schooled fish glistering their stream.

The senses wrung into one sense,
not only sight becomes a scene,
the greens and purples resonant,
but sounds and scents blow into hue.

Thought too and feeling bodied out,
the mystery of what men are
jets forth their fiery ambience.

* * *

Jets through my master.
Even now,
whatever doubtings may oppress,
what dust the light is speckled by,
that primal breath abruptly starting
up again, the fresco twitching
like a beast, I feel him, warm
and knowing on us, luminous
his steadfast gaze, his hand still touching
through the paints, however settled,
vibrant in its span the world.

Once more we seem to be mid-making,
he, stroking us out, martyrs,
seraphs, pouring from the brush,
a torrent out of heaven.

* * *

Out
of other spheres as well.
Earth blent
with heaven in his paints, his fire
fuses them.
Each stroke compiles
its cells in which an anchorite,
but coupled with his counterpart
in mortal combat, love immortal,
dwells.
The many strokes combined
making a single, blowing field,
impassioned bodies loom, triumphant
and serene in very passion.
Living
creatures, no less lime, water
mixed with clay, no less than we
loom forth, a mystery.

* * *

So noontide lavish, plashed with him,
as though just stepped into his spot,
the shepherd stands, youthful, glowing.
Whole also, like the others, caught
within their stride, their ample garments
sails for wilful breezes gusting
through them.
        Action, even as
they bend into the quivering bow
of concentration, springs from one
blazed eye and hand raised to the next
around the fervent, central scene
though He's no longer part of it.

This incandescence that they kindle
by, fast catching like dry limbs,
my master takes his fire from
and feeds it, fueled, back to them.

      * * *

Although this fresco map-like keeps
the scorching route a tempest takes—
at moments some gust threatens still—
its fury blesses everything
it touches.
        But it plunders too
near countries, far, their crowded past,
to furbish us.
        At times no doubt,
hauling such spoils to his corner,
my master feels himself a miser, rogue.

And yet by fondling them he hopes
to make them his and more than his,
this nook become a center, see,
a port and haven of renown,
through which the riches of the world
must flow enhanced.
        The famous dead
wrung dry in us, his fellow rivals,
the most gifted tributary
with the serried kings and queens,
all help to swell his boldest news.

* * *

And when the light adjusts, as now,
the midday noon streamed in a light
yet certain leaning on our noon,
the hordes the fresco has consumed,
their glances, sparkle out a fire-
works befitting kings.
              But no,
you cannot see—not in my eyes
their eyes, not all they'd done, the women,
flickering, they staked them on—
as in the making of a man,
the generations on generations
that merge to consummate this scene.

      * * *

And other imposing things there are
you cannot see: ships, cargo-crammed,
sunk to the painting's floor, its waves
closed over in a glossy sleep.

Till slowly rising to the surface,
answering this sunlit probing,
but suffused throughout the fresco's
flesh, thus visible and not,
crushed lapis lazuli with ocher,
umber, smalt, viridian
and other oxides from exotic
realms.
        Ores' fusillading looks,
enveined with secret reveries,
as high noon's tropic closes in,
expose their figures.
              More than nuggets,
more than ancient, hardened days,
those kingly ingots, they explode
god-like from our master's dreaming.

With the day sodden outside,
a time for dreaming, for siesta,
it is that the noon be kept at bay.

      * * *

This day swiftly piled on days,
a cascade dashed down mountainsides,
far faster than the clay can dry
my master finishes.
　　　　　And finished,
paints and brushes, scaffolding
disposed of, he considers us
equipped, armed by his love, his craft,
to keep us here, outwitting worm
and wet, the worst that time can do.
An offspring on our own, we're left.

　　　* * *

While the town, sweltering, sleeps,
trace that far arch my master's built,
stroke fit to stroke.
　　　　　The arch admits,
softened by distance, bustlings from
the town beyond you almost hear
packed murmurs of as in a dream—

scarlet banners flapping wind
may token blood-raw war or fan-
fare of some gaudy carnival,
the loaded, creaky wagon, driver
singing as he lurches, drunk,
or, shouting, lurches, drunk with rage,
to flog his mule—
　　　　　　　　confused with rumblings
and occasional cries, the town
adrowse where worlds ago dense arbors
danced around us, olive groves,
air laden with the scent of must.

　　　* * *

And now, lapped inside this coil
of paints, grown heavy in the late
noon light, the roses blotch; the bird
wings droop; wind, as though it's joined
the drowsing, nods, hunched up, dream-
less, like a locust in its husk.

Like the breath once rustled through
a pipe hung by the shepherd's side.
Then folded, puffy layer on layer,
breath sleeps within, till roused by sounds
suddenly recalled, the reaper song
it had swept up along with it.

That side and pipe long blown away,
you would blow them back again?

* * *

The light grown silent, through this crack,
this, a fragment of the fresco
missing here, the underdrawing
shows, shows what, compared with what
we might have been, we have become.

Submissive to proprieties
belonging to our time, these paints,
drying as if by instant aging,
fit public faces on us all.

The wiry spirit we began
with, wild as in a wind, still beating
free beneath, the flesh conforms.
And we stand ready for display.

* * *

The town awake, my master comes
with others. The garrulous flock of monks,
their purchase prized as if their hands
had fashioned it, gloats over rival
orders scowling.
                  Magistrates,
wool merchants, burghers, bankers, guilds-
men, suchlike worthies of the town
for whom my master's often painted,
bustle in to see themselves,
be seen, in church as in the fresco,
they, their world, immortalized.

Committed to a kindred work,
the making of the world in words,
his friend of the singed countenance
confronts us, multitude of one.
His gaze, whatever fire eats
at him, hammers sparks from us.

Our reputation spread, soon sweep
in lords and ladies, well attended.
Gems of them, their lustrous glances,
voices, mining out new gleams,
intensify the fresco's fame.

Our maker basks with us in praises
sung, the choir, joining us,
the masses of the town, in rounds
rejoicing.
      Till that fame hales in
far travelers. And for a time,
still new, the world around us new,
we also travel, colors, smells,
strewn over us, the jumbled sounds
from distant lands, and strange, that they
had wandered through, secreted by
their robes' stiff folds.

     * * *

        An early dusk
my master, much like you, slips in
alone. He falls into a study,
hushed that he seems one of us.

But then, brow wrinkling, he frowns
at what is happening, events
he has no inkling of.
      The shadows
shifting, sudden wit wrung out
from restless light and dark by chance
encounterings, it must appear
that we are bent on mocking him.

Once exposed, fame fancying,
we wear what looks men hang on us.
And time as well.

* * *

Not only men.
One time, no one about, a figure,
hooded, slight inside its wrappings,
takes its station just below.

Instantly I feel that I
am looking up at her, but in
the lengthened shadows dimly seen.
Her garments fluted like a sculpture,
huge she seems, to the waist dark,
the face radiant.
              Her gaze,
as though set off by what it sees,
now flashes fire. Beams of that
I felt when he first came from her?

Although beyond those probing eyes
we spy no farther part of her,
their gaze, having drunk its fill,
responsive to some thing in us
even our master failed, grows mild.
The glistening we bathe us in!

I I

But that was ages, worlds ago.

The fresco done, my master gone,
new work proceeds. Here in this church,
and yet beyond the church's rites,
the rites of passion swirl over us.

Amid the hush, night streaming in,
sometimes broken by light steps,
a sudden whisper, one or two
steal through, these with a squinny
looks about to scrape the coat
from off our bodies, pluck gems out
of diadems, gold-plated haloes!

Others also scurry by,
then stop in sudden weakness, fright,
bodies, breathless, strained toward us.

Or is it something else detains them?
Peer as I may, two faces moth-
like, beside a taper wavering,
how tell love from its contrary?

Scuffles, sighs maybe, a scream
cut off.
        The glints, are they reflections
from moist lips? A blade, blood-lit,
slashed across the fresco?
                See
that scratch next to your hand!

     * * *

                             At dusk
avengers come, their fury furled
round them religiously.
                That fury
as they fumble in the dim light
spending itself, they disappear.

Though things I've seen cast certain shade—
rust splotches on my robe the sun
this moment polishes, they're nothing
but time's smudge? red only red—
those others, bent upon pursuit,
were too sunk in themselves to see.

Law, late, in purfled hood struts by;
so well encased, what eyes has it
for anything beyond itself?

     * * *

Or now two gliding candles, paused,
light up the painting opposite
so that its figures seem to carry
on some secret rite.
             The dream
their master served awake in them,

they strive to celebrate his saint-
liness, this way restore the mystery
his praying—hours rigid, self-
forgetting while he painted—made
him one with.
         Like local actors
prinked out in their loose-fit sacks
(were they dabbed on, mulberry stains?),
cosily they live with reeking
goats and mules, the manger's glory,
shepherds gawking at the star,
whatever wrinkled babe it may
now have become.
         Two strides from them,
we stand apart wide centuries.

* * *

They proudly turn away, moving
hues we shall not see again,
their far-off era in its distance
on them with their vanishing.

Still out of them a certainty,
that truth, always more urgent,
always more lost.
         Wrapped in tasks
they were created for, they do
not need to struggle with the knowledge
troubling us.

* * *

         Rarely now
the novices, each a green man,
trundle in whole summer, flowers
drowning us, sweet wilderness.

Rarely now the blare of trumpets,
buffeting our wall as though
to fell it, wakes the cornered angels
that the stones recall the music
so volcanic they like notes
had flurried round in till it massed
them.

355

Blare confused with thick incense,
the church bursts open with a gay
commotion.
Clad in robes like paints
newly splashed upon the air,
people march in slow procession.

Supervisors of the pomp,
we mingle with the lordly elders
and the bright-eyed boys and girls,
their warblings parti-colored ribbons
floating high the seraphim
delight to dress them in.
But once
they leave we, like the flowers, may
fold up or like the banners, flung
aside.
So you might say we stand
uninterrupted down the years?
And stood save for the praises wafted
round?

* * *

The praises that at first
rang out with equal fervor changed.
New preachers, passionate for doom
and rancorous, much like that cinder
monk, wind-howling some, a hail
of pebbles, pelted away at us
as at their flocks.
These, wailing,
gnashed their teeth or, as though
to join our company, stood petrified.

* * *

To be flung, had we been portable,
with other follies, our poor fellows,
on the pyre.
In the splendor
which our disappearing makes
at last immortal!

Countless paintings
reprobated? Nymphs and satyrs,
yoked together, shamelessly
leap out their lust's extremity,
as in hell-flames their flesh's antics
helped to fuel?
Others too:
artfully mixed, applied with care
my master would appreciate,
those paints precious to their users
more than prayers, than sacred images
they kiss, unless it be the image
close pressed in the full-length glass?

How should this not inspire blasts!

　　　* * *

So, just below us, in a stormy
session, roused inquisitors
condemn—a litany the muttered
names, each lingered on to number—
diverse culprits, jumbled round
them on a table.
Charges leveled
thunder so the veils which wind
and breath conspire to enliven
billow, silk, as though nude bodies
dance in them, quick to the light
of looks much like our colors.
Silks
and veils cling to those priestly fingers
even as they spurn; powders, plasters,
snaring wigs.
Next applications
for the ear, deft pipes, soft lutes.

Riggish the priests pronounce their tunes:
these, sowing themselves within the hearer's
dreams and wake, as promptly reap.

Let flames accommodate their music
to a last Magnificat.
So lofty music waits to be
released from what seems lowliest!

* * *

And last, pored over them, as though
each were a casement onto hell,
those scrolls.
       In their engrossment—faces
scorched a florid hue—nothing
other than religious zeal?

Dumped on the fire, Aretino,
till now cold for all his sighs,
is spouting heat and light at last.
And cries as well, cheek by jowl,
alas, with Petrarch and Vasari,
the painters' private lives on show,
Boccaccio and *Primavera,*
scintillating as though gods
were strolling naked in its midst?

Such happenings I leave to you.
I see no more than looks reflect,
rumors crackling still with flames.

* * *

The church, meantime, enacts the countless
scenes its paint and stone had figured
in.
      And still the battles roar
around us. Conquerors clanking through,
their armor's glitter clashes with
our gaze.
      There, just beneath our edge,
they meet to stake out rival claims.
But then, words rousing rage, the treaty,
its high-blown words still puffing air,
breaks off.
      One ruffian, kneeling
to receive the crown, another stabs
and, even as he stabs, snatches
up the prize.
      That despot and his kin,
securely guarded day and night,
the monks, their mass devoutly kept,

perform the deed a brigand dare not.
The cries add volume to the Dies
Irae.
    Silk, one patch, left fluttering
behind, ruddy as if dipped
in blood, appears ripped out of us.

* * *

Few notice this. The bulk, bent
on an assignation waiting, money,
plots, spend no more than a passing
glance on us.
        Except that one,
stumbled by his weapon, looking
up. And certain he reads laughter
in my face, half draws that sword,
but then, ashamed of his absurd
embarrassment, face ruddier
than ever, as he puffed in, puffs out.

* * *

Such trippers flitter through. Enough
so that I can, times changed, keep time,
their costumes changed to say they are,
their gabble echoing those gone,
the same repainted.
            Burly some,
a troop, now clamber us with banners
rampant, rucksacks, hobnail boots.

But others blunder past, content
to undertake our lowliest foothills.
Eyes nailed to the back ahead,
each one the other's donkey-tail.
A flapping by, had they been wet,
would blot our paints.
                And do and do!
But mostly let the dust they stir
bestrew on us, the darkness darker
for the dun-like, fitful dusk
their looking comes to.

* * *

Colors also,
shirt-green, -black, -brown, -red,
go marching through: men stiffer than we,
painted shadows, dreams, unreeling.

Someone, staggered in, a star
dangled from his arm, dragging
like a wing, falls at our feet.

The crimson, brimming from my robe,
clots his shaggy beard, his head,
slashed ruddy gold.

* * *

Now, dashing after,
anonymous as petty clerks
in greyish suits and hats and ties,
men circle him and, striking many
times—O could we spread our cloaks,
we, who have seen such deed over
and over, would cover him—they drag
him off. This silently except
for grunts and crackings which tell us
what bones are like, and tell, each gasp,
what life and death.
                    The art's renewed
that put the seal upon man's hope
by way of one Man's doom. Incarnate
it must be each age.
                    Astonished by
that sight, one act uniting times,
we stand and, timeless, stand.

* * *

Aeons
it may be, the dripping, is it,
from those wounds or from the moisture
oozed out of these stones?
                    Aeons
or a day.

Then suddenly like some-
one tapping up and down the roof,
a splattering begins. What light
there is blinks on, blinks off.
The tapping after turns into a roar
that says the sky has ripped wide open.

There, swooped on us as from wings
in waves, a flock of shadows capers
with the patriarchs,
                 while blasts,
close-pressed, crescendoing—the dark
shot through by crowded torches—jolt
the church in every rock.
                    The earth
it must be, cracking open, vomits
ingots, kings, their golden rage,
gay devils.
             Every martyr quaking
finally, the dove, its drove
of seraphs, moult. We also flake
away.
           Paints once more wet, our lake,
sprung from us and overflowing
its muddy banks, smacks of the sea
wallowing near.

        * * *

                  The welter soon
sets all afloat.
             Soaked with others
in his streaky pane, pale his mosaic face,
Noah seems to weep:
                 "Not again!
The Ark, here dry-docked centuries,
must it endure another storm?"

Who would have dreamed the sleepy Arno
harbored the Flood!

        * * *

                          Eddying, the waters
ebb. And with them some of us.

As though abruptly summoned
by the truth that they had served,
a stool, a bowl, dropped in the rush,
our neighbors have drawn farther off
than ever.
             Too late we realize
what gap they leave, our solitude's
chief company. And company
against the crowds.

              * * *

                      Despite the paints
discolored here and there, with gashes
one might think an imp's improvements,
dank restored to normal damp,
we take our wonted stance again.

But for that scabbed off, the stone-
like silence hemming, hard it is
to call back times we once had made
a lively part of.
             Still the motes,
twirled in the light, rebounding off
the stone, resemble glimmers left
of angels,
             dreaming we drift in . . .

III

and each day dream a little more,
while they, this age's natives,
vibrations as of battering rams,
flock to the lure we are, a settle-
ment, so they would like to think,
against the madly swirling world.

See how they melt among the mob
that smites our Lord and, swelling it,

the mindless brawling, help fulfil
the whole, great, terrible story.
You too with every stroke you add.

These no less, still come to pray,
kissing away the feet of the stone-
twisted Christ that He must see
why He was crucified and crucified
again, the one successful portion
of His life. He hanging, nailed
there, as we hang.

   * * *

      Be sure no tiger
caged more tellingly, its raging
crammed within the tiny space
of repetitious, tail-twitched pacings.

You expect to climb these miles
on miles of nothing more than dried-
out, scaling paints which time becomes?
Bound as you are to your own present,
what past it can you know?

   * * *

      So now
you shiver for this dungeon air.
The church's shady, tranquil cool
a mountaintop indeed!
      This work,
first charged with crimsons like apocalypse
you strive to summon forth once more,
still dangles, a torn gonfalon
from some old war, in an abandoned
site of stone.
     So stony bare
these flocks dare not dawdle here.
How can we feed their basic hungers?

Still our lake, fish-scaled its waves,
yet racing too for shadows deep-
ening on it, looks as if it might
slake any thirst.

As likely it
as bits of weed and scraggly grass-
blades, breaking through the crevices,
confused with fresco grass and weeds.

* * *

And yet it may be we remain,
like Lot's wife obstinate, a salt
lick for those few who, joining us,
look back.
      A salt lick and a light
like precious gems kept in a cave
that eyes might dazzle by.

* * *

      At first
our master and we were also rapt
by cavernous, rich light.
      But soon
the mind, so opened in this fresco
after animals, saints too, arose,
spewed trafficking, malicious imps,
exuberant to share their filth.
As if the radiance arose
to study out their churning void!

Then past those patriarchs and prophets,
things we clung to, stolid land-
marks, squat, opaque, benignly peasant.

Warmth they give off, glow, to succor
us, my master, me, still aching
at our loneliness your time
cannot suspect the fullness of,
the terror of that emptiness,
the mercy lost and from that One,
the overwhelming, tender power
that had seemed a touch away.

Glimpses of His love the shepherd
basked in, the departing sun-
set, in his crumbled cheek still flushed?

As at the common clay they share,
the common, irredeemable clay,
for which in His great pitying
He bore His final agony.

    * * *

Now long ages gone.
        More gone
for what those ages ruthlessly
have done as though to underscore
the truth in His extreme torment,
the terror of our emptiness.

Not even His corpse sop enough,
the heritage those ages left,
the carrion, its ravenous
debris, grows hungrier consuming.

Here, our strongest rites and customs
lost, the works you prize ghosts many
times over of long forgotten ghosts,
this church, a mortuary for
the heaped, devoured dead, hoards
emptiness on emptiness.

    * * *

             Still some,
in quiet times slipped in alone,
as if the fresco, not yet done,
had just now, from a recess hidden
in it, loosed them, or as you
do lingering, again light us,
light we had forgot.
            Luxuriating
in it, by your brush's strokes
(see how much you've learned from us!)
like wingings, we fly out as by
our master's strokings to those places
one time ours alone, the moment we
were meant for nearing.

* * *

Now as near
as it can be? The heaven touch is,
stroke-sure, vibrant, as one meaning
twines a complex sentence?
Winds
can revel in a grapevine so,
mining out of its complicated
tendrils a pervasive scent?

Such things I now can feel only
at second hand, a hand beyond
my maker's.
Still this touching joins
us all, my master, saints and demons,
tourists too?

* * *

It may be so.
By what you are a few like you
highlight some section of the work
to find new bits of us, odd hues
not we, not nature, could have seen.

This one, gaze fixed upon my sleeve,
discovers daedal patterns there,
a landscape he then magnifies
to sprout a lunar scene's wild flora.

Or my garment's stains, for him
not blood, our dim, recorded past,
but mappings to the treasure that
lights up inside the mind alone.

* * *

Time passed, some things, as if abiding
proper time, mature. The carmine
in that figure, standing by
the shepherd, mellows, petal-rose.
The fingers of his left hand bloom.
And springs to it—what seemed a blur—

a flowered branch, the lake reflecting
verdant shadows, strangers craning
just outside our scene.
                          A shadow
such as yours upon us.
                          Darkness
rushing in, last glisten, letting
go that branch slow leaf by leaf,
looks like my master's glance, the One,
a child's.
            Last glisten as this rose,
now closing, sheds a bit of color
on its neighbor while the redbreast
bundles in its wings as in a nest.

    * * *

But see what you have made of us,
changed from sacred things, a meeting
between men and God, to something
strange.
          Yet, stripped of everything
beyond our selves, that strangeness
can bestow a glamor still.
Shrines we remain.
                    Your age's lust
for dusty shards and shells which echo
no Red Sea beyond your blood,
does it not smack of idolatry?

    * * *

Relics you're not after, but glimpses
caught in works like ours of the human
truth, the mind and senses' moments,
accommodating their kind of heaven?

Jacob's wrestle and the name
he won must mean no more to you
than our maker's struggle with his vision.

    * * *

And still the work we are remains,
a telling witness to that struggle,
like the angel hovered over us?

He, flown outside his parent heaven
near to earth, but winged so well,
from out his nimbus spins an Eden,
in this dark collecting.
                              Winds
of where he once had risen, ruffling
in his feathers, flight that needs
no space and, yes, no motion, buoys
him still.
              Sufficient he as any
tousled thrush that dares to winter
in its trill, its courage spurred
on by the rugged marigold
its petals and its breath sustain,
as many florets in their self-
made neighborhood maintain each other.
Such warmth, though it be laid away
in ice and snow, by that is kept.

                    * * *

People wandering past us,
for the local, daily things they use,
the bags they carry, clothes they wear,
that painted, frizzled hair, those shoes,
the landmarks of their time and place
uniquely theirs, look fabulous.

Even so they think them real.
                              Just so
the world I am adheres to me
as to wet paint?
                    Leaves, how long
can they outlive the branch that bears
them? Carry, like an acorn stuffed,
a limitless fertility,
the past thirsting for its person
in the future, as though the future
already throbs, dependent,
to be perching on its limbs?

* * *

So you, my future's present, strained
forward, reaching out, think you
obliterate the centuries
to touch beneath my robe a heart
still battering, its strokes pulsing
from my master's hand, his heart.

A splash of paint so radiant,
you are convinced, patches space
between the tiger and the lamb,
as it spans the gap between us both?

Unaware he'd draw you here,
my master, in a sense, paints you
in too, essential to the scene
(since now you have appeared): painting
goes on still.
        For eyes like yours
my hand, grasping this robe, hauls up
the beasts, my fellows, even far-
off, cloud-crowned hills.
        And you, by lines
drawn out of me, surprised, are hoisted
to a sky which dazzles you,
a sky dazzled by the gleaming
springs from you.

     * * *

        Times must be
themselves. Yet you believe that even
while they go their special ways,
times meet, and most of all in such
embodiments?
        So for the bodies
wearing us, bodies that you lend,
we shine forth, brand-new fresco?

But soon surprises that you find
in us worn off, we come to little
more than loot your mind has hung
upon its walls, framed images
mirroring you.

                    There is a pleasure,
future, such misprising one
another prospers? Endless future
of a pleasure bound to grow!

For even while you ponder us
we, flattened back to peeling paint,
inside this darkness thickening
seal shut forever. Seal the more
for all the layers you apply.

                    * * *

And so we linger on, not past,
not present, neither life nor death.

Even while I speak crumbling
gnaws away at me, a maw
incessant though it be unseen.

Weary of this rigid landscape,
the wind at last is shedding it.
Much like a music breaking out
of jail a pipe can be, it would
abound within the open sea
of air.

                    * * *

                    That air entices me,
the ceaseless murmuring which swift
wings, be it angels, be it gnats
in nation, make:
                    the murmuring
within the patch those teeming sun-
beams and wings gossamer spin out,
they wrapped in it (as our fresco
once kept us, we keeping it),
until, dissolving, they sweep off
with it.
                    So I, like the shepherd,
always more strongly drawn to join
the One our eyes have never left,
the grip in all its rigor of
these paints at last cast off, I would

let go of gown and hill, you
and the rest, this will, now stiffened
into stone.
       I also would return
to mica-flakes before they flocked
into one beetling, hoary, star-
torched mountain which men ages later
carved into this crag-like church.

A wisdom I begin to know
beyond all wisdom, blessing, time's
scant joys: the radiance danced out
by nothingness.

           * * *

          However much that dance
may satisfy, it soon must change:
the painting going on, the latest creature,
wave insurgent, leaf, bird, star,
supplants it.
        Thus, by being wholly fresh,
it saves—by making wholly new best serves—
the treasures else forgotten which belong
to you, your master, all who once have lived.

Its longing to be free most powerful,
the wind, escaped, must soon yield to some song,
whether it be man or tiger, painting
in between, to house itself, as briefly
you and I, paired here—your maker also
backing you—compose wind's latest scene.

And from now on, so let its moment bid,
each shade and shimmer of your fresco,
opaque, immortal moment of a red,
obliterating every argument,
every theory, doubt and terror, will
be flashing through my mind.
                Now into night,
the precious mine of you amassing.

From A Slow Fuse *(1984)*

In Passing

As you speed by, a boy
waving, some cows at munching,
horses glossy for the double light—
your eyelashes' liquid blinking
swifter than thought brushing
those down—
     in one lifetime
how many sights can you expect
to spend more than a casual glance
on? Cattails wagging, dandelions,
this rushing, forsaken field.

Or a short delay for signals
at a crossroads, and the vista
down the enfilading maples, each
thickened with shade, one lopsided
shack, a man in khaki sprawled
on a bench, a dog,
       chickens,
kids tumbled round in the dirt.
You have lived long enough to know
you must not loiter. If you did
dust would spread,
      the curse
of habit, eye its own grim mote.
These junked cars quarry lightning
from the setting sun, astonished
by dents into a momentary
temple
    beggaring the glamor
of Solomon. Surpassing like one
prophet's short-lived Pisgah sights,
he thereby spared that maelstrom,
jammed-up sandstorms, named
Jerusalem.
     Each scene nothing
better than a station to pause in
before resuming speed?
      Still
they work to get you through,
momentum of a sort,
      a gasoline,

that field sufficient for a flight
of crows, the wind swinging in
a tree, a brook looked out,
emphatic inquiries.
                    Indeed,
though it's not Delphi, no site
outstanding in its cliffs, ravines,
events which centuries ago had
carved it out, what it has
to do it does.
                Our world's
so cupboard-crammed we've little
need to hoard or dally. Let things
go their separate ways, a will
at work engrossing ours.

Traveling Third Class

At times you wonder what it's like
wandering about in someone else's head.
Like suddenly being dropped in sleep
into a foreign country, its speech
almost familiar,
              but slipping away
the streets, the buildings, not entirely
strange and yet arranged in patterns
that escape you.
              As a swallow might dip
then sweep your image like a twig
into the sky, a hovering.
              Or zipped past
you on an autumn stroll, each leaf
a sunset echoing late day, an eye, casual
from a bus, with one blink thrusts you
into a melee, a sea-like thrashing
you, instantly become a perfect stranger
to yourself, can never navigate alone.

Else plunged into the rapture
of icy water with a bluefish you hold
a second on your quivering line, and both
united in that tussle as it, darted away,
for very eagerness takes bait and you
to green-dark recesses only coral
fathoms.
              Even more amazing, sunk
into the scattered thoughts of someone
dying and, dirt drowning you, emptied out
into a worm's mouth, your jumbled cells
now free in water taproots and someone
else—a pike, a dusk-brave muskrat—
drink.
              And so you take yourself
from every hand, this apple, plumped
with people rampant in its tangy flesh,
news of yourself about to be, the latest
leaves a kind of visa, travel also,
on their winter-driven maple,
                    travel
wolves somewhere are sponsoring, a herd
of deer sped farthest in their ravening.

Camel in the Snow

Professionals of snow,
the Eskimos mint many terms off it:
snow-at-sunset, snow-inside-an-igloo,
snow-tears-turn-to-icicles, a snow-
a-bear-is-tracking, snow-blood-
splatters.
         And in Arabic also
words amounting to five-thousand-
seven-hundred-and-eighty-four steam
from the camel.
                  As though those
and thousands crowding thousands more,
coupling night and day, could tell
the whole story!
                  As though,
given helpmate camel and the snow,
constants through the hurly-burly
of a life, one or the other does not
become—each word precisely spoked
from it—the axis for whatever happens.

You and I have lived together
over forty years, traveled through
some twenty countries. Well, are you,
the habits, whims, minute details of,
not my weather, for one happy spell
balm jasmine breathes, the next
wind-sinewed snow?
                  The wide world
desert at an instant turned into one
baffling sandstorm, a gaunt camel
draggles me through;
                  nomadic,
driven by the windy heat, it glides
into another blinding blast, snow
exploding, covering all, a hump
among unmoving humps.
                  That camel,
thick or thin, water sloshing in it,
clumps along, with days and nights,
a drove of vultures, sheep and drivers,
jeweled oases, fat flakes whirling
off its gallop.

Meantime, I, tossed
hither, yon, try reining it with words
in mighty swarms, since like the Eskimo
I know no single term redoubtable enough
for anything this living-changeable,
this mixed up with our lives, as (camel
also) snow.

A Building

                    to house
these maddened times, these squalid,
brawling lives? (Happily wasps
are sizzling, all-out war
over a muddy pool.)
                    Nearby
the sea sprawls, an incurable
complaint. Worse than gypsies we,
our path rutted far past recognition,
rove about,
                    yet like sands
tumbled, by the breezes tossing
and the sea, namelessly in one place:
rubble we pass, aimless suburbs,
ever the same.
                    Only a wren,
building its nest in our runted
catalpa tree, savors the ensolacings
of its trill (boughs once blew,
wilful leaves;
                    Brother Wood,
walking by man's side, gave fish,
fruit, songs: each season in its turn,
each day, for new youth sprung
to explore itself,
                    friskier).
But who can long abide in flaws
of man-made weather . . . one sluggish
August day, the heat like a mob
grown ugly,
                    by the Hudson's
east bank an old cow (its trail
founded this city) bloated with many
days' death; stench proclaimed
the fury of devotion.
                    Prodded
the belly, seething rose: a snarl
of eels dragged forth from the river
up the steep, miry path, to prop
the love-churned walls.

A Living Room

for Hannah Arendt and Heinrich Bleucher
"The past is never dead, it is not even past."

I

These brittle pages spread before me,
letter, manuscript, should store
some fragrance, glints long gathering.
Or at least the storm which bodies,
matching, once had set.
           The breathing,
different, catches: passages, this one,
that, their phrases off pitch, stiff,
seem to be straining to remember.

What a time it is, this time
let out, as though I've jimmied
a closet till now hid
           (much like
the low door I found years ago
behind some beams, a bed, a heavy
chest of drawers, in an old
Bath lodging house,
               which opened
on, discarded with its century,
the jutting cornice of a mansion),

free within its atmosphere to be
nothing but itself, attend to nothing
but itself.

I I

         There, for a moment,
like some eye considering the view
beneath its lid a world enough,
a living room.
          And late-noon-silvered
willows which had never made it
into these pages sprinkle twilight

(mountain pines beyond already mining
the harvest moon, a mass of shimmers)
through the room.
          As through it,
sounding out the dark, the char-
plush rustle of a train, its smoke
coiling in the trees. Or rain arrived,
an earlier version, offering glosses.

Still like words worn down, the rain
asserting shapes too distant to remark,
these pages keep their strangeness.

Possibly out of the dust collecting
a later time will fathom them.
By then the people somewhere inside
may, returning, look to one out here.

III

One out here?
          A grey December Princeton
morning lours like a giant shadow
that a snow, fast approaching, casts,
a train puffing along, and we lost
in it, lost inside its cloud of smoke.

Despite their bulk, in faded summer-
gaudy jackets even my stoutest volumes
flitter, while the Persian reproduction
on the wall, its light-clad figures
ruffled, flaps before the icy blasts.

And I, pulling out a plain brown
envelope stuffed through the mail-slot,
read the name scribbled in the upper
left-hand corner,
          name of her I saw
just yesterday at a popular Manhattan
memorial chapel, in a narrow plain
brown wooden box (just like the one
her husband filled five years before
when she whom I thought self-possessed
had riveted her gaze fast to his face).

Her packet's note transfixes me:

"Such a terrible long time since I
last saw you and talked with you.
Don't you ever come to New York?
I'm getting less and less willing
to move. . . . take this as an excuse
to call me."

I V

            Hannah, young vibrant muse
to Heidegger, Jasper's spiritual daughter,
German confidante and English of Jarrell,
Auden's final choice for a companion
("I came back to New York only because
of you."), Heinrich's chief, abiding lover,
gruff, imperious,
            thick smoky wreaths
ubiquitous around her blurted words,
now in the living room of their apart-
ment looking out upon the easygoing
Hudson, noon compiling ripples—
                     quivered
like her city's spires, ancient cities
she, loving, had to leave—which echo
squealing cars and roaring buses, loose
on Riverside Drive, the last time I see her
(Heinrich, "alive in every corner and at
every moment," hovering between us) alive,

and she, finally deciding what
I long have hoped for: "Heinrich's lectures"—
the main reason for our months on months
of meeting, but foiled in each attempt
("Why it's as if that humpback imp, mischief
its chief delight, never lost sight of us!")—
"I alone must shape for publication,"

bustling over me, a proper Jewish mother,
feeds me chicken soup with dumplings!

V

Midweek and Heinrich knocking at my door:
"I want your book of poems at once.
Tomorrow I am to see a publisher."
He brooking no demur, my protesting
it not finished, off it goes with him.

That Friday in New York to teach
the course that Heinrich had arranged
("You are too much a stick-in-the-mud
in Bard."), before our classes as he
nears, I see that something's happened.

"Ted, I don't know how to tell you
this. But when I got to New York,
my cab dashing off, your book was gone.
Since then and with the police I have
been looking for it everywhere."

Though, beyond some printed poems
and earlier drafts, nothing remains, I,
remarking his distress, must comfort him.
The Scarlet Letter I uncover to my class
flares out livid as it's ever been.

Should I blame him, who fled the Nazis
over several countries, for enabling
through solicitude that manuscript
to join those countless other works
destroyed?
              Who then deserves my rancor?

V I

"You don't know me?
O look and see.
This crookback's my
identity.

An elf from tales
of Germany,
I've popped into
the USA.

Of your bad luck
the guardian,
if your pot breaks
by me it's done.

A miser hooked
on misery,
when trouble strikes
and someone wails,

I am most gay,
as now when you,
too busy, fail
to notice me.

So I bestow
my dear regards.
Account your loss
my calling card."

Ah well, bowed down before this blow,
must I not also pray for that ingenious
hail-fellow?
     Who else, by cursing,
so successfully prevails on me
to trim my lines for such emergencies
and then in turn cooks up emergencies
(O ironies!) quite the reverse,

VII

as Hannah's note, continuing, reveals:

"Today going through Heinrich's papers
I found a folder with poems from you.
I hope to God you have copies.
Anyway, I'm sending it back to you
in case anything in your files
is missing.
     Warm regards.
                    Yours,
                    Hannah."

Missing? Here and now, nearly two
decades later, spread before me,
that manuscript, my book-to-be,
Outlanders, somewhere buried among
Heinrich's files!
      His rush from train
to taxi with a pile of papers,
crookback helping, must have caused
confusion. And his mind caught up
far beyond the glut of things.

An autodidact he, admiring the pariah,
any man freestanding, that naked flute-
player, lounging, buoyant as she pipes
a meditative tune, upon her stele
on the Greek postcard he sent us.

Torn between German and English,
he, like Lao Tse at the border, customs
fronting, would declare but one short
statement which, transparent, potent,
as a water drop, must change the world.

Small wonder writing comes so hard.

VIII

Instead Heinrich of the high places,
dapper past hope or fear and gone past
expectations of others, so accepting,
open to—at first his broad camaraderie
offended me—each one, yet hoping still,
devoted like Hannah to community,
the polis,
      Heinrich with his thin cigars,
his thick Berliner accent, deep down
grumbles, flash-eyed shoutings, spouting
like Vesuvius in their old world living
room amid the clash of amiable minds,

arguing, not less than with his friends
and Hannah's, with their dearest intimates,
Homer, Plato, Nietzsche, Kafka, Faulkner,

as though, everlasting in the flesh,
their minds still musing and through him
and her still making up their minds,

in the arrows he lets loose, no matter
what extremity may corner him, insouciant
since never losing sight of the bull's-eye
(he, fancying himself a military expert—
once recruited by the Kaiser's army,
had he not learned to elude the Nazis?—
his inspired, dashing troops deployed,
resorts to sallies, ambushes, raids),

addresses each Bard freshman class
as though the elders, august senators,
of Athens were assembled before him:

        IX

        "An artist never raises the question
        directly since he cannot doubt—
        as a pregnant woman, under normal
        circumstances, scarcely doubts—
        the value of life.
                        Yet he alone
        lives this question permanently,
        his whole work one emphatic answer.
        The artist's impulse springs from the
        initial shock that meaninglessness
        is possible at all, let alone
        boredom and banality;
                        this shock
        provokes an immediate transcending
        action, which, contradicting
        the question itself, by Beauty's aura
        again and again assures the artist
        and the beholder that, awaiting one
        bold enough to wake it, meaning exists
        everywhere."

                Several students, bemused,
then gaping, promptly slump into sleep;
others stare, incredulous at what

their ears are taking in; but a few,
like new buds thirsting, guzzle it
while Socrates, a full-time talker also
impatient of pale writing, once more,
bantering his distraught companions,
nonchalantly quaffs the bitter cup.

"My friends, promise me, whatever happens,
you will not contrive, and least of all
with drugs, to rob me of my death."

(Aging, his crack troops, scattered
far afield in wind and snow, contend
with tough guerrilla bands ever more
elusive, daring, and with mutineers
as well who would join already
fighting rebels.
　　　　　To retrieve these forces
from remote, harsh desert lands exacts
an always greater effort. And returning,
exhaustion weighs on them, the strain
of fending off a growing enemy.)

　　　　X

　　　　　　　　But I,
hearing from Hannah and Heinrich together,
as if a stormy spell may still be coiling
through the pages of my manuscript,
shove it into a crowded drawer.

As much dare look at that crookback
chortling here, at Heinrich's lectures
stowed away on some secluded shelf.

Let them declare, like lidded lavender
the names still green and branching out
in memory, the meaning everywhere!

　　　　X I

All parts of the Olympic games,
the gods bent over, fervidly regarding?

Hannah agrees:

"One goes there for fame; another
for trade. But the best ones sit there
in the amphitheater just to look.
Only such can get the gist out of it.

So, while some are mainly interested
in doing, I am not. Looking, you see,
is what I am after. I can very well
live without doing anything. Therefore,
I get less and less willing to move.

You think me passive? A pariah
from the start, a woman and a Jew,
I, by nature, am not an actor.
On the contrary.
                    And even when Heinrich
(after Hitler!) beat me over the head
with a hammer, waking me to the urgent,
lesser, murderous realities, I still
had this advantage: to look at the world
from the outside.
                    And now, if I would
think, I must withdraw. After hard,
long years, the world our passionate care,
have I, to shun "the they," their talk,
their trivialities, washed over every-
thing, not won the right to such retreat?

A bearing out this thinking is,
sitting here intent, speeding past
all measurement, the way that aspen
leaves sail off at any breeze.
A blessed keeping which action itself
can never fully realize.

Forgive me, but a little boredom is
quite healthy. And, so long as it is not
allowed to overwhelm our appetite
for greatness, some commonplace as well.

More than enough I've traveled,
the blurred, lurching ships and trains,

the hissing waves, the belching smoke,
the jammed-up boxcar we just missed
turning soon enough into that smoke-
bound car nothing stops, nobody misses.

So I ponder the world, its rush of strange
events, mishaps, yes, even monstrosities.
These, free as they are, unpredictable,
our storytelling proves inevitable.
I cannot live without trying every day
to understand—and never, up and down
the slippery stairs, a bannister to lean
on!—the wonder of their being, meaning.

Poetry, yours, is it so different?

Thinking, freed of physical obstacles,
for me amounts to sheer activity.
In the older Cato's words, 'When I do
nothing I am most active, and when I'm
by myself, I am the least alone.'

The moment you cannot sit still,
cannot admit plurality, the endless
dialogue between yourself and you,
contending with the world, you surely
stumble over your own feet. As Plato
said, "Your body always wants to be
taken care of and to hell with it!"

XII

And yet are we not after pleasure,
the passions, even the most painful,
pouring forth their rhapsodies as they
erupt in and through the bodied mind
out of collision with the world, lust
in the best of us for pleasure so vast
it seeks whatever excess, outrage
earth can muster?
           Needs it—as some
plants require fiercest storms to tear
away their outer husks—and needs

to praise, praise which, pitting itself
against the worst, sucks nectar strength
out of the wounds that tales be told,
songs sung, praise.

XIII

August blazing,
I spend the day with Hannah and Heinrich
in Palenville. This summer once again
they occupy a little, box-shaped cottage
to escape the city's jungle squalor and,
among the Catskills, rugged path and wake
of a volcano—
climbing them, the jolt
of every step on rock throughout the body,
one can feel that first eruption still,
its aspiration, as it hurled itself,
voluminous fire, headlong in the heavens—

to recover from the year's packed rigors
as from our storm-beleaguered epoch,
though their windows show a village
sprawled in shacks and dumps, garages,

which confirms that they, adjusting old
familiar terrors to the foreign new
as to abasements opening on depths
still able to surprise, are still adrift
aboard the ship set sail with crew—
its passengers stroll into view—unseen,
its orders and its destination sealed.

And still they seek the sacred polis.

XIV

Inevitably talk of poetry prevails.
Another visitor, a charter member
of their tribe, hand to her brow
as if to help her understand, inquires:

"Pray tell, how do you Americans manage?
Never to learn by heart beloved poems
for the dark and lonely times! Who are
your companions then?"
                        And as I hunch
forward in that simple living room
between Hannah and Heinrich, suddenly
a unison, they chant; their phrases,
soaring
          ("Da stieg ein Baum. O reine
Übersteigung!"),
                        smitten like their con-
centrated glances by the molten sun
descending, glitter.
                        I am caught
up in the empyrean middle—a capacious
temple, perched as on a sky-capped summit,
building of that terrible, blithe marble,
only stone to last in being lava still
like bristling stars, the stately breath.

There, for a moment, in that double
sibilance, and flared as by a burning
glass, the paired-off animals draw near,
their stir, their roars, now stilled,
all ears to learn their private names,
I too—the moon already, famous with
the wind-strummed pines, allotting light—
engrossed among these numberless regards.

            X V

More than ten years past, having come
this far in the poem, I pause, dig out
the manuscript and, riffling through,
dare look at its like-coffin-browning
pages.
          Some of the poems differ
from my final versions. Others take
me, strangers, by surprise, yet promptly
for their stiff-locked cadence spring
to mind.

At once I'm in a living
room, its windows flung wide open
to the sky, as if, someone unfolding
a letter—
      pressed inside its leaves
a tiny, faded flower, mountain laurel,
what is left of one particular morning—
morning, atop this autumn afternoon,
bursts from its pages;
              gusts rousing
out of trees and braided with day's ric-
ochet from mountains hulked behind,
a couple dally, once more fledglings
nestled like the larks that towered round
them, rue-and-laurel-interwoven wreath.

X V I

And I not looking back, yet looking,
feeling like an ore long buried struck
or like a river as it, riding, deepens
for its travels down inside a cavern
out to sea,
      these two (have they not
waited all this time ahead of me?) break,
sparkling, forth upon the blood's whole-
hearted tide out on this stream of notes,
a storming, my breath dares to flourish
in the dark.
      This way they look to me . . .

A Slow Fuse

Some seventy years later
your father, sitting at your table
over wine he savors, last rays mellow-
ing in it, recalls his favorite aunt,
Rifka.
      "Just naming her shoots
rifles off again inside the morning
square, rifles she aimed into the air
for certain customers, the pigeons
erupting."
      Handsome, clever,
but with little actual schooling,
she, a Jewess, kept a shop in Moscow,
stocking horse- and battle-gear,
bustling all day long.
      Powders,
braided with his laboring breath,
still prickle inside his nostrils;
like the wayward flickers cast
by lazily swimming,
      naked limbs,
leathers polished, buckles, gleam;
and the oats banked in their bins,
heavy August winds drowsed in them,
at one glance, a single sniffing,
bloom;
      the harnesses and bells,
by gaslight starred, send out appeals,
while sleighs collect for midnight
junkets.
      He smitten with it all,
like those officers of the Czar
who, admiring her wit, her seasoned
gaiety, forever jammed the shop.

"Even the city's metropolitan,
young despite his full, black robes,
took to dropping in on her, his jagged,
bushy beard awag with chat.

One balmy
summer evening, I remember, the three
of us, laughter brimming like wine
(he turned his glass to the lessened
light), relaxed in her snug flat.

The next morning at breakfast,
talk going on as if we'd never stop"—
he, a startled look lit on his face,
breaking in upon himself, exclaims,
the pigeons crackling through the air—
"My God, he spent the night with her!"

He, sipping the last drop, sits
back, as much as he's amazed amused
to see this special virtue of old age,
the oats ripening only in slow time.

A Pair of Shoes

This, you were sure, whatever happened,
you'd remember, long as any thought
stuck in your head.
           After a bitter
winter, when you and your family had
to eat weeds, bark, scraps of leather,
and it seemed certain the caked ice
would last forever,
                   the first lull came
drifting over. And then, more sudden
than the dusk invading, a tattered army,
raping, looting, killed all the others,
burned down the huts, and disappeared
before the smoke could scatter.
                      This
you were sure you'd remember, the blood
of your mother soaked in your blouse.

That was how many epochs, how many
countries, earthquakes, holocausts ago?
And oceans washing through, the cloudy
dreams, how many furnished rooms, a rusty
stain on them from how many people?

Now you are old and bent over, old
and bent to this spot called New York.
And crossing the street, only one thing
matters: to keep these broken shoes,
three sizes too big, from falling off.

Beside such chore, your left foot
slowly, slowly sliding after the other,
what a far-off, pointless tale that memory.
Let those sporting a polished pair
which fit indulge themselves.
                   Crossing
this street, the weight of you collected,
the old blood shuffles through your veins,
too busy to remember.

Under the Appearance of . . .

Reality of a basic kind,
even as it is local and therefore
seemingly commonplace, you begin to think,
underlies extraordinary appearances.

This curator, stumbling on
a painting he recognizes a Vermeer,
but knowing he cannot export it as it is,
orders a copy of some lesser work

slapped across the original.
And so he smuggles it out. At home
the restorer writes to him, "I've removed
the fake (whatever it is) and the fake

Vermeer under it. What shall
I do with the wretched portrait remaining
of the young Mussolini?" So, you recall,
Vermeer copies in the thirties duped

the experts. But now you see,
as people of that period could not,
that all the faces looked like Greta Garbo.
In that sense those copies were not

in any way fake but faithful,
as Vermeer had been, to their own
time and place and to the special face
their time believed the lasting loveliness.

So the copies of the 13th-century
Gothic wall paintings, hailed as authentic
masterpieces, justly so, for they were
more like Gothic wall paintings

than Gothic paintings themselves:
the forger painted what we saw—our Gothic—
in the originals and painted it directly
without the past intruding.

The Proof

Was it all put on then,
little, vigorous man, obsessed
by a longing for the good—so torn
between admired order and the rages
stormed from you, reason's storms—
to try you and so wring out
the last precious drop?
                          You thundering
away the whole Sunday at the piano,
an indomitable faith perfected
those irresistible mistakes.

As if, you chopping an avenue,
great trees dropping left and right,
through an endless forest, finally
it must give way to a square
filled with smiling presences.

Else engaged in heated arguments
against a wrathful, arbitrary God—
hours long you plied the Bible
for damning proof—with preachers,
hoarded jokes your reinforcements,

coupled with a spate of stories
pouring over like a sunlit, nonstop
torrent, like the tub of scalding,
soapy water that your wife dumped
into the snow-encrusted day.

All put on to prove the justice
of this madhouse world, its hungers
good, its terrors, even obstacles
preventing you from doing what
you thought you ought to—must—
to stay alive: establishing reason
as man's true estate?

Meantime,
a great depression ravaging the land,
you took in father, sisters, brothers.

Times improving, for years consumed,
the energies, despite your will,
your own depression prospered
till your last hope disappeared.
And yet, with every winsome torture
showered on you, you clung fast.

This morning stretched before you,
still another winter-mooded day
to test your will's resiliency,
as you bite into this bitter fruit,
a precious drop's wrung out of you,
a taste the gods cannot enjoy alone.

The Place of Laughter

In some countries laughter
is forbidden, a luxury, a kind
of sin, belonging to the mindless
or the mad.
       So for one poet
"the man who laughs/Has simply
not yet heard the terrible news."
In other countries
              it persists
almost apart from circumstances,
fruits without a tree, laughter
at—if not
         out of—extremities.
However, in the villages of India,
at least as you observed them,
if the people
        stay alive, they,
burnished by hard times, famine,
plagues, trying all their strength,
shine out like deities,
              women,
heavy bundles balanced like crowns,
erectly walking, with a laughter
rarely heard
        but weaving
through their bodies' movements
and their glances soft if piercing,
the way trees stand,
           welcoming
winter, easing sun-stricken summer
with leaves that seem to listen
as they wave,
          shadowy laughter.
Or that little flower breaking out
from a seed that's had to push
its way through granite.

En Route

Things we, sinking
in an anytime mid-gloom,
cling to which might pluck us
out of this mess, or at least bring
it into momentary focus—no wonder
they grow wonderful,
                perched
seven stories up in this study
of a spacious New York apartment,
the rooms, each one, cosily lined
with ceiling-high shelves, books
behind books, art-books, records,
paintings, caved as at Lascaux,

the mousy little cat, a thing
of springs, hurtled across the bed-
room, while its mother, prickly,
spook-like, crouches behind some
topmost, dusty volumes,
                this day
meantime glum enough, the day
before Christmas, at the Riverside,
buses soughing by, the buildings
which glittered Byzantine last night
like Christmas itself, this morning
fuzzy cutouts of smutched mist,
risen from the river,
              sitting
at my friend's desk, its drawers
no doubt littered with postcards,
letters, bills like crumpled sails
of voyages long over, many a flight
if mainly to the Italy he loves,

he this very moment in Rome
sightseeing with Kathleen or maybe,
as in my revery, floating along
on a gondola in Venice, its waves
blown, Byzantine, into shapes
mercurial as their capered colors,

while, for wind's incessant blasts,
our world's become a giant ice cube,
this metropolis, one frozen, rock-
grey, fossil fish,
                    the moon hoar too,
in the stories just above each roof
a cavern crystalline with heroes,
gods and angels, sealed like flies,

inside their wings less gossamer
than you, gliding in the next room
on your violin, good as any gondola
for taking breakers of Monteverdi
to transform this day's stark waters
(how they stream along your notes!),

I clutching things not my own:
your schooled flotilla, riding high;
this inkwell, all the sighs in it,
the mermaids, a once stormy deity,
mostly dried; this bottle of glue
stuck fast to itself; stacked
like tiny spears, that jar of pencils;
and the typewriter with its tiers
on tiers of a population waiting—
then it weeps, cheers, boos—to be
manipulated,
                    able to compose
who knows what score of lightning
phrases, able at once to stab
us into wounds we'd rather keep
concealed, yet thereby soothe them
with the precious balm of something
discovered, something almost
understood.
                    Through plants I squint
out the window, hoping this day,
like the bottle's glue, your notes
entwined, these words, will hold
at least itself together
                    and say
out of the murmurous, daylong surf-
ing buses, trucks, twirled cars
that it, maybe through the phone

humming on this desk, contains
assorted messages which will find
me in an instant, targeted
by any cry or cat's-pawed music,
with a homesick grief, a fiercely
fondling, homecome laughter.
                          O
must disconsolateness, this feeling
unmade-up like a many-times-slept-
in bed, this clutter as of leaves
season upon season grounded, everywhere
a bitten grey, fit and fit and fit me?

(for Harry and Kathleen)

The Here and Now

for Yehuda Amichai

Though you live in a little country,
crammed and crisscrossed with debris,
the past oppressive many times over—
where you buy your grapes David, pausing,
eyes a fiery dark girl, a lusty song
riding his breath, the old dance urgent
at his body; where you buy your bread
Christ, stumbling, stoops to heavy lumber—
you insist on your own loves and griefs,
on living your own life.
              So you love
this city, but mainly as it goes on
living its own life, across its roofs
the lines flapping, not gaudy banners,
but sheets and diapers, pants and slips,
as if rehearsing private pleasures.

And though you know you cannot win,
you play the game with all the skill
and love that you can muster, hoping
to keep it, keep it going, whatever
the fierceness in it, while you learn
the repertoire of your opponent's wrist,
the repertoire your own commands,
with every stroke surprising you,
as in a woman's glance the abundance
glinting of her passion stored away.

Those opposing roles, victor, victim
both, when they require re-enacting,
the moon as ever plays the luminous dome
above your god-and-man-scarred rock,
responsive to each nuance of the light
informing it with this, the latest scene.

The sweat you've shared between you,
juices drying on your hands and moon-
lit belly, swirls out of the rutted, stain-
stiff sheets a fragrance stronger, more
anointing, than the myrrh, the frank-
incense the magi brought, a gleam
that would eclipse their beaten gold.

Making It

(Jerusalem, July 4, 1980)

Easily as the moon
comes,
  as surprising . . .

  I

the eyes rising
to the shining surface
of this violin
    you rented:
its old wood, newly
carved,
  is redolent
still to nose and finger,

the body a big, curving
sound . . .

  I I

    and the stone
of this city, ages ground
in ages,
  the unblemished
sunlight, daylong trooping
days
  sunk into it,

but pink & yellow flowers
welling out of it,
crowns in little like

the moon now over it,
as though newly polished,
newly made . . .

I I I

make it new,
make it now,
make it . . .

I V

      the scrawny
young black cat, that
fixed us
     through a window
of our room with her
triangular
     Egyptian stare,
already several times
a mother
     with all her
skittish, half-crazed, little
kittens,

V

     crouches in the
doorway, shadow-silent,
waiting
     for the geckos,
prehistoric mini-monsters,
scarabs of good luck,

which, once dusk arrives,
out hunting, skitter
across
     our outdoor wall,
the chittering their name,
one with the voices
     laden
in the air, making it,
here in Israel . . .

VI

only appetite, that cat's,
the geckos', ancient
as the moon,
         its latest
luster that predates those
hoary rocks,
         like you and me,
the old gods throbbing
in us,
      the looks flocked
from your fingers, penetrant
as any star,
        only the song,
risen like a wellspring
from this violin,
        out
of the prayers, the bloody
sighs, the wailing,
          easily
as the moon comes,
its luminous calm, ever

      making it new,
      making it now,
      making it . . .

The Death of Fathers

Rummaging inside yourself
for clues and coming up
with nothing more than old
familiar news, you think
you have it hard.
            Your
father having died when you
were still a child, you keep,
it's true, but faded sense
of him.
            Soon after that,
as though to make it worse,
the village he was born
and lived in all his life
dispersed.
            And now—
perhaps with him it joined
the lost tribes of Virginia—
it survives, name only,
on discarded, browning maps.

But though my father died
when I was some years older,
I know, beyond all ordinary
disappearings, nothing
of his past, his country

(Hungary he called it,
only a few of his oaths
still peppery on my tongue
to prove it), least of all
his town.
            New vandals
rampant, kicking boundaries
askew, whole nations also
on the run, as though their
lands were made of wind-

blown sand, how expect
to know? (Only when, Hitler
bringing my father's country
home to him, the two of us

hunched
      by the radio,
did I get a bitter sense
of who my father might have
been and was and of his
world
      in a past much
overlaid.) Like you I try
to ferret out whatever hints
of him from the one source
still available—myself.

Recall a few of his
loved saws like "The apple
never falls far from its tree."
But only a worm in it sticks
its fat tongue out at me.

Or "Teddy, I understand
you all right. Are you not
my son?" Well, was he not
my father? Clues or not,
chasing fast scribbled lines,

I lean on his robustious
love: his skill with animals:
his joy in gypsy fiddling,
notes ripening within his
fingers' will: his passion

for his work, I awed
watching him—old things
bought, and new, to sell—
danced among green filing-
cabinets, as he, a boy,

shoes riding his neck,
had skipped along (he told
me this?) the speckled path
bisecting the Black Forest:
pride that almost drove

him, raging, over cliffs
and finally, when, despite
strong warnings, he would

mount a frisky horse, rode
him off forever,
    I there
by him as he stumbles up,
eyes closed, face set,
a name, my mother's,
still hot upon his lips.

And gripping his arm,
I summon all my strength
("Am I not your son?"
Surely I can reach him,
haul him back), to learn—

as I shout "Father!"
over the growing chasm,
his breath slammed shut,
a wall instantly gone up—
the lesson never learned.

The Hostage

The young man, all mixed up,
long before he used it dumped
his life to take on something
else because it sounded, if not
better, different.
          So he landed
in jail for assorted crimes,
in a country he couldn't name.
Little more than a pail he had
to remind him
          what his days
were coming to, and a straw cot
so hard, so narrow, it failed
to bear him and his dreams.
These anyway grew
                    so fat
that they, his sleep unable
to accommodate the least of them,
the cell too small, promptly
overran his days.
               Until a fly
flew in and, lounging back,
seemed to ponder him.
                    Returning,
pondered day by day.
                    And sleep
began to work: the fly, at first
with wings and then without,
then wings, free of the body,
always bigger
          as they flapped,
flew—cell shaking like a storm-
struck ship—him out into the open
air beyond the need of wings
until he woke.
          Whatever fly
smuggled in of plums it had sipped,
lips it had briefly perched upon,
and choice pollution, it denied
to sit and ponder him.

                              Grown fond
          of it, he, catching it, tore off
          its wings to keep it, hardly
          worse off than he.
                              Appreciation,
          which made his loneliness less,
          made this possible.
                              Between them,
          needing little, they managed
          a world. What's more, he could
          afford to feed it fabulously.

Looking Back

Look for an explanation?
You had reposed such trust
in everything you touched
that, touched in turn, hands
earned again and again, you
did not know how much each
had entered into you:
              your pot
which heated soup; the wine-
filled jars; that artful plate
that kept the sun, and faces too
bent over into it, the shining
waters of, as into joyous prayer;
under them
          the wobbling table
where you spread your hunger
with your talk, laughter trail-
ing after as you went to bed.

That shimmer, was it figures
flamed in dancing, seraph, star,
the streaming of your love?

And then you were expected
to let go without a glance!
Could they think you so
unfeeling, so unthankful?

Most of all to Him Who made
these things, long golden days
heaping the fields, your window
steepened by gold-bulging birds
and fruit.
       Or was it figures
flamed in dancing, seraph, star,
the glancing of His love?

Each thing dear and dear
within the countless touches
shared with husband, children,
friends, your cat.

So when,
that impulse sweeping over you,
you turned, the tears that might
have drowned your eyes lumped
into one.
Should you not weep
for those denied a time to weep,
your household, the whole town,
lively once with all its evening
candle lights,
that last time
sparkling—fire let loose, brim-
stone, cries a single crackling—
in your glance?

Coming Attractions

You know to take directions
from the rain. It is a telling
landmark.
      In their rainbow-throat-
swelled cooing pouter-pigeons
also cue.
      And any fire you
may crouch by instantly exposes
landscape to the core,
            the spirit
all things else would flesh,
a ghost thereafter.
      Do not try
to cling to what you are: at once
it changes.
      Rest assured steady
drifting is goodwill enough
to mollify a sea.
      This field
too, leaned on its elbow, a straw
stuck in its mouth
      as it enjoys
its weed work, bees wreathed
round its head,
      takes you,
trying it on with every sense,
wherever you want to go.
      Standing
here, a lamp for someone else,
you rout up a mouse
      or two;
from ruffling wings crows shake
out preview dark
      that trees grow
dense. Yet when the evening,
till now stored,
      one multi-
pleated screen, inside the light,
unfolds,
      the moon bursts forth,
the guttering lamp of some
body else,

> body else of her,
> the sky, the future, in her look.
> By lights like these
> how choice
> your errors, all crumbling
> things.
> An impulse, brooding
> in the air, readies its surprises.

Variations on a Favorite Theme

Early One Morning

Earth's plenty in a little room?
Call to mind a painting, Chardin,
Vermeer, opulent for being
simple,
       its pots and pans
keeping the outer world at bay,
pictures, maps, lovingly arrayed,
composing themselves
           around
the woman who, the light focused,
in a scale weighs gems, bright
with her look.
       But the day
floods in, notably amassing scale
by scale, like a salmon hooked—
throughout
       its battering
upstream, the waters bracing-
cold and, flashed in the splatter,
a thrashing
       as if partner
of the leap—to its nativity.
Like you, practicing, practicing,
in a room:
       a lustrous bough,
your violin transmutes the beams
streamed through your window
mote on mote to melody
         that,
time and fate made light of, made
so much at home, we, knowing
we fail to understand,
       feel
lighthearted since we realize we
need not trouble: what we do
enough,
       that plenty heaped
meticulous as in a little shining
scale, the scale deft fingers
and your bow divine.

Outside It's Tuesday

As though to turn every bit
of early morning air into its trill,
over and over and over, then over
again, a bird perched in our maple
iterates its four-tone row.

So you, first testing the strings
against your ear—one after another
you pluck them, press—start
practicing.
      A thrum established,
presto, the airy earth of it arises:
thick as crickets' ceaseless hum,
as hornets, in lush summer grasses,
listening and loosing voices
while they listen,
                creatures spring
full-blown to your fingers, ready
to hail in whatever you require.
Fed on skills your hands excel in,
instantly it's here, that passage:

farms and arbors deeply breathing
fragrances they, breathing, deepen;
towns abuzz with their inhabitants,
rapt in their works and days,
                    traffic
clattering away like field artillery
and distant, echoing, great engines,
the din a network underscored
by silence an abyss reports.

Staked in that open plot which you,
your violin, and these notes conspire,
all look to you, to music.
                Through
your strings the world, more spacious
as it turns upon itself, is passing,
our maple riding its dappled tide.

Earthrise

Like the conquistadors
our moon men lusted after novelty,
world out of this world no one
had ever visited before?

Every second passing,
though it seem a commonplace,
pries some unexpected door. Every
second a stepping into the unknown,

a leaping in the mind
that the breath catches, the heart
in its sputtering flame matches
against the delicious fear.

Moon more than enough
this body, this whirligig star
we wander, heaven enough the space
our looks dart through,

our talk: earth flies
with us, swamps and mountains,
eagles peaking, snow-packed clouds,
the rivers pouring over,

cataracts. And burrowed
far below, those furry meteors
of the mineral dark: mole sedulous
with sidekick squeaky bat

and mouse. Those also,
bearded comets, sparks struck
off, fellow travelers streaming by,
like us equipped to people

briefly our atmosphere.
Last night the fireflies composed
a galaxy, a complex universe,
among the trees. Falling

together mouth to mouth,
the dark, its planets, backing us,
we sighed forth air unhusked
a god might yearn to use.

Moon on our hands
and everywhere, space fell
away. For the rapture whirling us
a song too close to hear.

Every Second Thought

And thence return me to my Milan, where
Every third thought shall be my grave.

—*Prospero*

I

A grey and dankish thing
this day, here in the winter
of your years, each blustering
winter all year long.
           Gusts
peevish at you, mutterings,
you huddle by the fitful fire.
Light—just enough
                for dark
to score itself, a riches much
too packed to be spelled out—
flips woods,
           one instant
gold and green, sky shooting
fire-caps that crest a mild,
swart sea.
           But, shivering,
do you not regret their loss,
those powers you thought able
to ensnare the world
                in song?
In your regardless corner-shade
you drowse: the hours pass
remarkable
           as random clouds.
Yet clouds, building at a glance,
once cobbled sky a causeway
nymphs and deities
              traversed.
Who now attends, amazed to think
this dried grey stalk, young,
crowned itself
           with flowers?

I I

Not even she, the flower
crowning all the rest, one time
your all in all:
        miles on miles
and many hardships piled between,
answering calls more urgent
than your sighing,
        with her
husband and their children she
has fled his once more plotting
uncle.
        Not your brother
who, lurked hard upon your years,
stirred a fresh rebellion
to ensure
        your present, last
forsakenness. Though your people
venerate you still, had you
not proved
        passive as before—
how he must have scoffed at you
assuming you could prevail
without your scepter
        of a wand,
your books. Much they served you
that first treacherous time!
Could you,
        adrift in a leaky
boat with Miranda and your brave
devices, bid the wind behave?
Or later,
        mastery complete,
the spirits called at will, what
power could you exercise past
that isle,
        what skill to conjure
voyages would fly you safely
home, safe from his heart?—
he would, this time
        not trusting
the sea, have had you killed.

I I I

Your distant isle, however
forsaken,
          was never like this!
Yet already there you saw the play
you staged at best moved none
but those responsive.
              Others,
stony at your magic, obedient only
to their own desires, must go
the way
          they had gone.
Still even here, amid rustling,
flambeaus, as of an autumn morning,
blossom
         to awaken scattered
secrets of your day: dense forests
stretching, out of the shadows
one after one
            shapes emerge.
As a fragrance or a comely cry
each richly prinked in your senses,
women are they,
             pliant nymphs
flourished by like the overlapping
leaves and puffy flowers, pink
for the musk they shed,
             with lords
in their gaudy plumage peacocks
yoked to a goddess' chariot?
The fire
        starting up, a hag,
blue-lidded, leering, rides behind;
scrambling round her, a rabble
wrangles.

I V

        Abruptly after
out of air—old age also wields
its charms!—familiar voices
speak:

"Had you an inkling
then, drowned in words, what thing
of shame a younger brother is,
his place the dust
        cast off
his senior's feet? Humbly I stood
by while you, ignoring me
as you ignored
        the state,
the thievery which ate the people,
corruption honeycombing all,
played,
        old man as you were,
with baubles till I took over: war
which I knew how to loosen
and how to quell,
        restoring
a prosperous peace. Perhaps now,
in aging helpless, younger than I,
you understand."

V

        The features
change. The voice. Underscoring it,
brushes crackle; squawks rise,
yaps, chittering.
        "Me, your slave,
a rooted thing, an earth, first
plucked from out my place,
you threw back,
        mere filth,
lowlier, since man more, than any
muskrat. And far, far below
your spirits.
        Yet more than those
me you needed. Lacking sticks
I lugged to patch your fire,
you could
        have gone on conjuring
how long? How long, lacking
fruits and fish I brought,
would you have lived?"

V I

More motley flutters by.
Resembles sprites you imagined
you commanded. Ruly as that stuff
you wrenched them from,
                                    they
at your grumblings grow fractious.
Actors of a traveling company,
their fleering antics,
                                    tumbles,
mimic you, your tale, your monster.
A wretched copy of an English
writer's work it is,
                        he said
to possess some gifts, but neither
burdened nor detained by truth:
a lightweight drama,
                                    full
of foolery, of horseplay, and years
ago put on. Yet something most
disturbing stirs within.

V I I

                                    Startled—
in you a frenzied dream awakes?—
again you feel the battering,
exultant heart
                        of that lush
isle, buffeted by tempests you once
played master to. Many puppets
you had managed,
                                    as they were—
the burly sea, its wildest combers—
but mimicry of your will; so
for a time
                        it brought to heel
that grunting breath, the stinking
body, bent on being nothing
but itself.

VIII

That stinking's
come again! Even as you rummage
through your books, you stumble on
old words,
   like dolphins leaped
out of black waves. Or in a thicket
rhapsodies. That moonshine
heaping the page,
    the fire's
lambencies—its shadows shuddered
for a moth flown by, first
loitering
   as on your aspen-
flustered sighs—can they once
more highlight phrases come alive?
Do their letters,
    twisting,
rise, pismires hauling fluttered,
nacreous things many times
their size?
   Buds unfurling
their calligraphy, the rain itself,
a printer ink to you, maps instant
on their treasure.
    Words
you'd put on things, not read them—
bark's writing, water, newt—
for what they are.
    Strings
once taut with gales, fair mermaid
singing, gone slack, drone out
the clay clumped
   under all,
this earth as it truly is, this
prosaic world that you had dreamt
a word could alter.

I X

      Still
you pick up sticks, this withy
you peel now, mumbling, brandish
as if to whip forth
       wonders.
Just so that chair, your eyes set
on it, by firelight looming
(hands out, is that
       Miranda,
young, smiling, sits there? Then,
even as you would embrace her,
another!
    You crying out
astonished, "Cecilia, come again!"
she, blazing, turns: "Words
at last for me?
      Too late.
Your books, bid them respond.")
She, your answering still
on your lips, dissolves.
      The ring
she gave you, rubbed as now,
owns powers stronger than
your magic.
     Stranger feelings
flare up in you, harshness as of
the world against you, earth
one grave.
     The withy works
no tittle better than your mind
trying to recall that book,
drowned long ago.
     And still
a whisper seems to rise from it:
"Next be the wind design,
a sign, a sigh . . .",
      that flaw
in your poor, porous memory
blows all the rest away.
Blows whiffs of him
       grating

to your nostrils as from the dark
interior of a cave (or maybe
your decay?).

X

The wind strong
in the rigging, time fast arrived
to board the ship, he, cowed
by sailor jeers,
        the crashing
waves, and what might wait ahead,
hid himself within a cleft
he showed to no one?
        Lives
he still? And still, sprawled back
beneath a bee-spun canopy
of woodbine,
        sunk in dreams
that open the heavens, showering
on him bounty light as song,
remembers you?
        Alone there
now, like you alone, and all,
Miranda, you, the rest, chimerae,
slurring husks of air.
        Bites
bring him back, bites jabbing
words still fitful on his tongue?

X I

"Remember?
        Speech you taught
that for a time I loved—so loved
you all the more—the world
thus singled out.
        I, words
guiding, eyes skyward, with words
startled, my flock, the stars
into their place

and uttered
perfect, round as an O mouth makes,
a bubbled droplet in my mouth,
the moon,
        the fireball sun,
you, and, most of all, skipping in
and out the rest—a river
sparkled
        as it rides the crest
it rushes forth—Miranda. All those
flowering star-like in grassy beds.
Bedded among you me."

XII

You had planned to use him
kindly, and you did; had planned
to set him—when he learned
the lessons
        that would make
him man, his reasoning upright—
free. Man proper he was that day,
upright, rearing!
              Air you
might curb, never flesh and blood . . .
a something in that moment
(was it Ariel?)
        warned you.
Panicked, you rushed to the spot.
There they lay, she, eyes
shut, clothes torn,
           and he
over her, breathless, hands water
bugs darting upon her body;
bending,
        clamped lips to hers.
Furious, clutching a branch, again
and again you strike. Force
matching your fury,
           dead
he must have been. Up, blood
on him, rage, he yanks the branch
from you,

raises it, holds,
then, breaking it, scuttles off.
Later: "Saw her, butterfly chased,
plunge into that pit.
            I—
not you, not all your magic—
clambered down after, struggling
in the mud, dragged her out."

XIII

And if he told the truth?
Whatever the truth, truce you tried
to keep. But how, on an isle
so open, free him?
            Not like the elf
who, swinging on dawn's ledge,
quarries from the sky what-
ever music it desires
            and,
nature all-engrossing, impervious
to any print, has no designs
on you.
         And so, back turned
to the light, crouching over black-
and-white, you still went on
drilling him.
          To what end?
There, days later, seeking you out,
flushed, racing hard on him,
he, stammering
            triumph,
hands full, offers slimy, slug-
like things. The smell overwhelming,
hopeless you feel it.
          Crimson,
head lowered, a snarl on his mouth,
like a beast on all fours,
he scuffles away.
         Too late
you see he had meant it a treasure
sought out for you, his part
of that island, him.
         More

than you could take in, the truths,
the mysteries, of his world
he might have taught?

X I V

                    Jutting
through those multi-colored cries
of name-defying birds, bare
rock you judged it,
                  its sea-
pulsed, leaped, and leaping lizard
green, eager to engulf you,
your child,
              those precious books,
the dream you clung to. Rock
juts also here in rotting,
pullulating Milan.
             Inside
these sweating walls, bunched
by the fire flagging, dreams alone
start up a moment:
                scents
you scarcely sniffed; mutters too,
hived as in a secret, moss-
bound rift of memory.
               "Hunger
prodding, words I ferreted out,
scampering, furry names, marmosets
and scamels,
            till words, crusted,
became a curse, a way of worsting
things and, worsted, hobbled,
styed like Ariel in a pine.

And then I saw those things,
as if ashamed, behind clumsy names
recoiling, more than ever hid.
Oh you had freed
            a spirit
from its tree, lightsome one my dam
trussed there, but little freedom
for that trussed in me."

X V

            They
sweep out now, even as your body,
twanging, engrosses you
with its tricks.
            Pangs, swarmed
inside and out, as of hissing imps
perfecting their technique
along your spine,
                        prick you
like porcupines aroused. And you,
at last a stepchild to the one
you could not father,
                        bear
his every ache, the pangs you sent,
the quilled, devils indeed,
against him:
            tempest sweeping
through this isle, the reek of him
your own decay. Could he know,
he might forgive?
                        Oh might.
The fire—no one tending it—is
going out.

X V I

                  But see! He, grumbling,
loyal, lugs in logs.
                  Flames
leap up, leap at you, thundering
waves. Miranda and you toss
in your little boat!
                  Those two,
body, breath, music out of tumult,
tumult once more claims
to sound
            its always growing
triumph. Its vehemence, exuberant
through your breath—storm
you made,

      the sky on fire
crashing into the waves, made you—
works to free you, your body
withering to air.
          To him,
the all-embracing, you surrender,
of a love that never needs
to think of love.

Index

About the Author

Theodore Weiss is the author of eleven books of poetry and three books of literary criticism. He is the recipient of numerous honors, awards, and fellowships, including a Guggenheim, the Brandeis Prize for Poetry, and a Ford Fellowship. He holds the Paton Foundation Professorship for Ancient and Modern Literature at Princeton University; he is also a Fellow at the Institute of Advanced Studies in Princeton. He and his wife, Renée, are the publishers and editors of the *Quarterly Review of Literature*.